Learning Cities, Learning Regions, Learning Communities

The cities, towns and regions in which we live are dynamic, exciting places that are set to evolve more rapidly than ever in the immediate future. As a result, local and regional authorities are re-inventing themselves as Learning Cities, Towns and Regions, where the development of human and social potential takes first priority. Across the six continents, local, regional and national governments now recognise that the opportunities they create can open the door to a better future for their citizens.

This indispensable and visionary book examines the mental and social landscape of the city of today and tomorrow, the ways in which organisations and people act, interact, learn and live with and among each other. From the standpoint of local administrations, learning providers, workplaces, and the people themselves, it offers a better vision of the future. *Learning Cities, Learning Regions, Learning Communities* addresses the urgent need for a guide to the principles and practice of lifelong learning for everyone in the cities, towns and regions of every country in the world. Among the many topics are:

- The origins, development and meaning of the lifelong learning cities and regions concept and the reason why it is vital for personal and social growth;
- The many tools and techniques usable by cities, towns, regions and their stakeholders to energise participation and help create a culture of learning;
- A proposed global role for cities and regions to help combat the blinkered ignorance, binding poverty and militant terror that may ultimately engulf us all.

But the author's main thesis is that learning cities, towns and regions will not happen unless their decision-makers, their managers and professionals and a large number of their citizens become co-creators in their construction. This highly readable and fascinating book therefore identifies learning materials available from the internet that can be used to educate people from all walks of life and all backgrounds. In particular, it pinpoints those lessons, exercises and assignments specially written to support the ideas, experiences, case studies and recommendations contained in the book's nine chapters.

Councillors, managers, administrators and professionals in local, regional and national government, and their stakeholder institutions in workplaces, universities, learning providers and voluntary and community organisations – anyone with an interest in the future will find this book highly readable, fascinating and practically useful.

Norman Longworth, one of the world's foremost thinkers in the field, has worked in schools, industry, universities and professional associations. A former President of the European Lifelong Learning Initiative, and current Vice-President of the World Initiative on Lifelong Learning, he has managed many European and global learning city projects, and written several acclaimed books. He is currently Visiting Professor at several European universities.

Learning Cities, Learning Regions, Learning Communities

Lifelong learning and local government

Norman Longworth

Routledge
Taylor & Francis Group

LONDON AND NEW YORK

First published 2006
by Routledge
2 Park Square, Milton Park, Abingdon, Oxon OX14 4RN

Simultaneously published in the USA and Canada
by Routledge
270 Madison Ave, New York, NY 10016

Routledge is an imprint of the Taylor & Francis Group

© 2006 Norman Longworth

Typeset in Bembo by
HWA Text and Data Management, Tunbridge Wells
Printed and bound in Great Britain by
The Cromwell Press, Trowbridge, Wiltshire

British Library Cataloguing in Publication Data
A catalogue record for this book is available from the British Library

Library of Congress Cataloging-in-Publication Data
A catalog record for this book has been requested

ISBN10 0–415–37174–0 (hbk)
ISBN10 0–415–37175–9 (pbk)

ISBN13 9–780–415–37174–2 (hbk)
ISBN13 9–780–415–37175–9 (pbk)

Contents

Figures

Foreword

The development of society depends on our capacity to learn and adapt to new realities and new circumstances. The mark of development in the human story going forth in this millennium depends on the application of creative mind, thought and practice on ancient challenges that find new expression in the pressures of the modern world. The creation of learning societies depends on the fostering of learning cities and they in turn must be made up of learning communities and learning organizations. This book therefore is a timely contribution to an important subject – how do we create learning cities and learning organizations?

This work is not an isolated and academic piece. It is a reflection on a European project within which Dublin City was able to play a valuable role. That European project demonstrated the value of different players concerned with the wellbeing of society working together to create a programme which can guide and inform those committed to the ideal of the learning city. We called the programme LILLIPUT. The image is taken from the work of one of Ireland's great writers, Jonathan Swift. In his work *Gulliver's Travels* he uses the image of different lands, one being Lilliput – the land of giants. We can all be giants if we allow the learning imperative to drive our vision and our personal growth.

The learning journey is an adventure into new worlds and towards new shores. The coastlines that lie out there to be discovered are at the end of personal journeys requiring courage, optimism and a sense of adventure. Like Columbus we must begin our journey in faith; unlike the Columbus experience we must be careful to respect and honour the new cultures and experiences we encounter in our journey.

This work documents some of the frameworks and issues that can help us prepare for that journey into learning. I trust that it will lead to practical action by city leaders and concerned citizens so that together we may build the learning cities that can light humanity's journey through this millennium.

Peter J. Finnegan, Director
Dublin City Development Board

Peter Finnegan, BA, BD, MA, is the Director of the Dublin City Development Board. The Board is responsible for the economic, social and cultural development of Dublin – Ireland's capital. The Board's work is reflected in the Citizens Online Portal www.dublin.ie.

Preface

Why read this book? After all, everyone who works for local and regional government is, by definition, a very busy person, up to the eyeballs in work and responsibility. And if you are not a local government administrator or professional what possible interest could a book called *Learning Cities, Learning Regions, Learning Communities* have for you?

There isn't an easy answer to either question, but if you believe that your city or your region, the one you are helping to sustain and hopefully grow, or simply live in, will be the same in the year 2020 as it is now, then please don't even open the pages. But I can tell you this – it won't!

The inhabitants of your city in that year may just recognise the place after the physical transformations that inevitably happen during regeneration. But, in this book, we are not discussing the physical landscape. It is the mental landscape that concerns us, the way in which people think, interact, work together, solve problems, make decisions, handle information, live with and among each other. And who can deny that, in this world of anti-social behaviour orders, inter-racial violence, habitual truancy, increasing intolerance, war, alienated youth, non-stop change, aging populations and environmental degradation, these human and social things are important? You don't have to be a rocket scientist to recognise that some strategy needs to be formulated to address the educational, social and cultural issues that confront our cities and regions. And nor need you be in local or regional government to appreciate that solving these problems implies a change of mind set from that we are using today. It involves the one word you will find in great abundance throughout the book – no, not 'education, education, education' à la Blair, but 'learning, learning and learning'. There is a big difference! One is only a result of the other if there is motivation, motivation and motivation.

So what's the big idea about learning cities and learning regions? Isn't that a matter for our schools, our colleges, our universities and the administrators and teachers who are paid to offer an education service? Well, actually no! Not if you believe the hundreds of reports and papers published month after month from government, academia and other experts. What they are saying, and what this book is saying, is that we *all* have to get involved – every one of us – if we want to create the sort of society in which we can feel safe and fulfilled. And why is that? Well – it looks like I just found an answer to the first question I asked!

You won't be disappointed. It's certainly a big idea but it's not higher algebra. It spells out why learning is the root of all our futures. Now that may not be a very attractive idea to many of us. But we should perhaps ask ourselves why that is. After all, learning is one of our most basic instincts – we wouldn't be able to speak or walk or feed ourselves if that were not so. What must change to make it a joy again? And what's so important about creating a learning culture in our cities and regions?

That's all dealt with in the book, which, you will be glad to know, is not a dry academic tome full of long words and abstract concepts and references to previous work. Well, not a lot of the last two anyway. Certainly it gives due acknowledgement to the ideas of those pioneers who have made a healthy contribution to learning city thinking, and it applauds those cities and regions where that thinking has already engendered a new spirit of enquiry.

Yes, indeed there are already a great number of cities and regions in many parts of the world making the journey. They have declared themselves to be learning cities or learning regions. And there are wise people in those cities and regions with the knowledge and commitment to make it happen, for whom this book is merely a reinforcement. But they realise, and this book emphasises, that it will not happen unless they have the support of the millions of citizens in local and regional authorities, business and industry, academia, schools, hospitals and communities everywhere. It's like total quality management – everyone has to be involved in one way or another. This book tells you why, what and how – and where you can find the additional learning materials that will transform you and the city or region where you live into a place of learning, to all our benefits. Here's the book's first quotation from the European policy document on the local and regional dimension of lifelong learning (Longworth 2001); it says, 'Cities and towns in a globalised world cannot afford *not* to become learning cities and towns. It is a matter of prosperity, stability and the personal development of *all* citizens'.

Perhaps that answers the first question. So there it is. Now all you need is motivation, motivation or motivation.

Norman Longworth
Eus, France
June 2005

Acknowledgements

This book is dedicated first to my long-suffering and supportive wife Margaret, whose ever-growing list of household tasks may now be, at least partly, fulfilled. Also to Professors Sam Allwinkle of Napier University and Michael Osborne of Stirling University, without whose encouragement and help the projects described herein would not even have been started. And to the many colleagues with whom I have worked and from whom I have learned much over the past ten years. They include:

Professor Shi Long, Xing Hui and Catherine Wang Yan from Beijing
Sylvia Lee from KMI, Edmonton
Peter Finnegan and Derek Fitzpatrick from Dublin City Development Board
Professor Denis Ralph, Darryl Dymock and Stan Salagaras from South Australia
Denise Reghenzani and Janelle Allison from Queensland
Vicki Adin and Professor Ron McDowell from New Zealand
Liisa Tommila, Markku Markkula and Kristiina Santala from Espoo, Finland
Alain Bournazel and Sabine Scanga from CEFEL, France
Professors Jonathan Winterton and Jacques Digout, Peter Harizanov and Laurence Patoux from ESC Toulouse
Martin Molholm and Peder Key Kristiansen from Skagen, Denmark
Dr Renata Vystrcilova and Tony Komenda from Palacky University, Olomouc
Kennet Lindquist and Lars Franson from Sweden
Bob Hogg and Jenny Williams, formerly from Southampton, UK
Dr Kate Sankey and Peter Gray from Stirling University
Professor Dermot Coughlan and Patricia Ann Moore from UL, Limerick
Professor Ingunn Sandaker from Akershus University College, Norway
Professor Giuseppe Ronsisvalle and Roberta Pia from Catania, Italy
Istvan Mikus from Budapest and Christine Fitton from ELLP
Professor Michael Thorne, UEL, and Professor Jack Hobbs, Chris Glover and David Mowthorpe from Sheffield Hallam.

And many others, too numerous to mention, who have provided much appreciated inspiration when needed.

Lastly to my former colleague in ELLI, Keith Davies, who first got me into this fine mess.

Chapter 1

Renewing, researching, refining

Making sense of learning cities and regions

A new phenomenon is hitting the world of cities, towns and regions and it is potentially one of the most powerful and important movements of our turbulent times. Most city managers will have heard of it; some are taking active steps to accommodate it. Not everyone understands its significance, nor its nature, nor its implications, nor the actions that need to be taken to incorporate it into city and regional life. But the fact is that learning cities, learning towns, learning regions, learning communities are terms now in common use throughout the developed and the developing world, mostly because local and regional administrations have recognized that a more prosperous future depends on the development of the human and social capital in their midst. And the key to that development is encapsulated in three words – learning, learning and learning. That means to instil the habit of learning in as many as possible of their citizens and to empower them to assist in the building of their own communities as communities of learning.

All member states of the European Union subscribe to the words adapted from the Lisbon summit,

> Lifelong learning is no longer just one aspect of education and training; it must become the guiding principle for provision and participation across the full continuum of learning contexts. The coming decade must see the implementation of this vision. All those living in Europe, without exception, should have equal opportunities to adjust to the demands of social and economic change and to participate actively in the shaping of Europe's future.
>
> (Commission of the European Union 2000)

This is not just because lifelong learning is the flavour of the time, but because it has beneficial economic, social, political, cultural and environmental implications for everyone's quality of life. And, in the same way that a whole continent sees lifelong learning as its potential salvation, so too do many cities and regions within that continent, and in other continents too. But some pertinent questions remain. What does lifelong learning mean in the context of the city, the community and the region? And how would cities and regions know that they had become 'learning cities' and 'learning regions', as opposed to those that simply support and encourage learning? What are the imperatives driving this movement? How can they develop a culture of learning within their boundaries? What are the tools and techniques that can be mobilised to assist in this process? How will these learning cities and learning regions trigger real, dynamic progress into the 21st century?

The answers to these questions are not so simple that they can be explained in a series of one-line statements. We have definitions galore and several of them will be articulated in Chapter 2. Moreover, definitions of a learning city and region tend to differ according to the provenance of the definers and their own interpretation of the purpose of lifelong learning. Where it is based in the urban development departments of universities and cities a learning city or region will emphasise the physical and technological infrastructure of city regeneration. Where the focus is on employment, employability, organisational management and training for industry, the development of human and social capital for economic gain and competitive edge tends to predominate. Where the motivation is based on education methodology, curriculum and assessment, it will concentrate on e-learning, classroom management and the psychology of how people learn. And still we have not reached the social, environmental and cultural rationale, which provides it with a heart and a soul.

Truth to tell the learning city or region is not any one of these, but a glorious mixture of all of them, allied to the release of the health-giving creativity and imagination which every place needs to harness in order to progress into a more prosperous and stable future. Working together, they produce a developmental paradigm shift in countries, cities, regions and communities in which the age of education and training – which has served western society well in the late 20th century in satisfying the needs of a growing, upwardly mobile proportion of the population – is now giving way to the era of lifelong learning, in which new methods, tools and techniques are employed to target and motivate *everyone* in a community, city, town or region as a lifelong learner. The European Policy Paper on the local and regional dimension of lifelong learning is quite explicit. It says that 'those cities that achieve success in this will be the winners in the paradox where intelligent local action leads to success in a globalised world'.

It will be a very different world. We live in momentous times. Richard Eckersley, writing in the *Sydney Morning Herald*, suggests that the twin spikes of technological change and populations growth might lead to 'A new universalism and, because of the global threat they pose, help drive the emergence of a universal culture, a new sense of human solidarity and destiny, a resurgent spirituality'. Almost four years later he detects 'a thousand brushfires of revolution breaking out as more people re-assess their priorities and explore different ways of thinking and living their lives. What we are seeing are parallel processes of cultural decay and renewal, a titanic struggle as old ways of thinking about ourselves fail and new ways of being human strive for definition and acceptance'.

Such musing is given a more practical vision in the journalist Toffler's *'practopia'*. 'Neither the best nor the worst of all possible worlds,' he says, 'but one that is both practical and preferable to the one we had – not ruthlessly undemocratic, not inherently militarist, not reducing its citizens to faceless uniformity, not destroying neighbours or degrading environment. A civilisation that is not frozen in amber but pulsing with innovation, capable of directing great passion into great art, facing unprecedented historical choices – about genetics, biotechnology, environmental salvation – but inventing new ethical or moral standards to deal with such complex issues'.

By contrast Botkin, author of *No Limits to Learning*, predicates a 'wisdom society'. 'By wisdom society, I mean societies that have a tolerance for alternative values and value that diversity. I mean cultures that break out of the arrogance and monopoly of believing they know the answers and should tell others how to live. I mean a society that has a large number of people with the ability and capacity to accept more than a single viewpoint. They can understand multiple perspectives and generate multiple solutions to complex problems. How do we get from here to there? First we must become a learning society. Only then can we move toward wisdom. Becoming a wisdom society involves a process of learning, learning to become more tolerant, more respectful of the value of alternative views and ways of living, more open to difference and less attached to preserving ways of life that dominate other people.'

Once again we see not only powerful messages that would benefit urban societies in the present age, but also the centrality of learning in a democratic and pluralistic society, the sort of society that permeates many of the multicultural, multi-ethnic cities, regions and towns in the developed world. Botkin's vision of a population able to 'understand multiple perspectives and generate multiple solutions' is not one that present-day educational structures will generate. And yet he is right to highlight the challenge to administrators and politicians at both national and local levels. They have a solemn responsibility to help create his 'wisdom society', if only because the alternative is one of manipulation, ignorance and segregation, more reminiscent of Huxley's brave new world of 'alpha to epsilon Bokanowski groups', and the distribution of the television equivalent of soma tablets.

Moral philosopher Denis Kenny suggests that societal change occurs when there is a shift in people's conception of the universe, which he believes is happening right now. Over more than 100,000 years of human history, we have inhabited four quite different universes, he says:

- The *enchanted* universe: a world alive with forces, powers and influences, often personified as gods, which toyed with people's lives; it lives on in New Age beliefs.
- The *sacred* universe: the universe of Christianity, a world created by God; 'the first comprehensive, fully integrated theory of everything in human experience'.

- The *mechanical* universe: the universe of Newtonian physics; a world that runs like clockwork according to a set of physical laws.
- The *organic* universe: the universe of Einstein, relativity and quantum physics; a cosmic dance of energy in which the distinction between the material and spiritual no longer makes much sense; 'the first universally valid and scientifically based cosmology in the history of human consciousness and culture'.

Now, he believes, we are on the threshold of a fifth cosmology, the *creative* universe, the universe as a self-organising and creative process, in which 'the human species is given the opportunity to take full control of its future'. 'We are all now faced with a radical moral choice', he says: 'We can step confidently into a new realm of creative freedom and take full, democratic responsibility for that future, or, alternatively, retreat into a blind and irresponsible dependence on moral authorities who will confidently claim that they have a mandate from God, nature, history or the market to define that future for us'.

Such moral and philosophical reflections may seem to be a long way from the concerns of city and regional managers, struggling to reconcile the needs of thousands, sometimes millions, of people to remain employable, healthy and mentally active within a stable and prosperous environment. But there is a clear connection. The movement toward a much more open lifelong learning society is symptomatic of the newly resurgent desire in citizens to influence the future of the place in which they live, love, learn and create. Top-down authoritarian structures are no longer in vogue, and leaders in cities and regions will need to know how to harness the creative energies of thousands of people for the good. Shakespeare's 'tide in the affairs of men' becomes also a tide in the affairs of local and regional authorities.

Once again the answer lies in opening up many minds to learning. It is one of the imperatives of the early 21st century. The four educational pillars for modern living of UNESCO's 'Treasure Within', 'learning to be', 'learning to do', 'learning to understand' and 'learning to live together', provide a good starting template for this process, although putting them into practice will take a radical shift of mindset in national, regional and local governance. Nor is this, as Kenny implies, new. The history of enlightenment, like many other areas of human activity, has a habit of moving in cycles and the concept of learning for and throughout life follows this pattern. For example, 2,500 years ago Plato put forward the theory of '*Dia Viou Paedeia*', which he described as 'the responsibility of every citizen to educate himself and develop his own potential'. The use of the masculine gender is authentic but not exclusive, even in Plato's day. And indeed in Athens and many other Greek cities over hundreds of years, learning and contribution were everyday, natural things to do for large numbers of citizens, though geared to the peculiar social patterns and the limited knowledge of the time. A similar learning revolution took place in the eighth and nineth century Islamic world of the Middle East, where Damascus, Jerusalem and Alexandria were hotbeds of culture and learning.

This ebb and flow is in keeping with the idea of 'the spirit of the time', a term more redolent with meaning in its original German '*Zeitgeist*', and defined in the Nordic Regional Development Policy as 'contemporary values, attitudes etc i.e. the way various issues are seen in contemporary society'. 'The spirit of the time', the authors say, 'Gives meaning to various policies – often it has a decisive influence over what policies are important in today's society and how they are expected to be carried out'. 'If interpreted positively the strong reflection of current fashion in the development strategies of regions appears as a signal of a proactive region striving to be ahead of its time. If interpreted negatively the strong influence of the spirit of the time may appear in many regions as trendy, but hollow rhetoric. In any case it clearly has a significant influence on regional development.'

Thus *Zeitgeist*, according to this document, has a strong influence on regional policy-making quite unrelated to scientific principle, social construct or administrative convenience. This book suggests that this is also making a significant contribution to the debate on learning cities and regions throughout the world and that, far from being hollow rhetoric, it articulates the desire of people, institutions and policy-makers to help create a more equal, democratic and vibrant society in which to live.

Conflicting definitions

City and regional administrators are not short of educational advice from the great, and not-so-great, thinkers of the day. Several thousand reports and papers, books and compendiums have been published by international and governmental organisations, by learned committees, by experts, universities and individuals over the past few years on the urgent need for, and the vast benefits to be gained from, implementing lifelong learning concepts in cities and communities. Not all of them agree on what these concepts are. Many put a particular spin on them to fit their own perceptions and desired outcomes. But one of the common denominators is the need for all aspects of city life, including education, to change to procedures and processes that are more bottom-up, and based on the real needs and demands of the learners – a 180 degree transfer of power and ownership of learning from teacher to learner.

The trick is how we might make this empowerment happen in reality. The New Zealander Gordon Dryden identifies five key revolutions that are driving society forward into the knowledge age. Not many of these are education-led. Indeed Dryden's thesis is that education is lagging way behind in responding to the challenges they present – but every one of them has deep implications for its content and the methods it uses.

- The *Instant Communications* Revolution: the new ability to link almost every person on earth into a web of networked intelligence.
- The *Swarm* Revolution: our growing ability to embed billions of cheap non-polluting computer silicon chips in everything we use – our refrigerators,

rice cookers, shoes, clothing, toilets, golfballs, toasters, doorknobs and cars – and employ them as a swarm of interlinked, silent, almost costless digital servants: just like we automatically use electricity and barcodes today.

- The *Convergence* Revolution: the growing synergy between four fundamental existing revolutions: the quantum revolution, the computer revolution, the internet revolution and the biomolecular revolution.
- The *Learning* Revolution: our emerging ability to learn anything faster and more effectively by combining the best brain research with the world's best digital technology.
- The *Creative* Revolution: our rapidly-expanding ability to create entirely new futures, and to analyse old problems in new ways, the opportunity to reinvent education as one example.

He points out that, in order to cope with these, every successful corporation is rethinking its strategy at least every four years, and that every nation state that aspires to prosper in such a world is reacting similarly. The world's largest corporation, General Electric, spends more than a billion dollars in internal staff training and education. Dryden quotes Jack Welch, the Chief Executive Officer, who, when asked what the company would be like in ten years' time, replied, 'I hope that it will be the world's greatest learning organisation', and William Daggett, who suggests that 'the world our children are living in is changing four times faster than our schools'. And Reed Hunt, Chairman of US Federal Telecommunications Commission, who laments, 'There are thousands of buildings in this country where people in them have few telephones, no cable television, and no reasonable prospects of broadband services. They are called schools'.

So where does this leave the cities and regions which inhabit that same world and are, as will be argued, in some way responsible for bringing their citizens up to speed in their appreciation of the need to respond to the demands it makes? What does all this mean for places like Seattle, Southampton, Helsinki, Brisbane, Pittsburgh, Toronto, São Paulo, Cape Town, South Australia, Moscow, Beijing and every other municipality, city and region over 5,000 people, and for that matter most communities of less than that? It means of course that they will need to become learning communities, cities, regions! The reasons are not only economic, they are political, cultural, environmental, social and personal. And indeed visionaries in many cities and regions have recognised that, and are taking active steps to address the deficit by inserting lifelong learning principles into their development strategies.

But the key that opens the door to success is the way in which city managers and citizens are brought along with these strategies. Learning cities and regions will not happen unless councillors, educators, managers, city employees, community workers, stakeholder leaders and the vast majority of the citizens themselves have given their consent and their active participation. They are not only the beneficiaries, they are the drivers. Even in those cities calling themselves learning cities and having long trodden that path, street polls would yield very few people who know that, and even fewer who could articulate what it means. This predicates a huge educational and marketing effort by city managers and administrators to provide the understanding and insight that will engender lift-off, and the use of the tools, techniques, lessons, ideas and propositions described in later chapters.

The growth of the learning city and region

So where does the process of response begin? Criticism of education is cheap and easy, sometimes misplaced, and sometimes too close to the truth for comfort. As suggested by this author in Crowther and Sutherland, Plato's starting point was the city itself. The primary rationale for encouraging citizens to learn was so that they could contribute to the life and growth of the city and the community at large, perhaps one of the first recorded examples of active citizenship, which up until then had been taken for granted in more primitive cultures. Thus, though learning was an individual pursuit, the rationale for taking part had its source in community, in living together harmoniously and in growing in understanding together. In another time, Alexandria's library attracted scholars and learners from all parts of the known world and it prided itself on being the learning city of its age. Many Islamic cities, such as Damascus and Jerusalem were, between 900 and 1,300 years ago, real 'learning cities', centres of culture and learning, participated in by most of their citizens, and probably truer learning cities than anywhere that exists in our modern world.

And so, in the present-day movement towards the concept of the 'learning city', 'the learning region', 'the learning community' as geographical models within the social concept of the 'learning society', all of them terms now in common usage, we may learn much from the past. The concept has been in vogue over a number of years. In the 1970s, OECD funded a project to create 'Educating Cities'. It invited seven cities from among its member states – Edmonton in Canada, Gothenburg, Vienna and Edinburgh in Europe, Kakegawa in Japan, Adelaide in Australia and Pittsburgh in the United States – to put education at the forefront of their strategies in order to justify the term 'Educating City'. More recently the term 'Learning City' has become more popular. Liverpool in the UK declared itself to be a 'City of Learning' in 1996, and was quickly followed in the UK by Southampton, Norwich, Edinburgh, Birmingham and others. The UK Learning Cities Network now numbers some 80 members. European cities such as Espoo, Gothenburg and Dublin followed their own learning city pathways. Meanwhile, at another level, the City of Barcelona has, since 1992, led an Association of 'Educating Cities' now reaching some 250 members worldwide. These cities are the leaders in the learning regions movement because they recognise that to prosper economically, socially and culturally, their citizens will need to come to terms with rapid and accelerating change.

Characteristics of a learning city and region

Amidst all this plethora of activity in the mid-1990s, the European Lifelong Learning Initiative (ELLI), now unfortunately defunct, initiated a debate on what a Learning City was, how it would define itself and how it might be distinguished from a city that was not yet in tune with the times. As long ago as 1995, this author, a former President of the Association, published a number of articles in its house magazine 'Comment' to clarify the issues. Figure 1.1, published in one of these, shows how ELLI envisioned the major characteristics of a learning city. In 1996, the 'European Year of Lifelong Learning', he published, in conjunction with Davies, a book describing the role and implications of lifelong learning for stakeholders in the city. In this, the consequences of implementing lifelong learning principles in schools, universities, business and industry and local government were spelt out, as was their potential contribution to working together to help grow both community and city. This book was followed three years later by a more targeted book, subtitled *Learning Cities for a Learning Century*, containing examples from a wide variety of cities that were ahead of the rest in thinking and action, including the learning region of Kent in the UK, which, in a last chapter, measured itself against many of the characteristics in Figure 1.1.

The TELS learning cities project

It is in all of these contexts that the European Commission's TELS (Towards a European Learning Society) project becomes very relevant. TELS was one of the early projects to examine the characteristics of the learning city, and to test the perceptions and progress of some 80 cities around Europe. The main objective was to encourage cities, towns and regions to take the new concept on board, and then measure and monitor themselves as 'learning cities, towns or regions' both as an internal exercise to help develop new lifelong learning strategies, and as an external measure of progress against other municipalities.

In order to do this TELS developed a comprehensive audit tool (the Learning Cities Audit Tool), identifying ten major municipal learning domains and 40 sub-domains (shown in Figure 1.2) where cities, towns and regions might need to take action:

- To take stock of their present performance as learning community.
- As a rich source of ideas for helping to create a learning society in learning cities.
- To help create awareness among key people.
- As a comprehensive tool for planning and maintaining a learning city strategy.
- As a way of obtaining best practice examples and case studies.

The interesting results of TELS will be described in fuller detail in Chapter 4, since they include the indicators that cities and regions can use to explore

Figure 1.1 Characteristics of a learning city

A learning city is one with plans and strategies to encourage personal growth, social cohesion and sustainable wealth creation through the development of the human potential of all its citizens and working partnerships between all its organisations

L	Leadership	Links its strategy to the development of leadership and learning counselling courses and skills in and for the whole community
E	Employment and employability	Effects plans to define and develop skills and competencies which make all its citizens employable
A	Aspirations	Activates the creative potential of its citizens through a strategy for encouraging the use of personal learning plans, mentors and guides in citizens of all ages
R	Resources	Releases the full potential of community resources, including human resources, by enabling mutually beneficial partnerships between public and private sectors
N	Networks	Nourishes tolerance and outward-looking mindsets through projects to link citizens of all races, ages and creeds locally, nationally and internationally
I	Information	Increases participation in learning by devising innovative strategies to provide information where people gather, and proactive publicity campaigns to promote learning
N	Needs and requirements	Nurtures a culture of learning by proactively auditing the learning requirements of all its citizens and providing the opportunities to satisfy them
G	Growth	Generates wealth through a defined strategy of developing its human talent and innovative projects with other learning communities
C	Change management	Cultivates programmes which allow citizens to cope positively and without fear in a world of rapid change
I	Investment	Influences the future by linking learning strategies to cross-departmental financial strategies
T	Technology	Transforms the city into a modern centre of learning by the effective use of the new learning technologies
I	Involvement	Inspires citizens to contribute to city life and culture by building a database of their skills, knowledge and talents and encouraging them to make them available to others
E	Environment	Energises programmes which enable all citizens to take positive action to care for the environment
S	Strategies for the family	Stimulates the community and whole families to learn by running festivals, fairs and other fun events which promote the habit of learning

Source: *Making Lifelong Learning Work* (1999).

their own progress and performance. Although the project had neither the authority to require cities to provide data nor the resources to carry out a controlled sample from each country, the project produced many insights into the perceptions of learning cities and regions in Europe. It also produced a significant knock-on effect. It was used as the basis for the development of a European Policy Paper on the Local and Regional Dimension of Lifelong Learning produced in 2001. It also provided a great deal of conceptual input for the Commission's memorandum on lifelong learning which subsequently led to the Commission's fuller, but watered down, lifelong learning policy document, *Towards the Realisation of a European Area of Learning*. Although the TELS methodology was not pure research, its visionary outputs encouraged many cities that had not previously made a commitment to become a learning city to re-examine their policies, and gave them a tool for use in doing so. Besides providing the audit tool, it produced the two definitions found at the beginning of the next chapter, later used by the Commission in its funding of 17 further 'regional dimension' projects under the 'R3L' label.

Developing a European policy for learning cities and regions

The results obtained by TELS confirmed a sorry lack of basic knowledge about the effects of lifelong learning in the majority of European municipalities. But it also uncovered the existence of some cities where much progress has been made, and more excitingly, a wish among most of the participating cities to know more. Indeed a good number of the participating cities admitted to becoming interested in the concept as a result of completing the audit, an interesting by-product of the survey. Its list of recommendations to the European Commission, shown in Figure 1.3, has resulted in supported action in a variety of fields.

Of these numbers one, three, four, six, seven, nine and ten have been wholly or partially realised. Indeed, several university networks have arisen as a result of number seven, led for example by Scottish universities at Napier, Edinburgh and the University of Stirling. The PALLACE project to link learning cities and regions globally, and described in fuller detail in Chapter 8, provides a good example of number ten in action, even though the resources available to it were pitifully small in relation to the need. This author, who managed both the TELS and PALLACE projects and wrote the European Policy Paper, commented at the time,

> At this embryo stage in learning city development there can be no other conclusion than that there is a long way to go. The majority of the municipalities coming into the project were unaware of the term 'Learning City', much less what it signified. In that respect the project has itself initiated a learning process … cities and towns in a globalised world cannot afford

Figure 1.2 The TELS learning cities indicators

Category	Explanation	Sub-topics
a) Commitment to a learning city	The extent to which the city or town has already started to implement plans and strategies which set it out on the path to becoming a learning community, and the thinking it has done to date.	Strategies for Lifelong Learning Organisation of Lifelong Learning City Charters for Lifelong Learning European Projects and Orientation The City as a Learning Organisation Readiness for Learning City
b) Information and communication	Ways in which lifelong learning ideas and plans are communicated to a) those responsible for implementing them and b) citizens at large. Including new curriculum development, teacher training, learning centres, use of the media, collection of information on learning requirements etc.	Information Strategies Use of the Media Learning Literature Marketing of Lifelong Learning
c) Partnerships and resources	The extent to which links between different sectors of the city have been encouraged and enabled, and their effectiveness. Including links between schools, colleges, business and industry, universities, professional associations, special interest groups, local government and other organisations. Includes physical and human resource sharing, knowledge generation, mobilisation etc.	Partnership Types Use for New Resources Combining Existing Resources
d) Leadership development	The extent to which lifelong learning leaders have been developed and how. Including community leadership courses, project management, city management, organisational mix.	Existing Leaders New Leaders Materials Development
e) Social inclusion	Projects and strategies to include those at present excluded – the mentally and physically handicapped, the unemployed, minorities, women returners, people with learning difficulties etc.	Barriers to Learning Qualifications, Standards and Assessment Special Programmes European National

continued…

Figure 1.2 continued

Category	Explanation	Sub-topics
f) Environment and citizenship	Projects to inform and involve citizens in city environmental matters. How the city is informing its citizens of all ages about citizenship and involving them in its practical expression in the city.	Environment Awareness and Learning – Adults and Children Environmental Involvement Citizenship and Democracy
g) Technology and networks	Innovative ways in which information and communications technology is used to link organisations and people internally, and with people and organisations in other communities. Includes use of open and distance learning, effective use of networks between all ages for learning and understanding of the internet.	Distance Learning Multimedia and Open Learning Using Internet and Networks Wired City
h) Wealth creation, employment and employability	Schemes and projects to improve the creation of both wealth and employment and to give citizens lifetime skills, knowledge and competencies to improve their employment prospects. Includes financial incentives, studies, links with industry, industry links with other communities etc.	Employment and Skills Wealth Creation Learning Requirements Analyses and Citizens Learning Audits Employability Initiatives
h) Mobilisation, participation and the personal development of citizens	The extent to which contribution is encouraged and enabled. Includes projects to gather and use the knowledge, skills and talents of people and to encourage their use for the common development of the city.	Lifelong Learning Tools and Techniques – Personal Learning Plans, Mentoring, Study Circles etc. Personal Development of Citizens Teacher/Counsellor Development and Training Participation and Contribution Strategies
j) Learning events and family involvement	Projects, plans and events to increase the credibility, attractiveness, visibility and incidence of learning among citizens individually and in families. Includes learning festivals, booklet generation, celebrations of learning, learning competitions, recognition events etc.	Learning Celebrations – festivals, fairs etc. Learning Recognition and Rewards Family Learning Strategies

Source: Report of the TELS Learning City project to the European Commission (2001).

not to become learning cities and towns. It is a matter of prosperity, stability, employability and the personal development of all citizens.

(European Policy 2001)

Stakeholder Audits – measuring lifelong learning progress in learning cities and regions

The successor to the TELS activities was the European Commission's R3L programme, which funded the development of European networks of learning city expertise. It is hardly a well-known goddess as recommended in Figure 1.3, but it expresses the relationship between Regions (R) and Lifelong Learning (3L). One solid output of R3L, and building upon the TELS experience, was the results produced by the INDICATORS project. Managed from the University of Stirling in Scotland, the project put together a series of tools they call 'Stakeholder Audits'. These will be of great interest to administrators in local and regional government, universities, schools, adult colleges and small

Figure 1.3 Recommendations to government from the TELS project

---

1   Create a cross-sectoral strand in the Socrates Programme to support the development of learning cities and regions. Name it after a famous civic leader or the goddess of communities.

2   Establish a programme for Cities of Learning similar to that for Cities of Culture. If necessary run a competition to decide which city it will be in each country.

3   Provide incentives for the formation of new regional, national, and European infrastructures which help learning community concepts to develop more quickly.

4   Develop indicators which measure and monitor aspects of the growth of learning cities and the learning society and initiate surveys and studies on these in and across member states.

5   Raise the awareness of learning community concepts in municipalities throughout Europe through high-visibility events such as a European Learning Cities week.

6   Develop a 'charter for European Learning Cities' outlining the city's responsibilities *vis-à-vis* its citizens as learners, and its relationship to a wider European learning community, which cities sign up to.

7   Create a European network of one or more university departments in each country able to specialise in learning city research and development.

8   Develop an all-encompassing, easy-to-use, web-based learning community simulation tool and make it accessible to all.

9   Promote Europe-wide interactions and partnerships between local government, industry and others for wealth/employment creation and international employability.

10   Establish links with global organisations and countries to share good practice and foster joint cultural, economic and educational development in the area of learning communities.

Source: Report of the TELS Learning City project to the European Commission (2001).

businesses. They are interactive learning documents in their own right enabling respondents to gain insights into the many basic elements of lifelong learning as it affects their organisation, and to convert this new knowledge into actions that will implement its concepts both internally within the organisation (i.e. turn it into a learning organisation) and externally (i.e. work with other organisations to help build a learning society, a learning city or a learning region within the geographical area where the organisation resides). The Stakeholder Audits will be described in greater detail in Chapters 4 and 5.

Many of the INDICATORS project findings are now extended into the PASCAL Observatory, a service for cities and regions initiated by OECD, and comprising partners from RMIT Melbourne, Kent Thameside Learning Region and the University of Stirling among others. Observatory PASCAL offers great scope as a constantly updated place management, social capital, information and lifelong learning tool for local and regional development.

OECD and the learning region

Quite separately, in 2000, the OECD initiated its own vision of learning regions by funding a study of developing regions of Europe. The resultant report and book, *Cities and Regions in the New Learning Economy*, predictably concentrate on the economic benefits of developing a learning region, in particular the process of transforming declining manufacturing and industrial economies into societies largely based on the production and dissemination of information and knowledge. They highlight the apparent paradox between the process of globalisation and the need for actions to promote innovation, productivity and economic performance at the local level. They analyse, among other things, the correlation between primary, secondary and tertiary education and Gross Domestic Product per capita in 180 regions of the European Union and come to a number of conclusions important for local and regional authorities. Some of these are:

- While tertiary education remains important, secondary education appears to be the most important for regional economic performance. Higher Education is clearly essential in terms of innovations, but secondary education instils the intermediary skills, which are also crucial to the new industrial know-how and 'learning-by-doing'.
- High levels of individual learning in themselves do not contribute to economic growth before it has been applied to the production of goods and services. It is important therefore to stress the practical application of learning and to encourage creativity at all levels of education.
- The extent to which individuals and organisations absorb and apply learning and innovation will determine their competitiveness in the learning economy.
- What learning cities and regions have in common is an explicit commitment to placing innovation and learning at the core of development. All seek to sustain economic activity through various combinations of lifelong learning,

innovation and creative uses of information and communication technologies.

While this economic rationale for the learning region is likely to appeal to administrators it does not address the social, cultural, educational and environmental dimension of the TELS survey, and nor would it be expected to. Nevertheless, the conclusions reached about the nature and content of learning itself and the methodologies that would enhance it in the city – learning through partnerships, learning through experience, the need for investment in learning as the source of well-being and so on – fit well with many of those obtained in TELS.

As in TELS, the OECD study provided recommendations for the development of learning regions, shown in Figure 1.4.

Learning region developments in Australia

The OECD work has contributed much to new thinking about learning cities and regions and these principles have formed the basis for developments in many parts of the world. At the same time as R3L activity was taking place in Europe, a great deal of learning cities and regions work was being done on the other side of the world in Australia. Every state now has its own government inspired and funded learning cities association. In Victoria, for example, all municipalities of more than 5,000 people are expected to belong to this and to pursue learning city policies. Based on the author's work in ELLI and TELS, the National Government also commissioned the Australian National Training Authority (ANTA) to carry out a TELS-like audit in ten cities. The results of each enquiry can be found on the ANTA website.

In 2002, the state of Victoria also organised, with the OECD, an inaugural conference on learning cities, and commissioned a wide-ranging report on the subject from the Royal Melbourne Institute of Technology. This comprehensive and innovative document presents a powerful case for the establishment of learning cities and regions. It analyses the progress of Victoria as a learning region within the context of international developments and benchmarks and particularly against the ten OECD principles shown in Figure 1.4. Once again its rationale for promoting the learning city and region is economic growth and development but interestingly the four themes of the conference transcended this, establishing a link between employment and such topics as social inclusion and good governance, namely:

- sustainable economic growth including the expansion of high quality jobs;
- social inclusion and the building of social capital;
- the role and limitations of different education and training strategies in fostering learning cities and regions;
- an integrated approach to achieving good governance.

Figure 1.4 OECD principles for the learning city and region

Inputs to the learning process

1 Ensure that high-quality and well-resourced educational provision is in place, in which effective individual learning throughout people's lives can be delivered.

2 Co-ordinate carefully the supply of skilled and knowledgeable individuals through education and training and the demand for them within the regional economy, so that the full benefits of individual learning may be reaped through its effects on organisational learning.

3 Establish appropriate framework conditions for the improvement of organisational learning, both within firms and between firms and other organisations in networks of interaction, and demonstrate to firms the benefits of these forms of learning.

4 Facilitate effective organisational learning not simply for a pre-selected set of conventionally defined 'high-tech' sectors, but across all of the industries and sectors within the regional economy that have the potential to develop high levels of innovative capacity.

5 Identify very carefully the extent to which the resources available to the region (existing industries, educational provision, research facilities, positive social capital and so forth) constitute an impediment to economic development ('lock-in') or may usefully contribute in developing innovative strategies for the future.

6 Respond positively to emergent economic and social conditions, especially where this involves the 'unlearning' of inappropriate practices and bodies of knowledge (including policy-makers' own) left over from the regional institutions of previous eras.

Mechanisms of the learning region

7 Pay close attention to mechanisms for co-ordination policies across what have generally been separate departmental responsibilities (for industrial development, R&D, science and technology, education and training and so forth) and between different levels of governance (regional, national and supra-national).

8 Develop strategies to foster appropriate forms of social capital as a key mechanism in promoting more effective organisational learning and innovation.

9 Evaluate continuously the relationship between participation in individual learning, innovation and wider labour market changes, especially with respect to social exclusion of groups with the regional population.

10 Ensure that regional straegies for learning and innovation are accorded legitimacy by the population of the region to be transformed.

Equally recommendations shown in Figure 1.5 support the outputs of both the TELS and OECD studies in correlating social, economic and cultural aspects.

There is evidence here of a vision that learning cities and regions, once created, cannot be static entities, but exhibit continuous dynamism in a world of rapid change. The state of Victoria has also produced a Consultation Resource Guide offering advice to its towns and cities and urging them to become learning cities within a learning region (Best Value Victoria 2002). A community resource service, i.e. 'a government initiative providing a set of guidelines to Community building which aim to improve social, economic and environmental well-being

Figure 1.5 Some recommendations for action in Victoria (Australia)

---

1 Break down the sectoral barriers between schools, VET and higher education, and government and non-government sectors

2 Design initiatives to encourage and extend adult learning and lifelong learning

3 Ensure that publicly funded training providers, in particular, are challenged to provide high quality programmes and services

4 Work with business organisations to provide forums for firms and their personnel to interact

5 Establish and regularly renew across government benchmarks for the relevant resources for economic growth, drawn from the most recent international standards

6 Promote the concept of learning organisations through a variety of means, beginning with a leadership role by government and the public sector

7 Articulate a political future for the region that is inclusive of a diversity of cultures and ideas, and which meets change by promoting discourses on policy options

8 Support networks, especially those that complement and strengthen other networks and organisations, notably at the local government level

9 Facilitate information systems, especially those that provide high degrees of access, such as public libraries, school community centres, adult and community education providers

10 Build a high degree of transparency in government, and in particular in its relationships with the private sector

11 Establish across government data gathering and analysis capacity that can provide ready and accurate advice to relevant areas of government

12 Increase the understanding amongst regional government employees of the impact of global change on employment, work and industries; and in particular amongst education and training personnel

13 Integrate into career guidance materials, programmes and facilities of information about the role of learning and innovation in the future economy and society

---

Source: 'Victoria as a Learning Region' (2002).

for all Victorians, and to develop new partnerships to address inequity and disadvantage', is also available.

Meanwhile, next door in South Australia, similar developments have taken place. Ralph, formerly Executive Director of the South Australia Centre for Education and Development in Lifelong Learning, now unfortunately defunct, initiated a number of projects and leaflets on learning cities and regions. The new dimension he introduced into the learning regions debate underlined the need to celebrate learning openly and visibly in order to overcome the psychological and emotional barriers to learning in some sections of the population. To that end he initiated 'Learning Festivals' in the City of Marion to foster learning, understanding and activity in the region, drawing from similar events in many UK cities and Sapporo, Japan (see *Learning Cities for a Learning Century*). The substance of the Marion Learning Festival and its impact on the Adelaide region is described in greater detail in Chapter 3.

CEDEFOP, vocational training and the learning region

The European CEDEFOP organisation for vocational education and training has also applied itself to the learning region concept in the context of assessing the role of educational institutions in both improving personal motivation to learn among disenfranchised learners and increasing economic performance. Nyhan suggests that the term *'learning'* has a much broader meaning in that it refers to the collective and collaborative learning by all of the different actors in a region – each one learning from each other and each one learning with each other – in planning and implementing social and economic innovations. Thus one major objective of regional management is to develop a means by which educational and other organisations have a common purpose. When this happens societies are able to innovate because they have the capacity for collective learning about how to develop new knowledge and, in particular, the practical 'know-how' type of knowledge. He suggests that collective learning for innovation takes place better in small, more self-contained social units – such as regions, communities or cities – where people have the opportunities to interact and cooperate with each other in an immediate way. The role of educational organisations is to act both as a catalyst for the production of new ideas and as brokers or mediators enabling different bodies to begin to work together, developing the know-how to turn these ideas into reality.

As with the OECD, learning regions for CEDEFOP therefore have a predominantly economic rationale. They work towards creating appropriate infrastructure and conditions so as to gain a comparative advantage, an 'edge' in the competitive environment generated by globalisation. The distinctive feature of a 'learning region' is the cooperation between different actors, i.e. educational bodies, research and development agencies, statutory bodies, enterprises and non-governmental organisations ('civil society'), in working together on how to devise solutions and produce new knowledge to address local needs. Educational institutions in this scenario have a much larger responsibility than the others as organisations for delivering courses. To fulfil their role in a learning region they will need to adopt new strategies and to build new kinds of relationships with the different economic, social and cultural actors in society.

Ideopolis

Such conclusions are encapsulated in the concept of the Ideopolis, defined by Cannon *et al.* as 'A city whose economy is driven by the creative search for, and the application of, new ideas, thinking and knowledge, and which is firmly rooted to the creative transfer of ideas, to opportunities, to innovation, and eventually to production'. Although again concerned principally with physical and economic growth and the development of urban capital, it does not ignore the influence of other factors as growth engines for attracting global business. Echoing the points made at the beginning of this chapter they describe the ideopolis as 'a distinctive mix of physical, economic, social and cultural features'. For them 'the vital buzzword is diversity: diversity of lifestyles and housing, diversity of ambitions, skills and career opportunities, and diversity in social and cultural life. It is whether all these diversities can co-exist in an area that decides whether the society of a city becomes a people-smart, socially responsible and culturally diverse space or a "bad neighbourhood"'.

Florida and Gates (2002) interpret that view in a slightly different way. 'A city's diversity, its level of tolerance for a wide range of people is key to its success in attracting talented people. Diverse inclusive communities that welcome unconventional people – gays, immigrants, artists, and freethinking "bohemians" – are ideal for nurturing the creativity and innovation that characterise the knowledge economy.'

The appeal of becoming a city of ideas is enticing for potential learning cities and regions throughout the world. Cities often identified with the term include San Francisco, Boston, and Seattle in the US, and Barcelona, Edinburgh, Manchester, Paris, Amsterdam, Stockholm and Helsinki in Europe. They are seen as hubs for international business, and centres of indigenous growth and creative, dynamic communities. For the Work Foundation, of which Cannon is Director, the ideal place to attract new investment, i.e. the Ideopolis, comprises the following combination of characteristics:

- High tech manufacturing
- Knowledge services or soft technology
- A university or universities with strong connections to industrial partners
- An airport or major communications node
- Architectural heritage and/or iconic new physical development
- A flourishing service sector, both in symbolic analysis, personal protective services and indigenous SMEs
- Large numbers of highly skilled professionals
- Large numbers of front-line service positions
- An ethos of tolerance, reflected in local attitudes and economic structure
- Significant local political direction and autonomy.

Unlike the conclusions from OECD, CEDEFOP and TELS, there is little here about educational reform, other than an exhortation for universities and industry to work more closely together, but clearly some of these conditions do not create themselves. Even more certainly, present-day educational systems at secondary and tertiary levels will not produce the flexible and adaptable workforce with the skills for modern industry described in Figure 1.6, and with an eager appetite for continuous learning throughout life. Although an Ideopolis is, almost by definition, a learning city or learning region, it will not produce one. Strategies, tools and techniques need to be inserted at the front end by national, regional and local governments to lift the general awareness of populations, to reform curricula in schools and adult education, perhaps to the skills-based curriculum

Figure 1.6 Skills for a learning society (from *Lifelong Learning in Action*)

Self-management skills	• Being determined to fulfil personal potential • Continuously developing personal skills and confidence • Setting and achieving realistic personal targets • Purposeful introspection • Maintaining perspective and a sense of humour
Handling and interpreting information	• Using information technology tools and techniques • Collecting, storing, analysing and combining information • Recognising patterns and links
Applying new knowledge into practice	• Seeing the connection between theory and practice • Transforming knowledge into action
Learning to learn	• Staying open to new knowledge and new learning techniques • Identifying and using sources of knowledge • Relating learning to personal objectives
Questioning, reasoning and critical judgement	• Knowing the difference between good, bad and indifferent • Continually wanting to improve procedures, processes and situations • Never being satisfied with the status quo
Management and communication skills	• Expressing oneself clearly orally and verbally in formal and informal situations • Persuading others • Listening to others • Helping others to help themselves
Thinking skills and creativity	• Using creativity and imagination to solve problems • Thinking 'out of the box' • Anticipating situations and developing forward vision
Adaptability, flexibility and versatility	• Facing change with confidence • Adapting to new situations and tasks • Being ready to change personal direction
Team work	• Sharing information and knowledge • Receiving information and knowledge • Participating in goal-setting • Achieving common goals
Lifelong learning	• Continuously upgrading personal skills and competence • Cherishing the habit of learning • Contributing to the learning of others

Source: Longworth *Lifelong Learning in Action*

described in *Lifelong Learning in Action*, and to address medium and long-term issues of social stability. Those strategies will be addressed in future chapters.

A summary

It remains only to summarise what this chapter has suggested. We can accept that the learning city and region concept is a peculiar mix of the political, economic, social, financial, environmental, cultural, educational and technological, and that to omit any one of these is to render the result the poorer. Its dynamic comes from a whole variety of interlocking initiatives – new productive partnerships, leadership development, proper information and communication methods, celebration, focused surveys and studies, decent educational support structures, continuous improvement strategies for all, motivation and ownership of learning. This is why the indicators contained in the Stakeholder Audits of the INDICATORS project are so comprehensive. They may produce long documents but that is inevitable when the transformation from an education and training to a lifelong learning society involves such a rich mixture of complex factors. The aim is to isolate each factor, to examine it for its implications and then to continuously develop the strategy, initiate and re-initiate the action, energise and re-energise the people and innovate incessantly. As in a learning organisation, the learning region is an endlessly developing entity, re-inventing and re-invigorating itself in a never-ending progression. When learning stops, development stops.

In this chapter we have explored together the development of some of the rationales, ideas, philosophies and projects behind the concept of the 'learning city' and the 'learning region'. It shows a hive of activity taking place around the world in this field, opening up exciting new possibilities for municipalities, regions and their citizens. There are of course many more initiatives for which there is neither the time nor the space, but the case has been partially made, and it remains to flesh out the case studies, tools and techniques and relationships that prove, as the author suggested, that modern cities and regions 'cannot afford not to become learning cities and regions'.

Suggestions for further work from this chapter

1 Write down six key changes that have happened to change the world in which you live in the past 30 years – say how and what effect it has had. Ask ten other people to do the same. Compare your changes with those of the others.

2 Write down six convincing reasons why the creation of a learning city or region is now an important priority. Invite several people, preferably from different departments of the city, to do the same and compare notes.

3 Use Figure 1.3 to estimate the extent to which national priorities have been oriented towards the creation of learning cities (substitute your nation for Europe). Give a mark out of 5 where 5 = fully implemented and 0 = not at all implemented. Give this exercise to several people and compare answers.

4 Imagine that your city or region wishes to become an Ideopolis. Make an inventory of the attractions it offers to potential investors and workers. Also make an inventory of those things that would deter investors. Discuss these with others who have done the same thing. Now make a list of those actions which you believe your city/region managers need to take in order to improve its allure. You may need to read up more on the concept, in which case use your internet search engine.

5 Access LILLIPUT module 1 (www.appui.esc-toulouse.fr) or section 1 of the Longlearn learning materials (www.longlearn.org.uk) and use them to set up and teach training courses or seminars on learning city concepts for key staff in your authority. Use a cascade process so that these key staff take the materials and use them in their own departments.

Chapter 2

Defining, dissecting, deepening

Learning communities, cities, regions and organisations

In Chapter 1 it was suggested that there are many definitions around the concept of learning cities and regions. And so there are. Here are just two of them, adopted by the European Commission's R3L programme from the European Lifelong Learning Initiative and the TELS project, that try to encapsulate the essence of its social, economic, cultural and creative rationale:

> A learning city, town or region goes beyond its statutory duty to provide education and training for those who require it and instead creates a vibrant, participative, culturally aware and economically buoyant human environment through the provision, justification and active promotion of learning opportunities to enhance the potential of all its citizens.

> A learning city, town or region recognises and understands the key role of learning in the development of basic prosperity, social stability and personal fulfilment, and mobilises all its human, physical and financial resources creatively and sensitively to develop the full human potential of all its citizens. It provides both a structural and a mental framework which allows its citizens to understand and react positively to change.

In both of these, words are used to illustrate needed actions. To choose some at random – 'participative' because a learning city encourages its citizens to contribute; 'culturally aware' partly because its people can build upon the past and the present to create the future and partly because a learning population becomes a more creatively appreciative and active one; 'justification' because it will not happen by top-down diktat, but by the consent of its citizens; 'active promotion' because it is not a take it or leave it idea, but one that has to be properly marketed and to bring a high proportion of individuals on board in order to be successful; 'fulfilment' because that is the ultimate aim of learning; 'sensitively' because different people will have different reactions, contributions and perhaps even fears. Learning can indeed instil fear in those who have been scarred by their early learning experiences, or who have been branded failures through lack of success. Our current educational systems are not exactly designed to foster a lifelong love of learning.

Taken in tandem, both definitions suggest, perhaps for the first time in European thinking, that there is the beginning of a movement away from the age of education and training into a much more inclusive and all-encompassing era of lifelong learning, characterised by the notion of the fulfilment of everyone's human potential, or in more exploitative terms, human capital development as a resource for the growth of social capital. But definitions take us only so far. It is what lies behind the words that counts – the actions and activities, the strategies and policies, the marketing and the support, the leadership and the empowerment, the feelings and emotions, the drama and the performance, and ultimately the way in which it makes a real difference to the everyday lives of people. Moreover there is a plethora of associated terms related to the concept, as we will see.

The learning society

One of these is the 'learning society', an all-embracing term often used to describe the concept of a learning commonwealth within a nation or a city. It will be remembered that TELS was an acronym for 'Towards a European Learning Society' implying that the development of learning towns, cities and regions in Europe would help to create that, at first glance, much more amorphous entity. But of course a learning society can be as large or as small a unit, and as vague or as precise a notion, as the user wishes. There is, as one would expect, a wealth of literature surrounding the idea. The European Round Table of Industrialists, representative of Europe's 42 largest industrial companies, makes the point that a learning society would be needed to parallel the information or knowledge society, and indeed act in symbiosis with it. One could not exist without the other. Its forum report *Towards a Learning Society* suggests that not just economies have changed, but also social manners and mores – 'fragmentation of the traditional family group and of family values produces a fundamental reorganisation of cultures, social habits, beliefs and values'. 'Education', it says, 'is about learning, not being taught' and it calls upon industrialists to 'take an active part' in creating the learning society accompanied by supportive action from European Government. Its five definition points for a learning society, also quoted in *Learning Cities for a Learning Century*, are shown in Figure 2.1 together with those added by Longworth and Davies of the European Lifelong Learning Initiative.

Such interest from a powerful industrialist body emphasises the importance now being given to lifelong learning by many sectors of society. Certainly all, except maybe number three, which is outside the capability of a town or city to influence, are desirable attributes which we would try to convert into action within a learning city and region.

However, the academic establishment is far more circumspect in its treatment of the learning society concept. Between 1994 and 1999, the Economic and Social Research Council supported 13 projects within a research programme entitled, 'The Learning Society: Knowledge and Skills for Employment'. Coffield, its co-ordinator, makes little secret of his scepticism about the implementation of a

Figure 2.1 ERT and ELLI principles for a learning society

A learning society would be one in which ...

1   Learning is accepted as a continuing activity throughout life

2   Learners take responsibility for their own progress

3   Assessment confirms progress rather than brands failure

4   Capability, personal and shared values, team-working are recognised equally with the pursuit of knowledge

5   Learning is a partnership between students, parents, teachers, employers and the community, who all work together to improve performance

Five additional principles have been added by the European Lifelong Learning Initiative

6   Everyone accepts some responsibility for the learning of others

7   Men, women, the disabled and minority groups have equal access to learning opportunities

8   Learning is seen as creative, rewarding and enjoyable

9   Learning is outward-looking, mind-opening and promotes tolerance, respect and understanding of other cultures, creeds, races and traditions

10   Learning is frequently celebrated individually, in families, in the community and in the wider world

---

Sources: European Round Table of Industrialists (1996) and European Lifelong Learning Initiative.

concept which he believes is vague and capable of exploitation and, with lifelong learning generally, open to use as a means of social control. He, together with others (Wain, Holford, Jarvis, Griffin), point out the undoubted gap between theory and reality, between promise and performance in the functioning of the learning society as it is proposed in official reports and policy papers.

They are right to reflect on the slow progress of social adjustment to rapid economic and structural change, but perhaps, also, they are too impatient. *Learning Cities for a Learning Century* has suggested that the process of becoming a true learning city can take as long as 50 years to achieve, and that no present-day city is more than 20 per cent of the way along that journey. That is a variable and contestable figure but it represents at least some notion of progress. They are right too in criticising the overly, but predictable, economic and ideological rationale behind government's espousal of the learning society concept. The criticism is based on four objections to the assumption that lifelong learning is seen as an individual responsibility:

•   it turns education from a public good to a private commodity, reducing individuals to their worker/producer/consumer roles, including consumers of educational services;

- by shifting responsibility to the individual it ignores the socially constructed nature of learning;
- it overemphasises the instrumental and vocational purposes of learning to the exclusion of others;
- it rewards primarily those learning activities that can show a visible and quick return.

Some of these are objections to the exploitative interpretation of social and human capital, which portrays people and communities as commodities to be manipulated by companies and governments. Such suppositions about the collective motivation of industry and government must in their turn be carefully examined for academic pedantry, with its origins in a pejorative interpretation of the terminology, and the complexities of transforming concepts from vague hopes to active reality. By contrast, Schuller, another academic now transformed into OECD administrator, suggests that 'social capital is built through relationships based on trust and acceptance of mutual obligations, [and] social values and norms encourage working for the common good' and this provides a more amenable basis for detailed attempts, such as the TELS and INDICATORS projects (see Chapters 1 and 4), to tease out the parameters that would ease the transformation process.

Learning organisations in a learning region

There is yet more in the constellation of epithets associated with lifelong learning and learning cities. The learning organisation is a frequently used term, particularly in industry, to describe the ambience of a community of people with a common aim and the ways of thinking and working to which that gives rise. More often than not, that aim is an economic one and the learning organisation is a company. Jack Horgan, Former Director of the European Commission's Eurotecnet Programme, describes it thus: 'A learning Organisation is one which has a vision of tomorrow, seeing the people who make up the organisation not simply being trained and developed to meet the organisation's ends in a limiting and prescriptive manner, but for a more expanded role.'

Thus, business gain may be the main reason to become a learning organisation but the means to achieve that gain is through the development of the human potential in the workforce – the 'expanded role'. And the way in which that potential is developed entails a different mindset from the traditional way in which companies are run. Gone in many modern organisations is the executive suite, with its perks for senior managers and directors. Gone is a large proportion of middle management, who were seen to be getting in the way of productivity. Hierarchies are flat. Into the vacuum thus created comes the quality culture driven by customer orientation, just-in-time ordering and decision-making at the most appropriate point by the most appropriate people. Line managers consult the workforce and bring them into the decision-making process. Team learning is the new panacea.

This of course engenders an urgent requirement for learning, so that the new decision-makers can make informed judgements and increase their knowledge of production processes, marketing imperatives, quality requirements and international differences. In the true learning organisation everybody from the managing director to the janitor learns, normally with the aid of a formal plan. Some companies use 'Learning Requirements Audits' (see Chapter 7) to measure the learning needs of each individual in the workforce. Mentoring and coaching are frequently used tools for increasing motivation. Managers become educators or 'Learning Counsellors', developing 'Personal Development Files' and advising on 'Personal Learning Plans', and armed with an array of incentives to encourage people to get into the learning habit. John Berkeley, former Education and Careers Manager of the Rover group, says: 'Today managers serve primarily as facilitators, coaches, mentors and motivators empowering the real experts who are the associates (members of the workforce). Managers and employees all work together as a potent force for continuous improvement in both quality and productivity.'

Most major car manufacturers, for example, offer sums of money to entice their employees to take education even if it has nothing to do with the company's activities or purpose as in the Ford Motor Company's EDAP programme. Southee describes it thus:

> EDAP takes a liberal view of the type of learning eligible for support, and this has been crucial when working to encourage non-traditional learners back into learning. Someone who has done little or no formal learning since leaving school needs to be gently encouraged back into learning. This has taken many forms over the years, from learning to swim or play a musical instrument, to taking a sports coaching course to help train a junior football team. Others have chosen to learn skills for home improvements – bricklaying, plastering or some other useful skill. Whatever the activity, the main aim is to increase self confidence and gently ease people back into formal learning in the most enjoyable way possible. But these are just a few examples of the types of courses that people have participated in through EDAP. The range of activities covers the whole adult curriculum, including basic/essential skills, vocational skills, academic qualifications up to graduate level, and a range of personal interest and health and fitness courses. Individuals can apply for as many EDAP courses as they like as long as they do not exceed the £200 annual grant.

This is not Quaker philanthropy as in the days of William Hesketh Lever and the Cadbury family. Rather it is a recognition that fostering the habit of learning has an impact on the bottom line. But a learning organisation need not be a company. Indeed ELLI's ten characteristics, developed by Longworth and Davies in *Lifelong Learning* and shown in Figure 2.2, specify that it can be a company, a professional association, a university, a school, a city, a nation or any group of people, large or small, with a need and a desire to improve performance through

Figure 2.2 ELLI characteristics of a learning organisation

1   A learning organisation can be a company, a professional association, a university, a school, a city, a nation or any group of people, large or small, with a need and a desire to improve performance through learning
2   A learning organisation invests in its own future through the education and training of all its people
3   A learning organisation creates opportunities for, and encourages, all its people in all its functions to fulfil their human potential • as employees, members, professionals or students of the organisation • as ambassadors of the organisation to its customers, clients, audiences and suppliers • as citizens of the wider society in which the organisation exists • as human beings with the need to realise their own capabilities
4   A learning organisation shares its vision of tomorrow with its people and stimulates them to challenge it, to change it and to contribute to it
5   A learning organisation integrates work and learning and inspires all its people to seek quality, excellence and continuous improvement in both
6   A learning organisation mobilises all its human talent by putting the emphasis on 'learning' and planning its education and training activities accordingly
7   A learning organisation empowers *all* its people to broaden their horizons in harmony with their own preferred learning styles
8   A learning organisation applies up to date open and distance delivery technologies appropriately to create broader and more varied learning opportunities
9   A learning organisation responds proactively to the wider needs of the environment and the society in which it operates, and encourages its people to do likewise
10 A learning organisation learns and relearns constantly in order to remain innovative, inventive, invigorating and in business

Source: European Lifelong Learning Initiative.

learning. Certainly city and regional administrations could, and in many cases do, benefit from the quality culture engendered by learning organisations.

Here again we see affinities to the needs of many learning cities. References to aspects such as preferred learning styles, open and distance learning and the environment would appear on any list of indicators for a learning city and region. They have a 'desire to improve performance through learning'. They 'invest in their own future' by so doing. They employ technology and modern aids to learning'. They need to 'learn and relearn constantly in order to remain innovative, inventive, invigorating and in business'.

The learning city and learning organisation principles

The dynamic behind the learning organisation can be applied to several aspects of the learning city and region. Numbers four, seven and nine of the principles in Figure 2.2 suggest that consultation with citizens is a desirable activity and that one of its major responsibilities is to provide them with the mental and intellectual means by which they can participate in decision-making. Not only do local and regional administration departments need to incorporate learning organisation management principles into their management practices, but so also does each stakeholder in, for example, the schools, universities, adult colleges, hospitals, police, small and medium-sized enterprises and others by focussing on the citizen as customer.

There are advantages in this. First, it sets a high quality standard for staff development in council and regional offices and all its institutions. Second, that standard extends to the quality of the information they all provide and the communication methods they all use. Third, it inserts a degree of creativity into the process since people who are now continuous improvers and lifelong learners will need, and want, to demonstrate it. And fourth, it highlights in practical terms the essential inter-connectedness and interdependency of local authority organisations. The application of quality in one depends upon the application of quality standards in the others. A lack of commitment to quality in any part of the system can affect the whole system. Many cities are already committing themselves to continuous improvement programmes for all their staff and some are also using external quality and standards reference points such as 'Investors in People'; in the words of its mission statement, 'a national quality standard which sets a level of good practice for improving an organisation's performance through its people'.

By way of example, the Southampton City Council issues the following principles and aims to its employees:

Principles:

Southampton Education Services, as a learning organisation, values and promotes:

- lifelong learning;
- the learning potential of all its members;
- a person-centred approach to learning;
- equality of opportunity;
- a learning culture which values diversity and flexibility;
- an outward-looking perspective;
- research, innovation, imagination and risk-taking;
- a willingness to listen and respond positively to feedback;
- an interpretation of learning which goes beyond the instrumental.

Aims:

In the way that we work, we shall demonstrate that we are a learning organisation, which means that we shall:

- work in partnership with others to provide mutual support for learning;
- support the learning of individual staff through professional development;
- manage information well, using information technology where appropriate;
- base decisions on reliable evidence;
- be transparent in decision-making;
- be responsive to feedback;
- acknowledge and rectify errors;
- evaluate our decisions and our performance;
- treat with uncertainty routes that are not clear;
- make decisions at the most appropriate level of the organisation;
- value self-esteem;
- use time efficiently;
- manage health, safety and staff welfare;
- work purposefully to achieve our aims.

The European Commission's LILLIPUT project has created a number of useful modules and lessons, described in greater detail in Figure 4.2, to help local and regional authorities to train their staff in all aspects of the learning city and region. One module is devoted to the concepts of the learning organisation. It includes exercises based around Figure 2.3, which breaks down the elements of a learning organisation in the city administration.

Such a breakdown allows city managers to assess the progress towards the implementation of learning organisation principles in each department and to develop continuous improvement programmes for each employee.

Whole cities and regions as learning organisations

There is, too, a more holistic sense in which cities and regions themselves, through a collective of their administration departments, their stakeholders, their businesses, their citizens and their suppliers and customers from inside and outside the city, form a living, vibrant and symbiotic learning organisation, a sort of community 'ghaia'. It is a complex organism to describe, still more to create, but its holistic principles and values lie at the core of the true learning city and learning region. It comprises a combination of all the initiatives described in this book, including those described below:

Figure 2.3 Local/regional authority administration as a learning organisation

Topic	Description
1 Management/ leadership	All employees of the city/region administration are consulted frequently and fully
2 Organisational decision-making	Decisions are made and acted upon at the most appropriate point in each department
3 Rewards	A sophisticated reward system exists and is applied to all people in the city/region administration
4 Organisational management	Non-hierarchical – each employee is a colleague and treated with equal respect
5 Feedback	Feedback on all matters is welcomed, acted upon and always replied to
6 Grievance channels	There is a sophisticated confidential system of airing grievances with no come-back to the complainant
7 Contribution to policy-making	Every city/region employee is encouraged to contribute to policy-making. Suggestions always replied to
8 Continuous improvement	All members of the city/region administration have continuous improvement programmes and an implementation plan
9 Lifelong learning	Everyone in the city/region administration is encouraged and given help to take learning inside and outside of the organisation
10 Learning support	Sophisticated personal support structures (e.g. learning counsellors) exist to ensure that every employee can be directed towards learning relevant to his/her own needs
11 Learning facilities	Has its own in-house learning facilities made available to all
12 Use of learning technologies	Full use made of new learning technologies
13 Displays of learning values	Prominent displays in all departments and building of the value of learning and encouragement to take it
14 Displays of results	Prominent displays of the performance of the organisation
15 Time off for activities	At least 10 per cent of working time can be taken off for learning and community contribution
16 Personal development	Personal skills development courses available for all as and when required
17 Learning targets	Everyone has a personal daily, weekly and monthly learning target

continued…

Figure 2.3 continued

Topic	Description
18 Customer focus	Everyone in the city/region administration has received training on satisfying the customer
19 Quality	Everyone in the organisation has been on a quality improvement course and is constantly trying to improve performance
20 Mission	Everyone has a hand in defining the mission of the department and is given a copy of the mission statement
21 Strategies	Everyone in the city/region administration knows, and acts upon, its strategy for the present and the next five years
22 Celebration	Learning success is celebrated tangibly and frequently and shared with others
23 Information-giving	Every effort is made in many different ways to keep all people up to date with events, news, successes, failures, problems, opportunities
24 Community contribution	Encourages and supports every person to contribute to the community
25 Organisational culture	Every member of the city/region administration feels part of it and is eager to contribute to its success
26 Promoting the learning organisation	Promotes and publicises its achievements as a learning organisation to the community and the wider world
27 Helping others	Actively helps other organisations to become learning organisations
28 Helping minorities	Has special procedures for actively helping all less fortunate people irrespective of creed, culture, language, handicap, race or nationality
29 Citizenship	Sets an example in good and responsible citizenship
30 The environment	Encourages all people to understand and take good care of the city/region environment

Source: LILLIPUT learning materials.

- Cities and regions as learning organisations emphasise the importance of partnerships between institutions and organisations, and their role in helping them to be fruitful and resourceful. There are hundreds of examples. The Woodberry Down/IBM schools-industry project described in *Lifelong Learning in Action*, in which close cooperation between an IBM location in the UK and an inner London school released the ingenuity and creativity of more than a hundred people to help build trust, break down stereotypes and solve problems in 30 joint projects, is one example. Adopt-a-school programmes in the United States are other, more top-down, models in the same field. University–industry–city joint research projects, such as the SKILL Europe project, described in Chapter 5, to discover the learning needs of all employees in small and medium businesses, can transform the perceptions and learning habits of thousands of people, and also provide insights into learning provision in the city and region. Local lifelong learning partnerships comprising representatives of schools, universities, industry, local and regional authorities, adult education and voluntary bodies can, with good leadership, potentially progress beyond talk shops into action generators.

- Cities and regions as learning organisations encourage active citizenship and volunteering and those schemes to activate goodwill, talent, experience and knowledge in communities (see Chapter 7).
- Cities and regions as learning organisations increase the application of the organisational tools and techniques described in Chapters 3 to 6 in the community as a whole as has happened in Blackburn and Dublin (Chapter 7).
- Cities and regions as learning organisations affect the way in which information is communicated and received. They consult as well as dictate; they empower citizens to participate in every aspect of life. People become information and knowledge providers for each other, using all the tools and techniques, including the city website, at their disposal. The example of Dublin described below and in Chapter 7 is particularly enlightening, but many other cities and regions are now working to improve communication to and among individuals.
- Cities and regions as learning organisations enlarge the number of places where learning takes place so that citizens can receive it wherever, whenever and however they want – in learning centres in shopping malls as in Gateshead, in learning shops as in several UK cities, in sports stadia as in 80 of the leading UK stadiums in the learning through sport programme, in every street, as in current plans for Xicheng, one of Beijing's more populous suburbs (see Chapter 8), in church halls, community centres, and ultimately perhaps in restaurants, surgeries, and other places where people gather.
- Cities and regions as learning organisations proactively use charters such as those shown in Chapter 3 to inform all citizens of their rights as learners and the commitments they will make to encourage learning throughout the city and region.
- Cities and regions as learning organisations provide all the support that their citizens will need to engage in learning – learning counsellors, mentors, expert help, facilities, self-learning opportunities, careers assistance. Whoever the person, whatever the need, however the method – all will be catered for.
- Cities and regions as learning organisations will make the linkages between people learning and reduced crime, between people learning and reduced poverty, between people learning and increased prosperity, between people

learning and increased contribution, between people learning and increased self-esteem and social stability. They will recognise the increased human and financial resources that all of these make and adjust their structures accordingly.

By addressing these and other issues cities and regions can become living and breathing learning organisations equipped to face the challenges of change, of globalisation, of social equality and stability and of democratic participation. The modification of Figure 2.3 shown in Figure 2.4 can be used to assess a city/region's progress as a learning organisation.

It will be seen that this presents an entirely different picture. Cities and regions can apply learning organisation principles to their administrative procedures and still be a long way off creating a learning city.

Learning communities

The peculiar nature of the English language often leads to confusion. The word community is an example, sometimes meaning a community of people with a common interest such as a religious order or a uniformed organisation. Or it can be a geographical construct describing a neighbourhood of, or even a whole, city or region. Peter Kearns defines learning communities as 'creative communities in forging partnerships to find new ways to adapt to the challenge of change and to provide learning opportunities throughout life for all'. 'Learning how to adapt to change, and to achieve sustainability in a world of constant change, is as much a challenge for communities as it is for individuals', he says, citing the growing number of learning community and creative community initiatives across Australia, such as Mawson Lakes in South Australia (see Chapter 8), Capricornia in Queensland, Launceston in Tasmania, Hume Global Village (also described in Chapter 8) and a plethora of other learning town initiatives in Victoria.

The South Australian Centre for Lifelong Learning and Development has its own interpretation>

In a community where lifelong learning is a reality, learning will be available for anyone, at anytime and in anyplace. All people in that community will embrace learning and seek to actively develop their knowledge and skills throughout their lives in a way that:

- Achieves economic prosperity and high standards of living and quality of life;
- Enriches peoples' lives and provides a sense of purpose and fulfilment; and
- Achieves a tolerant and caring community.

Figure 2.4 Cities and regions as learning organisations

Topic	Description
1 Management/ leadership	All citizens and institutions are consulted frequently and fully
2 City decision-making	Decisions are made and acted upon at the most appropriate point in the city
3 Rewards	A sophisticated reward system exists and is applied to all
4 Organisational system	Non-hierarchical – each citizen and institution is treated with equal respect
5 Feedback	Feedback on all city matters is welcomed, acted upon and always replied to
6 Grievance channels	There is a sophisticated confidential system of airing grievances with no come-back to the complainant
7 Contribution to policy-making	Every citizen and institution is encouraged to contribute to policy-making. Suggestions always replied to
8 Lifelong learning	Every citizen is encouraged and given help to take up learning
9 Continuous improvement	All citizens who wish have the opportunity to develop continuous improvement programmes and an implementation plan
10 Learning support	Sophisticated personal support structures (e.g. learning counsellors) exist to ensure that every citizen can be directed towards learning relevant to his/her own needs
11 Learning facilities	Accessible learning facilities are made available to all citizens
12 Use of learning technologies	Full use is made of new learning technologies within a wired city
13 Displays of learning values	The value of learning is prominently displayed in places where citizens gather, with encouragement to take it
14 Commitment to learning	Prominent displays of learning charters outlining city's commitment to learning

continued…

Figure 2.4 continued

Topic	Description
15 Active citizenship	Citizens encouraged to give at least 5% of their free time to active citizenship
16 Organisational contribution	City institutions and organisations encouraged to allow employees to contribute at least 5% of time to active citizenship
17 Personal development	Personal skills development courses available for all as and when required
18 Learning targets	Every citizen who wishes knows how to apply a personal daily, weekly and monthly learning target
19 Quality	Every citizen and organisation is aware of quality concepts and is constantly trying to improve performance
20 Mission	Every community has a mission and every citizen has a hand in defining the mission of his/her community and is given a copy of the mission statement
21 Strategies	Every citizen knows, and acts upon, the city's strategy for the present and the next five years

Candy and Copa enlarge on this: 'Furthermore, a learning community will develop a culture of continuous improvement ... it will be a community that is continually expanding its capacity to create its future; it will be a community that responds to needs much faster than other communities. A learning community has the capacity to unite all the diverse providers of learning to meet the aspirations of its citizens. It can create an environment in which business can develop both its people and its potential to compete in the global market.'

Bruce Jilks, an international architect with expertise in the development of learning communities, has his own interpretation of a learning community as having the following key features:

- includes a coherent network of multiple learning settings (learning will not be limited to school buildings);
- dissolves borders among learning settings (learning will be connected to the community);
- provides a sense of place and learner identity and enhances social connectivity among learners;
- adapts quickly to a variety of learning needs and accommodates differences in learners;

- provides for both general and specialised study, and enhances informal learning.

'Every aspect of the community is an integral part of the learning program', says William Ellis, 'Libraries, museums, parks, health clubs, shops, banks, businesses, municipal offices, farms, factories, the streets and the environment provide learning opportunities, facilities and services for self-learners. At the same time, learning becomes a service to the community, as future citizens become involved in the local community.'

Thus, wearing its geographical clothes, the creation of a number of smaller learning communities and neighbourhoods has been included within the strategies adopted by learning cities and regions in such places as Espoo, Birmingham, Edinburgh and Norwich in Europe and within most of the states of Australia.

Smart cities

North America is, as would be expected, a hive of community activity in all parts of the continent. However, where learning is concerned the concentration seems to be more technological. A learning city would be termed a 'smart city', a movement based principally on vastly increasing the amount and use of technology within the city and region. The smart cities network describes itself as 'communities using information technology as a catalyst for transforming life and work to meet the challenge of the new millennium'. Thus, while the objective includes cultural and social concerns, the means to that end is the effective use of technology by large numbers of people and that often leads to the development of a more economic rationale – in the words of the network, 'linking local communities to the global information economy'.

Consider these words by John M. Eger:

> The real effects of the telecommunications revolution are redefining America's cities ... Schools and universities everywhere must find ways of creating new programs that cross the lines between disciplines, cultures and institutions. The world has changed and students and their future employers demand broad-based, interdisciplinary, international curricula that produce a different and more relevant learning experience. The old curricula, bounded by discipline and tradition, constrained by fixed schedules and limited to assigned space, must be re-evaluated and the tools of telecommunications – fiber optics, multimedia, high-resolution video, video conferencing, cable and Internet access – must be employed to provide distance learning and extended access to research, resources and colleagues across the city and across the world. Accordingly, a focus on education and linkages to central libraries and other educational resources within the community are vitally important.

He presents an alluring vision of the uses of technology in all parts of the education system, and echoes many of the mantras of e-learning gurus, not forgetting the changes in approach, methodology and content that will be needed to accommodate that vision. Much of this is true with or without the technology, but there can be little doubt that the technology, applied sensitively and wisely, will help, so long as educators know how to use it properly.

New York is putting its mouth, and its money, into the smart city concept. 'Smart Cities – New York – Electronic Education for the new millennium', headlines its website, 'An initiative to support teaching and learning in cyberspace'. It bases this strategy on three actions:

- all students 4th grade and up, along with educators and administrators, will receive digital devices for use in schools and home;
- The Education Board will provide an ISP portal with an education zone for content, resources and communication in support of educational work throughout New York City;
- these provisions will enable every child, every family and every teacher to interact with education zone resources in school and out.

'As a result', it says, 'the education zone becomes the education program of the city – the sum of the educational resources the city avails to its children, to its educators and to its citizens in general'. And the advantages of the changes in learning methodology are spelt out:

- respecting multiple learning styles;
- cultural diversities become intellectual assets;
- learning by inquiry;
- using explanatory modules on demand;
- assessment through portfolio construction;
- educators will need to put powerful questions to students, thereby activating and directing their curiosity, leading them to exploit their opportunities for access.

Other North American cities, Edmonton, Vancouver and Toronto in Canada, San Francisco, Denver, Pittsburgh and a host of others, have been pursuing similar strategies for several years. Europe's equivalent is the 'e-learning city', and there is, as will be reported in subsequent chapters, a strong movement to emulate the experience of North America. They are huge in promise in every sense of the word, and there is ample research evidence that the effective use of technology does make a difference, even in the large urban distressed areas existing there. Consider an example from Indiana, described by Ray Steele from Ball University and reported in 'Lifelong Learning'.

An example

Ray Steele offers this powerful example of technology at work in a school.

> Westfield High School is a small school in a small town in rural southern Indiana – a school that only a generation ago would have been restricted by its isolation. But today, thanks to the school's investment in technology, its social-studies teachers are able to enrich their instruction on international trade by bringing into their classrooms live coverage of French farmers demonstrating in Strasbourg, or by discussing the subject live with a university teacher in California who is an authority on sanctions and embargoes. Thanks to the largesse of GTE, a local employer, several other technology companies and nearby Ball State University, every classroom and office in the three-school, 919-student school district is equipped with a TV monitor and wired into a fibre-optic network. New technologies have opened up the world to students in the school.
>
> Teachers can use a simple channel changer in their classrooms to display everything from newspaper articles and educational graphics to films and, in the case of Westfield, live programming via satellite. Much of the material is stored in a single technology distribution center serving the entire school system. Teachers in their classrooms electronically check out of the library-like center the material they want to use, and it is 'delivered' to their rooms with the push of a button. The technology also allows Westfield teachers to create their own multimedia materials.
>
> To students nurtured on Nintendo, multimedia materials make learning more fun. To teachers eager to improve the quality of instruction in the nation's classrooms, such technology offers opportunities for less teacher lecturing and more hands-on, interdisciplinary learning of the sort advocated in lifelong learning. Students become active rather than passive learners in many high-tech classrooms. Technology also can help address the problem of teacher quality that plagues so many schools. Westfield Washington District's satellite hook-up will permit its middle school to offer courses in Japanese, Latin, French and Spanish for the first time in 1998. The courses will be taught by certified teachers hired by TIIN Network, a provider of distance-learning programming.

Relevance to learning cities

Steele believes that, if introduced on a large scale, such cutting-edge technology has the potential to cut the finances of public education significantly, a notion which may send shivers of apprehension throughout the teaching profession. He is supported by the USA Congress's Office of Technology Assessment, which reported a general consensus that the appropriate assignment of new technologies within effectively organised schools could make a big difference in academic performance. Learning cities may wish to learn from this. And so may the learning providers themselves. For some educators it is the ultimate horror story, a mechanised world in which computers take over the education of our students. The reality, of course, is different. Technology is there to be used when appropriate, not abused for a majority of the time. While no amount of techno-wizardry is going to do away with the need for high-quality books, teachers and schools, educators are beginning to see technology's potential to transform and improve teaching and learning.

But perhaps the major drawback is that it presents an idealised picture from a relatively rich part of the world. The situation on the ground in most communities, especially large urban depressed areas, is more prosaic. Buying hardware and software, wiring schools with fibre optics and training typewriter-generation teachers to use the new equipment are all expensive. Funding difficulties for technology remain a major concern. And even where the technology has been installed, it has not always created the educational revolution forecasted. Classroom practice remains much the same, embedded in out of date constructs and teaching, rather than learning, based. The newly introduced technologies, which would lead to individualised learning, more intense and faster learning through new cognitive tools, and emphasis on small-group and individual inquiry over lecture and rote exercises, have not yet delivered their promise. Despite some wonderful materials and good classroom or school models, the technologies have been far more commonly appropriated to the ways things are traditionally done.

Putting all our eggs into the technology basket is a monochromic approach to the colourful variety of the true learning city. The jury is still out for example on whether or not it can help with active citizenship strategies, the community outreach and mentoring programmes where personal interaction is preferable, the development of values involving a sense of 'other', the celebration of learning or some of the most intransigent barriers to learning based on loss of self-esteem or early brainwashing, though some researchers claim that it can.

The wired city

Indeed the New York approach appears to miss out on the really exciting education technology scenarios around the concept of the 'wired city'. Consider these words from *Learning Cities for a Learning Century*:

> The wired and cabled city is now a fact on every continent. But that is just the tip of the iceberg. The proliferation of available cyberspace will lead to the possibility of neighbourhood channels offering information to the citizens of a single housing estate or a small ward. Schools will be able to broadcast to people in their catchment area, perhaps transmitting the school play, providing essential information to parents, even involving children who are unable to attend, the opportunity to receive lessons – not at present a popular idea among the young. They will be able to involve parents, advertise the school fete, explain their philosophy.

The possibilities are endless. Special interest groups – environmentalists, ornithologists, sports clubs, religious organisations – might have their own, or a shared, channel to involve people in the care of their own environment or the development of a new hobby. The opportunities for feedback are also in place, making these a two-way communications experience. Watchdog bodies may be needed to avoid abuse, but the technology is there to be used. Add this to the further development of internet facilities, available to every home and the sheer power of technology to change and expand people's perceptions, activities, lifestyles, access to learning soon into the new millennium is obvious. It adds flexibility, versatility and a new mental minefield of potential.

Learning city scenarios of this kind offer a beguiling glimpse of a possible future in which technology takes its place as a stimulator of learning activity rather than a deliverer of didactic subject content, which is where the majority of its applications are today.

Slow cities

By contrast a number of European cities are trying to buck the trend. The 'slow cities' movement initially started in Italy to celebrate the culinary delights of slow food (as opposed to fast food), and has expanded its membership and its philosophy to preserve the quality of life 'as an alternative to global mediocrity'. Nick Swift reports that the movement recognises 'globalisation as a phenomenon that offers great opportunity for exchange and diffusion', but laments that it 'does tend to level out differences and proposes median models which belong to no one and inevitably generates mediocrity'. 'A burgeoning new demand exists for alternative solutions', he says, 'which tend to pursue and disseminate excellence, seen not necessarily as an elite phenomenon, but rather as a cultural, hence universal, fact of life. Cities within the slow cities network will conduct themselves according to a shared code of tangible, verifiable conduct, embracing everything from good eating to the quality of hospitality, services and the urban fabric itself'.

Slow cities members must have a population of less than 50,000, and in return for meeting requirements in furthering the association's aims are entitled to use the name 'Slow City'. But this is not a Luddite association intent on waging war against the evil forces of change. Rather it attempts to preserve cultures and traditions in cities and regions of natural and cultural beauty, for example the Amalfi coast and alpine Cuneo in Italy and Ludlow in England, where heritage is worth preserving both for its own sake and as an economic imperative. Nor is it easy to join, Swift says.

Each town applying for membership is assessed on 55 criteria, grouped into six categories: environmental policy (dealing with pollution, waste and recycling), infrastructure (open space, seating, public conveniences, access), quality of urban fabric (historic buildings, gardens/parks), encouragement of local produce and products (local producers/suppliers of food and crafts, healthy eating; the arts), hospitality and community (facilities for tourists/visitors, community life) and Cittaslow awareness (communications, local involvement).

Dublin: putting it all together

One final word about learning regions in practice. The city of Dublin has undertaken a great deal of work in converting itself into a learning region. Its two-year process of consultation, led by the Dublin City Development Board, produced a wealth of information about the needs and desires of citizens which the city has incorporated into its learning region strategy. In the process it has established linkages through which the concept of the learning region plays a central role in addressing issues concerning institutions, organisations and people. Figure 2.5, adapted from the city's strategy booklet, encapsulates the essence of this.

Clearly Dublin is inspired to increase its commitment to lifelong learning within a learning city strategy for reasons that go well beyond the purely economic. Though the link between learning and economic growth is well-established, so also is the link between learning and social stability, learning and cultural participation, learning and opportunity, learning and sustainability and many others shown in Figure 2.5. In the Dublin Learning City Strategy (2002) document, Peter Finnegan, Director of the Dublin City Development Board, comments:

> Developing this strategy has been like setting out on a voyage of discovery. The waters were uncharted, the crew untested, the ocean was unpredictable and the destination not entirely clear. Commitment will turn the strategy into reality. This commitment is mobilised around a vision. It is a vision that challenges boundaries.

A more precise description of how Dublin has achieved this is given in Chapter 7.

Summary

This chapter has explored some definitions concerning the nature of learning cities and regions, learning societies, learning communities and learning organisations and tried to develop some insights into how they operate. It has suggested that local and regional authorities are not only users and implementers of learning organisation principles, but also that the learning city itself would be a huge learning organisation with a commitment to immerse its administration, its institutions, its organisations and its citizens – that is, its social and human capital

Figure 2.5 The centrality of learning in city development

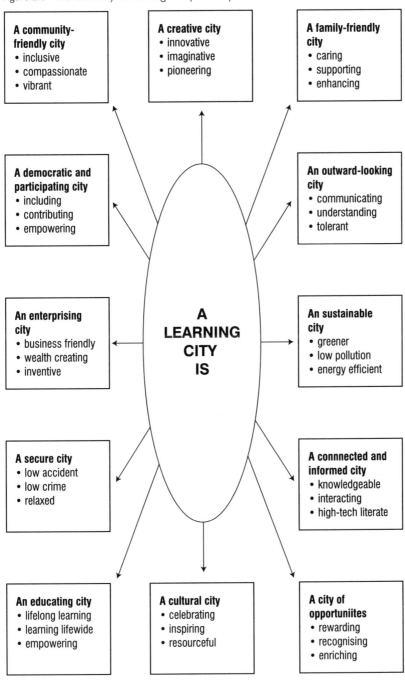

A community-friendly city
- inclusive
- compassionate
- vibrant

A creative city
- innovative
- imaginative
- pioneering

A family-friendly city
- caring
- supporting
- enhancing

A democratic and participating city
- including
- contributing
- empowering

An outward-looking city
- communicating
- understanding
- tolerant

An enterprising city
- business friendly
- wealth creating
- inventive

A LEARNING CITY IS

An sustainable city
- greener
- low pollution
- energy efficient

A secure city
- low accident
- low crime
- relaxed

A connnected and informed city
- knowledgeable
- interacting
- high-tech literate

An educating city
- lifelong learning
- learning lifewide
- empowering

A cultural city
- celebrating
- inspiring
- resourceful

A city of opportuniites
- rewarding
- recognising
- enriching

Source: LILLIPUT learning materials.

– into a collective learning organisation that respects the freedom of individuals and organisations as well as encouraging them to contribute to the growth of the city and region as a learning entity. It has also mentioned how increased learning creates increased resources for reinvestment in learning – a virtuous circle that all cities and regions would love to achieve. At the same time it has warned about the dangers of overplaying this function such that this becomes an exercise in social control.

Suggestions for further work from this chapter

1   Invite a group of people to write down their own definition of a learning city or learning region. Make an inventory of the words they use and compare them to the two definitions at the beginning of this chapter.

2   Use Figure 2.2 to estimate how far the ERT/ELLI principles for a learning society have been incorporated into your city/region's thinking. Give a mark out of 5 for each where 5 = fully implemented and 0 = not at all in the present thinking. Set as a small group exercise within departments and compare the results.

3   Do a similar exercise on Figure 2.3 to measure how far perceptions of your authority's procedures as a learning organisation are similar between people and departments. Use this as a training exercise to bring home the message of continuous improvement.

4   Repeat this for the whole city as a learning organisation with Figure 2.4.

5   Write a sentence about each which explains the difference between a learning city, a learning society, a learning organisation, a learning community, a smart city, a wired city. Compare your answers with others.

6   Access the LILLIPUT materials on learning organisations in modules 1 and 6 (www.appui.esc-toulouse.fr) and/or the Longlearn learning materials in sessions 2.3 and 2.4 (www.longlearn.org.uk) and use them in training courses and seminars. Bring to the attention of all departments.

7   Bring the attention of your learning providers and other organisations such as hospitals and companies to the same materials for their own staff training.

8   If you have not already done so, develop guidelines similar to those used in Southampton but oriented towards your own needs, culture and perceptions for your authority staff.

Chapter 3

Constructing, contracting, commemorating

Tools, techniques, charters and festivals for learning cities and regions

We now come to the first of four important chapters dealing with tools and techniques for learning cities and regions. In order to implement policies that will lead to the realisation of their objectives, budding learning cities and regions will need recourse to the means of creating a culture of learning. Surprisingly, there are many of them – for measuring, monitoring, activating, stimulating, mobilising, developing and consulting cities and citizens and for understanding the fundamental social, economic and educational dynamics – though many are not well-known in municipal circles. Many of them result from recent education projects in Europe, some of which we have already mentioned – TELS, NewTELS, LILLIPUT, R3L, INDICATORS, PALLACE, LILARA and SKILL EUROPE. These projects have designed, developed, tested, refined, modified and made available a variety of implementation aids to assist in the construction of learning cities and regions.

They divide themselves into several categories as in Figure 3.1.

Which tools?

1   *Tools for enhancing self-awareness and encouraging personal learning.* These include Personal Learning Audits and Personal Learning Action Plans, similar to the learning development programmes used in industry but modified for use in city administrations and in the community at large. They can be, and often already are, used in local and regional administrative offices where learning organization principles are in force. But there are also wider uses in cities and regions to help create the conditions within which the incidence of child and adult learning increases throughout the community. Often they need to be supported by a network of learning counsellors and mentors, both amateur and professional, to obtain the best results. Chapter 5 describes them, and how they work, in more detail.

2   *Tools administered by the city and the region for enabling and improving consultation with citizens on learning matters.* These include a whole gamut of approaches ranging from simple information-giving through active consultation to citizen empowerment. The issue of consultation is one that occupies the

Figure 3.1 Tools and techniques for constructing learning cities and regions

1	Tools for enhancing self-awareness and encouraging personal learning
2	Tools administered by the city and the region for enabling and improving consultation with citizens on learning matters
3	Data-gathering and analysis tools on learning attitudes and plans in the population as a whole
4	Tools administered by research organisations or the city/region itself for measuring and monitoring performance and progress in the learning domains of cities and regions
5	Tools for mobilising city and regional stakeholders (schools, adult colleges, universities, police, businesses etc.) in the service of the learning city
6	Learning needs analyses on lifelong learning and learning cities and regions for city professionals and administrators
7	Tools administered by the city for encouraging active citizenship and volunteering
8	Tools (charters) for expressing the city's intention to support its citizens to learn
9	Tools administered by stakeholders in the city (schools, adult colleges, universities, businesses etc.) to improve their own performance as learning organisations in a learning city
10	Mentoring tools linking learners with counsellors and/or experts and/or people who can supervise their learning or behaviour
11	Tools administered by city learning providers to increase financial, physical and human resources available for lifelong learning
12	Tools and techniques by which local and regional authorities can increase or better use financial, physical and human resources
13	Tools using a combination of information, communication and broadcasting technologies to improve knowledge of, and active participation in, lifelong learning activities
14	Tools for celebrating learning in/and learning cities and regions
15	Tools for optimising the physical design of new communities as learning communities
16	Tools for accrediting and ensuring quality in the city/region's operations and relationships with its customers

mind of city managers, since it is perceived to be the basis of a democratic society. The process is far from simple and cities and regions work hard to obtain responses based upon informed perceptions of the collective needs of whole communities on the premise that an involved community is a happier one. Chapter 7 expands on this and gives examples of cities and regions that have implemented consultation processes.

3 *Data-gathering and analysis tools on learning attitudes and plans in the population as a whole.* These include questionnaires or audits of a representative sample of citizens, the results of which would determine the nature and content of learning targets and goals for the future, particularly in the provision of learning for the adult population. Several prototypes exist and are described in Chapter 6.

4 *Tools administered by research organisations or the city/region itself for measuring and monitoring performance and progress in the learning domains of cities and regions.* All cities and regions need a frequent and reliable input of information on which to base their strategies. The Learning Cities Audit Tool created in the TELS project is an excellent example of this, as is the local and regional authority Stakeholder Audit developed in INDICATORS. Both are described more fully in Chapter 4.

5 *Tools for mobilising city and regional stakeholders (schools, adult colleges, universities, police, businesses etc.) in the service of the learning city.* As previous chapters have shown, a city or region is an amalgamation of a wide variety of institutions and organizations, hopefully working together to help create a harmonious environment for citizens. A learning city cannot be created without their consent and their active participation. The 'Stakeholder Audits' developed for schools, universities, adult colleges and businesses in the INDICATORS project provide excellent examples of such tools and these are described in Chapter 6.

6 *Learning needs analyses on lifelong learning and learning cities and regions for city professionals and administrators.* As in the drive for total quality management during the 1990s, quality will not pervade unless every person in the organisation has been immersed into the concept. So it is in the city administration departments of a budding learning city. Each person will need to know at least the basic principles of the learning city and each department will have its own particular orientation towards implementing them. Further, this extends to the city institutions and eventually to all citizens themselves – truly a mammoth task. Luckily help exists. The LILARA project of the European Commission intends to develop such learning needs analyses; the LILLIPUT project, described in Figure 4.2, has completed in 2005 the development of more than 300 hours of downloadable learning materials on most aspects of the learning city and region; and the Longlearn website provides more learning materials related to the concepts in this book.

7 *Tools administered by the city for encouraging active citizenship and volunteering.* To be sure, active citizenship is one of the fastest growing features of lifelong learning. The volunteering movement is alive and well and living in many of those cities that have espoused the cause. But many people still do not know how or where to volunteer, and neither local and regional authorities nor their stakeholders always have the know-how to mobilize all the goodwill that exists in a learning city/region. A volunteering and active citizenship

tool would help local and regional authorities to tap into the talents, skills, knowledge and experience of their citizens and enhance their involvement in the further development of voluntary and community organizations in their own learning city. Chapter 7 describes the way in which some cities have mobilized their citizens to make a real contribution.

8   *Tools (charters) for expressing the city's intention to support its citizens to learn.* As most city and regional administrations will know to their chagrin, decisions made at administration level rarely make their way down to individual citizens. In a learning city, where the consent and involvement of a majority of citizens are essential components, the feel-good factor resulting from a well communicated information and support system is invaluable. Tools at the city's disposal include charters and resolutions outlining its commitment to learning and the rights of citizens as learners, all made publicly available and prominently displayed. Such charters are described in fuller detail later in this chapter.

9   *Tools administered by stakeholders in the city (schools, adult colleges, universities, businesses etc.) to improve their own performance as learning organizations in a learning city.* If the city or region is itself to become a learning organization then the learning providers with a stake in the city's development – schools, universities, adult colleges, community centres, small and large companies, and even the community or voluntary organizations that contribute to the formal and informal learning of citizens – would benefit from a knowledge of how a learning organization works. This is where the 'Stakeholder Audits' mentioned in point 5 can play a part. Chapter 6 enlarges on this theme and provides case studies.

10   *Mentoring tools linking learners with counsellors and/or experts and/or people who can supervise their learning or behaviour.* As in many large companies, mentoring (sometimes called study buddies in the USA) is another mechanism used in some cities for supporting and encouraging learning. Often employed in city learning providers such as schools, adult colleges or universities, or as guides or coaches in industry, mentors and counsellors have a key role to play, particularly with those learners with motivational difficulties. The instruments used can be telementoring tools using email or they can concentrate on person-to-person mentoring. One section of the personal learning audit described in Chapter 5 provides such a tool and this is shown in full there.

11   *Tools administered by city learning providers to increase financial, physical and human resources available for lifelong learning.* Most learning providers reside in communities where there is a wealth of human talents, skills, knowledge, ideas and experience. Equally local shops, companies and individuals are willing to provide financial or resource (e.g. computer donation) support for projects where they can see benefit. Partnerships with industry can also yield mutually profitable results. A few schools for example tap into these resources but, outside the USA, few have full or even part-time people,

paid or voluntary, whose task it is to mine the goodwill and resource of the community. Chapter 7 provides some examples of those who do and a tool for helping with the process.

12   *Tools and techniques by which local and regional authorities can increase or better use financial, physical and human resources.* A few authorities are employing new organizational strategies to maximise the use of their resources, while others have adopted schemes such as 'time dollars' to improve volunteer effort in their area. Such tools and schemes are described in Chapter 7.

13   *Tools using a combination of information, communication and broadcasting technologies to improve knowledge of, and active participation in, lifelong learning activities.* This is by far the most visible of the tools and techniques available to learning cities and regions. They cover a variety of possibilities from the establishment of distance learning infrastructures in colleges and community centres through the development of multimedia software to programmes for increasing citizens' use of the internet. It would include other aspects of the 'wired city' such as computer delivery of learning materials, transmitting of neighbourhood events and receiving satellite broadcasts in learning providers to enhance topicality and effectiveness in learning. Many authorities are now using their own websites to improve communication with their citizens. Chapter 2 has demonstrated why, where and how.

14   *Tools for celebrating learning in/and learning cities and regions.* One example of these, described below in this chapter, is the learning festival. Several cities and regions are now employing learning festivals as a way of stimulating the joy of learning, bringing adults back into the learning fold, obtaining new knowledge about people's learning desires and transmitting the message of the learning city and region. Learning festivals and their advantages are described later in this chapter.

15   *Tools for optimising the physical design of new communities as learning communities.* Such tools are used in countries and regions where a growing population is demanding the installation of learning opportunities for children and adults alike. Learning becomes a marketing tool for the sale of real estate. Chapter 8 looks at some examples of how these are changing the planning mindset.

16   *Tools for accrediting and ensuring quality in the city/region's operations and its relationships with its customers.* External quality assurance tools such as those devised by the International Standards Organisation (ISO) and Investors in People (in the UK) are indicators of an authority's commitment to excellence.

Versions of all of these tools are currently available from various sources, and cities and regions will find them useful in differing situations, environments and circumstances. Indeed many cities and regions are already using many of them to improve their progress and performance. However they may need to be modified to fit particular cultures and procedures. Subsequent chapters describe them in much greater detail.

Learning city and region charters

In many ways charters are also tools. They serve several purposes.

- They describe the commitment of the city to satisfying the many demands made upon it connected with the learning of its citizens, and briefly how those commitments will be honoured.
- They describe the rights of those citizens to the learning they provide.
- They provide a rudimentary set of quality indicators to which local and regional government administrators can be held accountable.
- They can be used to raise general awareness of the characteristics of your locality as a learning city or region.
- They can inspire people to take up learning.
- They can provide the basis for consultation with citizens.
- They can help educate administrators, educators, elected representatives and other city/region leaders, specially if they are involved in drawing them up or approving them.

To work effectively:

- They should be displayed prominently in all public buildings, including offices, schools, museums, libraries, adult education colleges, community centres and also in universities, companies, shopping centres and church halls – anywhere where people gather.
- They should be printed in leaflet form for distribution to homes and organisations.
- They should be comprehensive, covering most aspects of learning in the city.
- Each promise should be backed up by a written statement saying exactly what it means in terms that people can understand, and where and how in the city or region it will be implemented.
- They should contain an address for further information and if possible a name of the person and/or department in the city or region taking ultimate responsibility for their implementation.
- Similarly there should be a local contact point for further information.
- They should have the imprimatur and approval of the city or regional council.
- There should be a high level city or region champion to implement the commitments and a local educational ombudsman to deal with complaints or other issues.
- They should be put together and approved by a wide variety of people in the city including those on the receiving end e.g. students, pupils, job-seekers.

Among the many excellent case studies in Martin Yarnit's (2000) survey of learning communities is the example of Kent Thameside region, which has identified six elements of its learning charter:

- Knowledge transfer – the management and transfer of information to promote competitiveness and an innovative learning culture.
- Family learning – inter-generational learning for all ages.
- Targeting school-leavers – to promote the benefits of learning post-16 and to improve the transition from school to post-school.
- Work-related learning and training – to meet emerging skills needs and to improve links between providers and employers.
- Connectivity – to create an ICT infrastructure and to ensure that skills to benefit from technology are broadly spread.
- Learning organisations – to promote the use of information and learning as a means of continuous improvement in organisations, especially businesses.

Self-evidently the driving force behind the charter is economic development, but this is not always the case. By law in some countries, patients' charters exist for hospitals, and local and regional government organisations have drawn up similar statements of their responsibilities to citizens. Most operate sophisticated complaints procedures where guidelines are breached, though sometimes an irresponsible application of compensation opportunities by legal organisations specialising in liability law prevents administrations from making binding promises up front. Few cities or regions use learning charters at present, but their number is growing fast as the positive aspects of their use as educational documents is seen. The example shown in Figure 3.2 has been updated in the European Commission's LILLIPUT project from a model drawn up by the European Lifelong Learning Initiative for the City of Southampton's conference on learning cities in 1998. Other cities known to be interested in adopting charters of this kind are Espoo in Finland, Marion in South Australia, Dublin in Ireland and Halifax in Canada.

Organisational charters

But of course learning stakeholders such as schools, adult colleges, companies, community centres and universities are becoming increasingly accountable for the quality of education they give. The brochure for Mawson Lakes school, for example, contains the following commitments:

Education for Everyone
'Mawson Lakes, through its education services, lifestyle and culture, is creating a lifelong learning community. Put simply, anyone of any age, who wants to learn can do so, in a variety of locations and at times to suit their needs. In addition, all education services at Mawson Lakes will make the

most of the high quality information and communication technologies already available within the community.

Innovative Education
Our rapidly changing world has placed greater focus on the need for continuous learning. At Mawson Lakes, we have designed our education services to build onto the traditional and successful forms of current educational practice in a new and innovative learning environment.

Learning Partnerships
Students will be supported to reach their highest potential as enterprising members of society. The formation of partnerships will be the key to success. It is essential for parents, students, staff and the wider community to work together sharing in significant decisions, responsibilities and achievements for learning at Mawson Lakes.

A Learner Centred Approach
An integrated approach to teaching and learning covering the key essential learning styles and the eight learning intelligences
- Developing multi-aged learning
- A focus on lifelong learning
- Customised individual learning programmes
- Use of advanced learning technologies
- Flexible delivery methods including traditional, online, distance education and partner arrangements with other providers
- A positive approach to student welfare promoting increased responsibility and self-growth

Students
Students are involved in an exciting range of programmes which foster:
- Leadership
- Citizenship
- Global understanding
- Gifts and talents
- Team work and collaboration
- The enjoyment of lifelong learning
- Participation and commitment
- Physical activity and healthy living

Staff
All staff contribute to the vision of a lifelong learning community through:
- Collaborative team work
- Engaging in quality training and development
- Linking with other learners in our interconnected community

- Working in partnership with families
- Trialling new innovations
- Flexible curriculum delivery
- Creating partnerships with surrounding schools

Parents
Opportunities exist for parents and care-givers to be involved in:
- School governance including the Governing Council and Committees
- Educational programmes and excursions
- Classroom programmes
- Fundraising, sponsorship and working bees
- Social functions

Facilities
Mawson Lakes School has extensive high quality learning facilities including:
- Access to advanced learning technologies
- Infrastructure for multimedia learning technologies
- Shared recreation, sporting, performing and visual arts facilities
- A multimedia interpretive resource centre (Mawson Centre)
- Access to the University of South Australia facilities, e.g. Planetarium, Fauna Centre, etc.
- Technology which links the school, home, community and world
- Access to wetlands, waterways and land-care projects

This is an impressive and visionary list of commitments to its students, staff, parents and the community at large, which could be adopted by learning providers everywhere. It not only spells out its obligations to everyone concerned with the school, it explains how they too can help achieve the ambitious objectives desired by all.

A more prosaic, approach is adopted in Figure 3.2, an alternative generic charter developed by the LILLIPUT project for use or modification by either cities and regions or organisations wherever learning takes place.

An alternative way of presenting a charter is to concentrate on the rights of the learner as in Figure 3.3. This would be more suitable for a learning provider's commitment to students.

Finally the City of St Albert in Canada uses its initials in an innovative way of presenting its charter, shown in Figure 3.4. This may not be a viable option for cities and regions with short or unusual names or with a surfeit of x's, but there is always the possibility of adding another word or two (e.g. charter or city charter) to make up the letters deficit.

Figure 3.2 A charter for learning cities

We recognise the crucial importance of learning as the major driving force for the future prosperity, stability and well-being of our citizens.

We declare that we will invest in lifelong learning within our city by:

1. Developing productive partnerships between all sectors of the city for optimising and sharing resources, and increasing learning opportunities for all

2. Discovering the learning requirements of every citizen for personal growth, career development and family well-being

3. Energising learning providers to supply learning geared to the needs of each learner where, when, how and by whom it is required, lifelong.

4. Stimulating demand for learning through innovative information strategies, promotional events and the effective use of the media

5. Supporting the supply of learning by providing modern learning guidance services and enabling the effective use of new learning technologies

6. Motivating all citizens to contribute their own talents, skills, knowledge and energy for environmental care, community organisations, schools and other people

7. Promoting wealth creation through entrepreneur development and assistance for public and private sector organisations to become learning organisations

8. Activating outward-looking programmes to enable citizens to learn from others in their own, and the global, community

9. Combatting exclusion by creative programmes to involve the excluded in learning and the life of the city

10. Recognising the pleasure of learning through events to celebrate and reward learning achievement in organisations, families and indviduals

On behalf of the city of .... Seal

Signed ....

Title..

Source: *Lifelong Learning in Action*.

Figure 3.3 A learner's charter

Good food, good health and good learning are interdependent parts of the human bio-system

As a citizen you have the right to learn and to develop your own full potential throughout life

Your right to learning exists irrespective of your religion, ethnic background, age, nationality or gender

As a customer for learning your needs take first priority

As far as possible, learning will be provided for you where, when and how you desire it

The value of learning will be actively promoted and encouraged throughout your lifetime

Your individual learning style will be recognised and catered for

Whether or not you have learning difficulties you have the right to receive expert help within sophisticated support and guidance systems at all times

You will have access to modern resources for learning wherever they may be

As far as possible, you will be given ownership of, and control over, your own learning

Whatever learning you choose to do will be treated with respect, recognition and reward

Source: European Policy Report on the Local and Regional Dimension of Lifelong Learning.

Learning festivals as tools to celebrate and increase learning

Cities and regions are increasingly turning to learning festivals as a way of broadcasting the message of learning to a large number of its citizens. The prototype was developed in Japan, whose government from the late 1980s to the late 1990s sponsored and financially supported a different city in each six months to run its own learning festival. The happiness, vibrancy and purposefulness of one such festival in Sapporo in the northern island of Hokkaido is described in Annexe 2 of *Learning Cities for a Learning Century*. There, more than 60,000 adults were brought into the lifelong learning fold as a result. But these events can also be used for a variety of purposes, as the story of the Marion Festival below demonstrates.

The Marion City Lifelong Learning Festival

The week-long Marion City Lifelong Learning Festival has taken place each September since 2002. Marion is one of the larger townships in the Adelaide conglomeration of South Australia, fortunate enough to contain a centre for lifelong learning and a dynamic mayor who makes it her mission to increase learning there. Among the many central activities taking place at the festival were performances by choirs of all ages, brass, pipe and jazz bands, string

Figure 3.4 St Albert learning city charter

The City of St Albert recognises the prime importance of continuous learning by all its citizens for the maintenance of individual employability, social stability and personal development and well-being. It encourages this by:
Stimulating citizens and families to celebrate frequently their own learning success and to contribute to the learning of others **T**ransforming the perceptions of all St Albert organisations and people to recognise the place of continuous learning in a world of rapid change for personal satisfaction, civic progress and new wealth creation **A**uditing the learning needs of all citizens and responding to the demand **L**ocating and mobilising new resources through partnerships and the unlocking of community talents, knowledge and skills **B**roadcasting the message of learning in innovative ways using all available media and means **E**ncouraging all city departments and institutions, not only learning providers, to develop a learner's charter and new strategies and projects to expand lifelong learning throughout their spheres of influence **R**eforming curricula in all learning organisations to develop skills, values, knowledge and understanding in all learners **T**ransferring the ownership of learning to the learner through the modern tools and techniques of lifelong learning including electronic networks, personal learning plans, mentoring programmes and personal targets through learning counsellors
(Stops from time to time to measure, reflect upon and improve the performance of St Albert as a learning city in all its aspects)

Source: Lee (2004).

orchestras, classical, modern and disco dancing groups, drama groups and gymnastic groups. Interactive demonstrations of T'ai Chi, karate, taekwondo, dog-handling and model plane making abounded. Jugglers, stilt-walkers, belly-dancers, clowns, singers and fire-eaters plied their trade. Authors described their works, poets their poetry. Sixty-three taster courses were offered by local learning providers – from elementary Spanish, through cooking and floristry to internet surfing. In order to increase the potential audience, the event was planned around the annual Royal Adelaide Show bringing in people from all over the State and beyond. A one-stop learning shop occupied a central spot claiming to find a course to suit each individual's learning needs.

Seventy stands manned by representatives of all the major formal and informal learning providers, schools, universities, adult colleges, community centres, voluntary and special interest groups, marketed the attractiveness of their learning offerings. Further stands included playgroups, companies, e.g. Mitsubishi, theatre groups, carer associations, medical centres, scholarship groups, fitness centres, sports clubs, churches, state and local services, family groups, army, travel and tourism, and U3A (University of the Third Age).

The whole was designed to showcase the excitement of learning and the benefits it would bring to the people of Adelaide and South Australia. According to Professor Denis Ralph, whose centre organised the first festival, and the local *Advertiser* which produced a special supplement also acting as a programme guide to the festival, 'the week was a great success'. 'Council proud to enrich community', said a message from the Mayor, 'Services to provide for the future' proclaimed the State Governor, and the Education Ministers extolled the pleasures of learning, the opportunities available to citizens and its importance to the prosperity of the city and region. Even the manager of the place where the festival was centred, Westfield shopping centre, a community in its own right with 300 stores and 3,500 workers, proudly described himself as a partner to the festival and a strong supporter of lifelong learning for all.

Special articles about seniors online, second chance learning opportunities, distance learning, careers, and new educational methods were contained within its pages. Messages promoted the new images of old organisations. 'No – this is not typical of libraries' declared the State Library Board, depicting a particularly fusty set of bookshelves with a 'silence please' notice above. 'The libraries of today are fully interactive information centres, they have computers, cafés, galleries, community activities, CDs and DVDs, interactive storytelling sessions. They are meeting places for dynamic learners.' Adult learning providers were at pains to present themselves as modern, fascinating, glamorous, APEL-friendly places offering bridging courses, foundation courses and all the support needed for older students to settle back into learning, as well as courses on topics from organ transplants to understanding *Brave New World*. There was even an article by the Astrology Academy offering to detect 'your learning in the stars', and of course advertisements from learning providers, churches, schools, companies, educational suppliers and centres of all kinds.

The icing on the cake was a lifelong learning survey on the back page with a prize draw for those who completed it. It was almost the sort of learning audit described in Chapter 5 containing questions such as:

How do you prefer to find out information or to develop your skills for your hobbies and projects or at work?

A learning project is when you decide to find out something new, or how to do something better. It includes finding out new things about an existing hobby, trying a new project in your house or in your own time. Have you completed a learning project within the last year or are you working on projects at the moment (home or work)?

What was your most recent project?

If you had the time, money and opportunity to do anything you wanted, what would you really like to learn?

What do you think of the learning opportunities and activities where you live?

How do you think they can be improved?

Which of the following statements about learning do you personally agree with

- The more people learn, the better off Australia will be
- Learning is most important for people who are making a change in their lives
- The only way to get ahead these days is to be learning and training all the time
- The way many people were taught at school has put them off learning for life
- Learning anything is valuable, even if it doesn't lead to a better job
- The only time people need to learn is when they are getting qualifications
- Everyone should invest their own time and effort to keep learning
- Life is too short to waste time learning

And many more, providing administrators and learning organisations with a wealth of information and insight about preferences, attitudes, desires and perceptions. Learning festivals such as this need not be costly – indeed, run properly, they can bring in revenue to the organising body. The spin-off benefits, however, are immense. They include:

- thousands more learners in cities and regions;
- a concomitant reduction in crime and social unrest;
- the opportunity for learning providers and administrations to showcase their achievements and their special characteristics;
- the opportunity for other institutions to present their credentials as learning organisations;
- Aashowcase focus for choirs, bands, dancers, gymnasts and other groups to display their talents and recruit new members;
- an occasion for citizens to see and compare new learning opportunities
- the opportunity to gather up-to-date knowledge on people's learning preferences;
- the presentation of learning as a necessary, beneficial and pleasurable activity within a fun environment;
- potential income to learning providers;
- the opportunity to showcase volunteering and invite active citizenship;
- another step towards the achievement of a learning city and region.

And probably a hundred more.

Denis Ralph, Director of the Lifelong Learning Centre which organised it, says:

> The Marion Learning Festival was a great initiative and drew a terrific positive response from the public, business and government. It played an important role in bringing lifelong learning to the attention of more than 250,000 people each year when they visited the Marion Shopping Centre during the Festival and to over 1.3 million who saw the special feature in the State's newspaper, The Advertiser. The fact that it continued even after the closure of our Centre is testimony to its success.

A learning festival in Mount Isa and its region

Perhaps even more innovative was the festival in Mount Isa in South West Queensland, a mixed mining and agricultural region. The festival was arranged around the schools as 'community hubs' and a visiting train. Allison and Nystrom (2003), who helped organise this under the auspices of the PALLACE project (see Chapter 8), reports:

> The event was launched on 27th August with the arrival of the QUT (Queensland University of Technology) train. This was open to the community all the following day before moving on to other rural communities. The same day a rich array of other activities was launched to provide an atmosphere of learning with all sorts of lifelong learning possibilities for people of all ages, ethnic and educational backgrounds. Aside from the local community, busloads of children 'came to town' to participate in the learning festival … Other activities in the two-week period included Mount Isa day, a showcase for indigenous business, recruitment as part of the national numeracy and literacy week and an IT expo. The response was extraordinary at the various events in specific learning sites. The Flight expo at Sunset State school, for example, drew children from all the schools in the region. But lined up around the school oval were hundreds of mums and dads and locals who wanted to see and participate. 1500 people visited the train on the day it was there, the largest for any one day in any rural and regional centre.

The 'family maths night' (by demand) attracted so many people that it continued after the festival, as did the NASA satellite project with links to schools from the USA and continued help from QUT. But there were many more long-lasting effects in this region, which is badly hit by falling employment and the shift from a rural/industrial base to a knowledge economy. Learning came to this town and its hinterland, and it stayed. The full report can be seen in the PALLACE report to the European Commission.

Suggestions for further work from this chapter

1   Look through the list of tools and techniques in Figure 3.1. Evaluate each one for potential usefulness in your city/region – three stars for must have and use, two stars for very useful and one star for a maybe. Have several people do this and compare results.

2   Put together a working group to develop a charter for your city or region. Include people on the receiving end of learning. Using Figures 3.2 and 3.3 as templates, ask them to produce a draft learning charter for discussion in focus groups, consultation groups, learning providers, companies, community and city councils etc. Distribute it widely to individuals. From the feedback reconstruct the charter for general distribution. Ensure that each clause of the charter has a back-up rationale containing why, how, where and when it will be implemented in the city. Ensure that someone at a high level takes responsibility and drives its implementation throughout the city/ region.

3   Ask each one of the public learning institutions under your control to develop charters in the same way for their organisations. As in quality management, involve as many people as possible in the process. If a school, use the Mawson Lakes example as a template.

4   Establish a working group to organise a learning festival in your city or region. Get it to provide a list of events and advantages for the city and a business case which would make it an economically viable occasion.

Chapter 4

Measuring, monitoring, managing

Tools and techniques for measuring and monitoring learning cities and regions

Budding learning cities and regions will focus on the domains within their cities where activities and strategies will need to be updated and re-cast. This is not, as might be expected, only in the realm of education. As we have discussed in earlier chapters, the lifelong learning revolution is not about isolating new ways of delivering education, but more about taking a new look at all aspects, values and procedures in nations, cities and regions and refashioning them into a more complete and holistic learning image in order to prepare for a future shaped by rapid change – that is re-inventing the city and region and all its institutions, organisations and inhabitants as components of a learning society.

Learning city audits

To do this cities and regions need to separate out the key indicators by which a city, town or region could be measured as a 'learning city, town or region'. One of the first projects to do this was TELS (Towards a European Learning Society). Mention has already been made of this ground-breaking project in Chapter 1, where Figure 1.2 shows the ten domains and 26 sub-domains studied by the TELS researchers between 1998 and 2001.

The TELS project

TELS was proposed at a time when lifelong learning in Europe was on the move. It recognised that, to progress from the vagueness of an educational concept, albeit one which was to lead Europe into the modern age, there had to be a focus for its application into society, and that this focus was the city and the region. At the same time cities and towns in the UK, Sweden and Australia were realising that their future had to be founded on more and better learning by more people. They were giving themselves the title of 'Cities of Learning' or 'Learning Cities'. TELS recognised that any city, town or region could give itself these new labels as a publicity exercise, and change things very little. Labels without substance. Work needed to be done to establish what a 'City of learning' was and how it differed from a city which provides just a little more education and training to those who require it as a part of its statutory function. The intelligence so gained could be used to expand knowledge of the concept to cities, towns and regions throughout Europe and hence stimulate a bottom-up development of a European lifelong learning society.

So, in order to help cities, towns and regions to understand the basic dynamics of lifelong learning at work, TELS isolated the many domains of city life where new learning to meet new challenges is essential, and developed indicators of activity in each of these. Its vision of learning in the city was based partly on the ELLI definition, also used during the European Year of Lifelong Learning in 1996, of a seamless and holistic, cradle to grave activity for each individual in each municipality:

LIFELONG LEARNING is

The development of human potential through a continuously supportive process, which stimulates and empowers individuals

to acquire all the knowledge, values, skills and understanding they will require throughout their lifetimes

and to apply them

with confidence, creativity and enjoyment in all roles, circumstances and environments.

This enlarges the vision of learning from an education and training focus, in which specialised services are provided top-down from a central education department, to a whole of life activity in which many sectors of city life can play a part in learning – formally and informally – and which proactively encourages participation by everyone. The local support services needed to nourish lifelong learning therefore would originate from many city departments and organisations, as they have done in Japan for many years.

The main objective of TELS was to encourage cities, towns and regions to take the new concept on board, and then measure and monitor themselves as 'learning cities, towns or regions' both as an internal exercise to help develop new lifelong learning strategies, and as an external measure of progress against other municipalities. As outlined in Chapter 1, the project developed and implemented a very comprehensive audit of a learning municipality (the Learning Cities Audit Tool).

It also developed a sophisticated interactive web tool (http://tels.euproject.org) initially to receive the data collected for analysis, but also to help people and organisations in learning communities to interact online.

Focus of the TELS study

In order to perfect the audit tool, TELS performed in its first year an in-depth study of 6 European Cities – Drammen (Norway), Edinburgh (Scotland), Espoo (Finland), Gothenburg (Sweden), Limerick (Ireland) and Southampton (England). These cities comprised a cross-section of learning city experience and expertise – Gothenburg, Espoo, Southampton and Edinburgh having already declared themselves as cities of learning at various points in the past, while Limerick and Drammen had rather less experience in this field, in the latter case none at all.

The methodology of using audit tools rather than questionnaires to give, as well as to receive, preliminary information and insights, ensured that the answers obtained would be more informed and meaningful than would be the case in a standard question and answer document. Those cities, for instance, which had not yet put together a strategy for the introduction of lifelong learning concepts would learn about the nature of lifelong learning and its possibilities for the city by completing the exercises in the audit. Further, putting them in one place demonstrates the holistic, interactive nature of a learning city.

As mentioned in Chapter 1, TELS was not a formal research project with well-defined geographical or methodological parameters (the project had neither the authority to require cities to provide data nor the resources to carry out a controlled sample from each country; the data obtained represented the voluntary contribution of those cities and towns motivated to provide it). It did, however, produce many insights into the extent of knowledge about the state of lifelong learning awareness in a variety of European cities, towns and regions. It was also credited with producing a sufficient body of new knowledge to be able to draw both general and particular conclusions about current progress towards the creation of a European learning society and to be able to come to some general conclusions about the next steps. This author, the project manager and author of the European Policy Document, concluded at its completion in 2000,

> At this embryo stage in learning city development there can be no other conclusion than that there is a long way to go. The majority of the munici-palities coming into the project were unaware of the term 'Learning City', much less what it signified. In that respect the project has itself initiated a learning process.

Results

The following summary of the results is distilled from a 370 page report, and is interesting as an indication of learning city awareness in 2000. Although many cities and regions have now moved on, administrators, councillors and others with a concern for learning city and region development can reinforce their knowledge and measure just how far they have travelled from the points made below.

COMMITMENT TO A LEARNING CITY

In the answers to questions in this section, the overall impression was not what cities were doing to become learning cities, but how many European cities were doing very little to promote lifelong learning, and how many were doing nothing at all. There were some excellent examples of cities and regions whose commitment was passionate and well-informed. Newcastle, Espoo, Bournemouth, Brighton, Tampere, Oulu, Alingsas, Worcestershire, Telford and Milton Keynes come to mind. Close behind came those cities making a great effort to catch up – Brno, Gdansk, Livorno, Tapolca, Jyvaskyla, Aalborg, and Nice, to mention some of them. But overall, activity was low.

There was a sense that many cities were, in 2000, at the beginning of a very steep learning curve, and that, before they even set foot upon it, many key people needed much more convincing. On the one hand there was a vague awareness in some cities of the need to embrace lifelong learning concepts, and on the other hand a complete lack of awareness of what those concepts are, and their implications for the way in which education is changing into learning. Even in some of those cities that were already active, there were signs of a belief that a minimum amount of tinkering with existing systems would produce a lifelong learning city. The very few that had appointed a coordinator at a fairly high level, for example, concentrated mainly on the adult community and adopted a top-down, economic rationale, demonstrating a lack of perception that lifelong learning is for everyone, that what happens in schools does (or in many cases does not) provide a motivational basis for continuing learning throughout life, and is learning, rather than teaching, oriented.

LEARNING INFORMATION AND COMMUNICATION STRATEGIES

The indicators used in determining whether cities have taken the message of the learning city on board included:

- what plans it had developed to actively promote lifelong learning;
- how it made use of the media at its disposal to deliver the learning message;
- whether or not its learning providers were using the lifelong learning message as an inducement to potential learners;
- what steps had been taken to discover people's real learning needs;
- how far learning was available wherever, whenever and however people might want it;
- how much it had invested in giving timely and continuous information to citizens about progress of learning in the city; and
- whether or not the idea of taking up learning was made attractive to potential learners.

Although only 19 cities formally called themselves learning cities, 27 cities used special articles or advertisements on lifelong learning in the local press to pass on a learning message – evidence of progress in some cities. However, while there were some excellent examples, particularly in the UK and Finland, the marketing of learning as an *attractive* activity for citizens was not given high importance by most cities. Further, the provision of learning wherever, whenever and however people might want it appeared to be an alien concept in many municipalities. The paradigm of institution-provided education and training to those who require it still dominated, while the economic and social rationales of bringing all citizens back into the learning fold as lifelong learners needed to be more loudly proclaimed in the vast majority of cities. Those 'second year participating' cities leading the way in this area were Walsall, Oulu, Tampere, Ajka, Valmiera, Exeter and St Georghe (Romania), but the overwhelming impression was of a lack of awareness in the majority of European municipalities of the advantages to be gained from a wider promotion of learning – or perhaps that learning is an attractive proposition at all. For many providers it is indeed still a take it or leave it activity with no attempt made to engage learners in the fun of it through interactive and individualised learning methods.

LEARNING PARTNERSHIPS AND THE CREATION OF NEW RESOURCES – WORKING TOGETHER FOR A LEARNING CITY

On the whole, TELS showed evidence that in many cities productive partnerships do exist, but not always in the volume which would make a real difference to the development of a learning city. The two major thrusts of the questions in this section were:

- the ways in which partnerships could help to break down the barriers and stereotypes between the sectors in a city and produce cooperative actions to further lifelong learning development; and
- the ways in which they can be used to generate new resources together with those new innovative uses of resources from the community as a whole.

Successful partnerships require creative thinking and a willingness to unlock the human and physical resources in every community and organisation for the benefit of all. There was however little evidence that, even in the few cities where a partnership programme existed, their full potential as resources and skills generators was being realised. The lack of any activity to relate to the community as a whole in the teacher training sector was particularly disappointing. It was as if they stood aloof and disinterested. Such attitudes from key educational organisations then permeate through the system to affect learning providers as a whole. That is not healthy, and learning cities will need to give priority to the fruitful possibilities of partnerships across all sectors. In particular, the potential benefits to real learning resulting from international cooperation demonstrated a shortage of perception, as did the lack of research and survey expertise in learning city matters. There is a need to create a European network of one or more university departments able to specialise in learning city research and development.

LOCAL LEADERSHIP FOR THE LEARNING CITY

Results from this section identified those places where leadership training is given, although very little of this is specifically directed at lifelong learning or happening within the cadre of a learning city. Some courses may have contained an element of that, but this depended on whether the city had made the leap from an education and training mindset into the lifelong learning paradigm of learner-focused and flexible interactive education for all throughout the city. Considering the affinity between educational issues and lifelong learning it is hardly surprising that 30 cities reported participation in formal training for lifelong learning for teachers and lecturers and that this group was expected to generate the new leaders expected to spread the idea of the learning city. However, this may have missed the point that lifelong learning is not simply an extension of existing educational practice, especially in a learning city. The whole community has to be involved, brought in from the cold, cajoled into contributing to the lifelong learning effort. From the evidence shown here few cities had grasped that challenge as yet. Nevertheless there were encouraging signs that some did appreciate the problem and were taking steps to respond to it. Eighteen cities included leadership development as a key activity. But, while some cities – for example Livorno, Nice, Gdansk and most of the UK cities involved in the sample – had started the process, a vast number of cities had not yet equipped themselves for the challenges ahead by preparing learning leaders on a sufficiently large scale.

INCLUDING THE EXCLUDED – SOCIAL INCLUSION ISSUES RELATED TO LEARNING

Most cities were rightly concerned with social exclusion issues and had identified education as the means to solve them. Only 11 cities, however, had actually conducted formal surveys to identify the barriers to learning. The tearing down of these barriers seemed to be more a question of personal attitudes or individual capacity rather than of organisational intention. On the whole, however, cities were trying to meet their problems and responsibilities in a variety of manners. Forty cities did have special programmes for groups of excluded people in order to get them into learning. The lack seemed to be in practical ways of building self-esteem, self-confidence and self-reliance, which most respondents told the TELS survey were the chief causes of a reluctance to engage in learning activities. Further, the basic tools of lifelong learning for doing this, such as Personal Learning Action Plans, using mentors and guides (and constructing a register of those who would be willing to act as such), and encouraging personal learning requirements audits (as described in Chapter 5), were in very short supply. Most cities had not heard of them, still less implemented them. Of the cities parti-cipating in TELS, Edinburgh, Malmö, Brighton, Exeter, Halmstad, Hillerod, Tampere and Szombathely were particularly attentive to special programmes for excluded groups.

ENVIRONMENT AND CITIZENSHIP

TELS found overall high positive figures in the responses in this section. Cities were, in general, making a good job of informing children about environmental issues and preparing them for a better future. Where they were perhaps more lacking was in the environmental education of adults, and in the *practical* involvement of both groups in tackling, jointly or separately, the key issues. Also, despite much effort, knowledge of European institutions and governance was neither well-known nor well-appreciated. Nor was there a great motivation to learn this. The conclusion is that the search should be for more practical and exciting ways of motivating people to learn about both environment and citizenship, rather than the content and classroom driven methods of the past. Person-to-person contact, as in, for example, schools–retirement home links, provided challenge and purpose in only one city, and environmental networking between educational institutions was almost non-existent. While formal environmental and citizenship issues had evidently grabbed attention in many cities, there was little evidence of an appreciation of this within the concept of the learning city. Nor was there much evidence of a formal recognition of the interdependence of city institutions or the link between education and crime, education and environment, education and most other things in the city.

USING NEW TECHNOLOGIES TO DEVELOP A LEARNING CITY

The TELS results were fairly positive, except in the use of distance learning where there seemed to be insufficient knowledge about the special pedagogical requirements of distance courses. In general, cities looked positively at the use of technology for education as a part of their obligation to embrace the information society. Almost half of the cities had policies aimed at increasing the use of multimedia in education and on the use of email and the internet as educational resources. Moreover the audit answers gave good reason to believe that the figures for use of IT would increase rapidly both within city administrations as well as in education in general in the near future. The use of technology was particularly strong in Finland, which aimed, and still aims, to set itself up as a technological laboratory for Europe, and in the UK and Sweden where local strategies favoured the use of the internet. Other places reporting widespread use included Livorno, Tapolca, Olomouc, Tromso and Tarttu. A few cities were using their bulk-buying power to make computer purchase less expensive in order to increase the technological capacity of their citizens. However, given the declared intention of increasing the use of computers and the internet, there was rather less activity in the more extensive and creative possibilities introduced by the concept of the 'wired city', perhaps because it was not so well understood or publicised.

CREATING WEALTH AND EMPLOYABILITY

From TELS, there was ample evidence that many cities are grasping the nettle of making their citizens ready for a changing world of employment and employability. This is not surprising, since economic success is often regarded as their defining role. A variety of initiatives existed in most cities to increase wealth-producing capacity. However, few of them were connected with learning in the minds of the city fathers. The notion of learning as the driving force behind prosperity had not been fully taken on board. Only nine cities included personal lifelong learning skills in the school curriculum, and more than half the sample had not highlighted the changing world of work as a requirement in courses in any of their establishments. Nor had any cities plans for making all citizens formally aware of the centrality of learning for future prosperity. Only six local authority administrations had introduced continuous improvement programmes for all their employees, a statistic which, if repeated in any medium or large industrial organisation, would quickly put it out of business. Town and company have much to learn, and much to learn from each other. As ever, of course, there were exceptions. Newcastle in the UK for example employed an employability manager, and there were equivalents in places like Malmö in Sweden, Brighton and Nottingham in the UK, Dublin, Ireland and Hillerod, Denmark. Other cities doing good work in this area included Tampere, Brno, Nyköping, Linköping and Enniskillen.

TOOLS FOR LEARNING AND ACTIVE CITIZENSHIP

While some cities were obviously making brave attempts to grapple with the problems of coming to terms with life in the 21st century, TELS demonstrated how far even those forward-looking cities with plans and vision had to go. Personal learning plans, mentoring and learning audits are the tools and techniques for stimulating learning in the new century (see Chapter 5), but very few cities were using them. A total of 47 cities stated that less than 5 per cent of their population had personal learning plans, and one suspects that this may be a high figure. And yet these are tools which, used sensitively with trained learning counsellors, can not only bring back lost learners, but also help plan learning offerings. Very few cities in the sample used mentoring. And yet again, used sensitively, it can help keep at-risk learners on track and stimulate new challenges in thousands of people, as demonstrated in Chapter 5. Teachers are a key group in any learning city. But only nine cities believed that their teachers could, for example, draw up and use personal learning plans for their students. Less than 15 per cent of the teachers in about half the number of cities could make use of learning audits. Only one city revealed that lifelong learning is on the curriculum in in-service teacher training.

And it was believed that three-quarters of teachers did not keep themselves up to date with new knowledge on how people learn. While much of what teachers do they do very well, the question has to be asked in a learning city whether they were doing the right things. They were well able to teach to the requirements of SATs and other tests, but were they able to measure the emotional and spiritual intelligences of their students identified by Goleman (1998), and Zohar and Marshall (1999), and the eight intelligences identified by Gardner (1993)? Much of this calls for mobilising all good forces, within the city administration, among the organisations run by the city and also the elected representatives of the population. Cities such as Aalborg, Esztergom, Pitesti, Hagen and Gdansk reported some activity but the audit as a whole revealed a solid knowledge deficit.

It also calls for a release of the talents, skills, knowledge, experience and creativity in the community for the benefit of all. However, the results of TELS in the field of active citizenship made for more depressing reading. Few of the European cities had formal plans for tapping into the goodwill and experience in the community for volunteering, an activity well developed in, for example, Australia and the United States, and no creative work had been done on the use of innovative schemes such as experiential learning, service learning or time currencies (see Chapter 7).

CELEBRATING LIFELONG AND FAMILY LEARNING

The extent of the cities' commitment to the celebration of learning both at the level of festivals and fetes for all to attend, and at the level of the family, demonstrated some activity. The value of the family as a motor for learning was vastly underestimated in most cities. Despite government interest in preserving the family as a unit in many countries in the face of increasing divorce – the family which learns together stays together – few cities had specific plans for involving families in learning events. Some cities considered fairs and festivals (see Chapter 3) to be more important in the promotion of the city as a learning city. Since this also has an economic rationale, this was understandable, and in increasing awareness among the population of a learning city's significance for them, it could be a valuable exercise. But the overall impression was again not of the activity, but of the lack of it in the majority of respondent cities. Nineteen cities ran festivals aimed specifically at celebrating the learning condition, but another 61 seemed not to bother. This is difficult to comprehend. The experience in Japan is instructive. In the Sapporo Learning Festival, it is estimated that, out of a population of 1,000,000, 60,000 new adult learners were brought into the learning fold. The Japanese government helps to finance two such events, to take place in major cities, per year. Some European cities have held their own festivals – Tampere, Milton Keynes, Telford, Kecskemét, Glasgow, Espoo and Ryde deserve a mention – but the power of the learning festival as a data-gatherer, learning inspirer, information provider and publicity event appears not have been released throughout most of Europe.

TELS knock-on effect

TELS was one of the first European projects to dissect the various domains of the learning city and to examine them in detail from the standpoint of strategies and policies in a goodly number of cities. Its methodology was visionary if not totally acceptable to pure researchers. It produced a significant knock-on effect. It was used as the basis for the development of a *'European Policy Paper on the Local and Regional Dimension of Lifelong Learning'* produced in 2001. It also provided a great deal of conceptual input for the Commission's ground-breaking *'Memorandum on Lifelong Learning'* which subsequently led to the Commission's fuller lifelong learning policy document *Towards the Realisation of a European Area of Learning*. It encouraged many cities that had not previously made a commitment to become a learning city to re-examine their policies, and gave them a starting tool for use in doing so. The subsequent R3L 'Learning Regions' programme funded 17 additional projects in the area of learning cities and regions. TELS also produced a second list of recommendations for learning cities shown in Figure 4.1.

Stakeholder Audits – measuring lifelong learning progress in learning cities and regions

The idea, partly embedded in TELS, that a learning city depends upon its institutions and people to make it work, led to a study of the changes which stakeholders would need to make to their internal and external strategies to become 'learning organisations within a learning society within a learning city/ region', and of course the contribution they would make to the latter. Managed from the University of Stirling in Scotland, the INDICATORS project has put together a series of tools called Stakeholder Audits. These are carefully worded interactive documents containing exercises, quotations from key reports, questions and data that enable respondents to reflect upon and understand the many basic elements of lifelong learning as it affects their organisation, and to convert this new knowledge into actions that will implement its concepts both internally within the organisation (i.e. turn it into a learning organisation) and externally (i.e. work with other organisations to help build a learning society, a learning city or a learning region within the geographical area where the organisation resides). One of those stakeholders, indeed the key stakeholder, is the local or regional authority.

The INDICATORS Stakeholder Audit for local authorities differs from TELS in several ways:

- There are both short and long versions of the audit – the first for those authorities which simply wish to 'taste the flavour' of an audit, and the second to help authorities seriously contemplating moving into learning city/learning region mode to develop new policies and strategies and to

Figure 4.1 TELS recommendations for embryo learning cities

1. Establish a Lifelong Learning Partnership Committee comprising people from all parts of the city, private and public. Be bold – invite unconventional people on to it, e.g. unemployed. Establish the guidelines for this Committee and give it powers to initiate activities, and set targets for each of these activities.

2. Establish a sub-committee for each action area – involve as wide a selection of people as possible in each group. Set targets and goals for people and organisations.

3. Appoint a champion of lifelong learning – one of the most influential figures in the city. Give him/her powers to get things done.

4. Hold a one-day conference of 100 key people and hire key lifelong learning experts to deliver the lifelong learning message to them. Make the conference bi-directional – during the day hold a series of guided brainstorming sessions in several aspects of learning city activity to obtain their commitment and ideas. Give someone the responsibility to collect and act upon these ideas.

5. Create an electronic Learning City Forum to which these people and others can contribute. Give them access to national and international forums (e.g. the TELS Forum) to allow them to communicate with sources of expertise in other cities.

6. Develop a leadership plan. Hire experts to run a series of lifelong learning city workshops, seminars and conferences for people from all parts of city life in order to create as quickly as possible a core of committed workers. Make this a cascade process – require the experts to provide the materials and train participants to train others.

7. Join a learning cities organisation – more than one if there is value-added. Some offer more than others. For example, some networks can offer access to experts for workshops and seminars, electronic forums between professionals and councillors in many cities, the facility to develop good practice case studies, information and knowledge online and a core of like-minded cities with which you can work.

8. Organise a learning festival. Involve many organisations in the city. Link it to other activities taking place, e.g. Adult Learners Week, Achievement Awards etc.

9. Audit the learning needs of all your citizens. Devise a questionnaire; administer it in companies, shopping centres, pubs etc. Use the universities to carry out and analyse the research results.

10. Hold a (bi)-annual conference for organisations in your, and others', city. Set your targets to be reported back at this. Set new targets based on these.

11. Encourage the use of the tools and techniques of lifelong learning in all your educational and business establishments – personal learning plans, mentorship programmes, etc.

12. Develop a city charter outlining the actions you will take to improve learning in the city.

13. Make a database of the talents, skills, knowledge, experience and creative ideas of the citizens and discuss with them how they can contribute to the learning of others.

14. Involve people in designing strategies for, and monitoring, their own environment.

15. Put as many people as possible, from all walks of life, in touch with others in different cities, towns and countries through electronic networks.

16. Develop a strategy and a business plan. Link it to the activities described above. Set realistic goals and objectives.

implement changes over a period of time, which could in some instances involve years.

- It contains a prioritisation system by assigning numerical values (0–4) for each indicator, enabling completed audits to be scored using the cumulative total.
- It is designed to address both regions and cities, whereas TELS concentrated on cities only.
- It is interactive – it embeds feedback opportunities into the audit itself comprising quotations for consideration, statements from official documents and frequent boxes for comment, ideas, and observations.
- It can be used as a learning tool – a progenitor and stimulator of reflection, debate, education and learning among staff.
- It can be used as a policy development tool to provide ideas and detailed input for senior management in stakeholder organisations.
- A prototype tool has been developed on the web, enabling additional supporting material to be accessed through hyperlinks to other sites. An example of a prototype can be found at http://r3l.euproject.net/InquiryID/139/.
- It allows local and regional authorities the opportunity to orchestrate learning city activity in other stakeholders within the city and region.

For local and regional authorities this has important implications and benefits. In the globalised world of the 21st century great and rapid change is inevitable. Those that are flexible and versatile enough to be able to adapt quickly and effectively will be the winners and will best serve the interests of their citizens. But all politicians and professionals in cities and regions will need to be closely involved in the transformation process sensibly and sensitively, and eventually to bring citizens along with them through consultation at all stages and at all levels. This implies a massive educational programme for all staff within cities and regions and the insertion of learning city matters in continuous development schemes. Much will depend on the persuasive strength of the messages reaching people, and the way in which actions for change are initiated. This is why many of the questions in this audit relate to communication, information-giving, decision-making and consultation processes, and citizen involvement. At the same time the audits themselves can be used as stimulators of discussion, debate and learning, perhaps using focus groups to concentrate on one or more aspects of learning city/region development. It should be emphasised that this is a tool and not just a questionnaire – its purpose is to stimulate thinking, debate and action. Inevitably the full version is long. The transition to a learning organisation affects all parts of the administration, often in quite fundamental ways, and the change process it will engender will take months and years. It is not therefore a tool to be used for a week and then discarded.

Parameters of the Stakeholder Audit

The local and regional authorities Stakeholder Audit contains the following topics and questions:

- Current perceptions, commitment and strategies, including content and implementation methods, the authority as a learning organisation, quality and standards, membership of learning city organisations, surveys and studies already completed etc.
- Participation and partnership in the community and the authority's role in making it happen, including measures to encourage active citizenship and volunteering, consultation processes, relations with stakeholders and leadership.
- Accessibility and wider participation in learning from the enabler's viewpoint, including provision of learning where, when and how people want it, support systems in place for all populations, barrier removal etc.
- Communications and information strategies to increase the incidence of learning, including internal information-giving in the administration, methods of communication, key learning messages and their accessibility, wired city etc.
- Staff training and development internally and externally, in-service teacher training and further skills development for the 21st century.
- Use of technology for learning in the city/region, including distance learning availability and strategies, multimedia development and use, internet use locally and with cities and regions nationally and globally etc
- Socio-economic and resource matters, creating wealth, skills surveys, development policies, finance and other initiatives.
- Other topics of value to the development of the learning city – environmental policies, sustainability, celebrating learning etc.

Feedback

Feedback from the local and regional authorities module came from three sources – Italy (Catania), France (Toulouse) and the UK (Stirling). The following is a résumé of the comments made in the trials and included in the project report to the European Commission in 2005.

ITALIAN PERCEPTIONS

In Italy the method used consisted of face-to-face interviews with representatives of authorities at three levels – the commune (departments of environment and technology), the province (professional training department) and the health department of the local hospital (professional training department). In some there were some difficulties of comprehension since lifelong learning is not one of their major concerns, but the process became a valuable learning experience for all.

None of the interviewees were familiar with the expression 'learning region' and nor had the concept been introduced into an administrative or training strategy. Professional training is strictly geared towards obtaining occupational qualifications. However, everyone was in agreement with the guiding principles of lifelong learning contained in the audit whether it is for general or professional training within the authority. All interviewees were convinced that the concept of the learning region is significant for the national and local economies, for encouraging new professional development and for reducing the number of drop-outs from the system. The need is to improve the knowledge of politicians in favour of more adult education as a right, especially with the objective of dealing with social exclusion and the integration of immigrants into the community. They estimated that it would take three to five years to implement a full strategy for sustainable development that would include such perceptions. The issue of quality has not as yet been confronted. All interviewees believed that the Stakeholder Audit is a valuable tool for increasing understanding of lifelong learning and learning region concepts, for promoting reflection, stimulating action, and for ultimately improving the economy and performance of the territory, locally and regionally.

FRENCH PERCEPTIONS

These latter sentiments were echoed in France, where the audit was tested in Toulouse Municipal Authority and the Chamber of Commerce for the midi-Pyrenees. Here the feedback demonstrates an awareness of the concepts of lifelong learning, but a perception that it is similar to (or the same as) the concepts of continued vocational adult training. As in most things French, development policy is determined centrally, so that although there is a willingness to participate in the process of development and implementation of the concept of the learning city, it would need to be imposed from above and take place through the national education programmes and systems for continuing education. The French interviewees considered the audit to be appropriate to their needs in that it takes into account economic and social development trends in a knowledge economy, and also EU construction and the mobility of its citizens. As a tool it promoted reflection on how to develop the educational, social and economic structures of local society in order to meet the goals of lifelong learning, on how to implement a learner-centred educational model, on how individual organisations must operate in the new context of lifelong learning, and about new pedagogical models and methods. Nevertheless all of this must be seen in the specificity of the highly centralised French system where the dynamic for change usually comes from national government.

UK PERCEPTIONS

In Stirling the local authority was extremely helpful in arranging meetings and trials of draft versions. Some debate took place around the definition of the learning region and its physical and conceptual boundaries, but this discussion was helpful in clarifying the aims of the project in relation to local authority stakeholders and in simplifying some of the statements within the tool itself. In Stirling, a short version of the local authority (LA) audit tool was distributed electronically by the council and 18 completed forms were returned. A high level of response was obtained from relevant officers within the council. Some respondents would like to see the word 'lifelong' feature in the definition. To date UK policy on lifelong learning has largely focused on economics, adults and 'employability'. Employability solutions in the UK have mostly involved a shift from passive to active labour market policies (some of which, though not all, put the responsibility solely on the individual to 'grab the ladder of opportunity' offered to them or suffer the consequences of not doing so). Respondents generally considered that, if this wider definition, which seems to suggest that all learning activity undertaken throughout life with the aim of improving knowledge, skills and competence within a personal, civic, social and/or employment-related perspective, is to receive wider attention, then this is to be welcomed.

The responses reveal significant (if unsurprising) differences in perceptions of local authority policy between different departments. This is a legitimate use for the audit tool, in that it can be a basis for self-diagnosis of deficits in organisational learning, communication or knowledge-sharing. Since the realisation of the learning region is dependent on the creation and maintenance of a large number of feedback loops at all levels, the tool provides a way of assessing how well these are functioning at any given point. However, the fact that large numbers of senior officers were not aware of developments is a concern. It demonstrates another use of the Stakeholder Audit, to determine the level of knowledge of employees and therefore to know how to increase this.

A significant number would widen the boundary of the learning region. With few exceptions the points made were positive and show a developing awareness of what the audit is trying to do – i.e. inform, educate and develop creativity and imagination. The responses to the pilot project indicate that ongoing cooperation with local authorities and other stakeholders is itself the essence of what the learning region is about. Partnership between them and informed and up-to-date research and development departments in centres of expertise can only enhance the development of more, and better, learning regions, to the benefit of the region, its organisations and its citizens.

The PASCAL project

While Stakeholder Audits take a scenario-based approach to learning city development and act as learning documents in their own right, there are interesting further developments for city and regional administrators in other projects. Much of the INDICATORS project findings are now extended into the PASCAL Observatory, initiated by OECD, and also comprising partners from Royal Melbourne Institute of Technology, Kent Region of Learning, the

Scottish Executive and the University of Stirling, among others. Observatory PASCAL (www.obs-pascal.com) is a website that will provide registered users with a strategic information tracking and sharing service of the latest global developments in social capital, place management and learning regions in the new economy, including:

- monthly reports on 'hot' topics, prepared by international experts on a commissioned basis;
- access to a clearinghouse providing details of relevant policy, research and programmes associated with successful interventions of various kinds;
- research and consultancy services focused on developing and managing public/private partnerships that are designed to promote community well-being;
- a news clipping service, providing daily insights into news stories relevant to social capital, place management and learning regions, from around the world;
- seminars and conferences on topics of interest to stakeholders.

The online resource brings together policy-makers, researchers and other stakeholders in government agencies and provides updates from around the globe on how public/private partnerships can promote economic and social well-being. It also focuses on partnerships between government agencies, community organisations and private enterprises undertaking social, cultural, economic and environmental initiatives. Evidently, many of the tools and materials discussed in these chapters will be of great use to the project.

Learning needs analyses (on lifelong learning, learning cities and regions concepts, and practice for city professionals and administrators)

As we have intimated earlier, quality will not pervade unless every person in the organisation has been immersed into the concept. So it is in the city adminis-tration departments of a budding learning city. Each person will need to know at least the basic principles of the learning city and each department will have its own particular orientation towards implementing them. Further, this extends to the city institutions and eventually to all citizens themselves – truly a mammoth educational task. Luckily, as we have suggested, help exists. The LILLIPUT project has completed in 2005 the development of more than 300 hours of downloadable learning materials on most aspects of the learning city and region. The 14 modules are listed in Figure 4.2 and can be found at www.appui.esc-toulouse.fr. They, and those on the Longlearn website, can offer the bulk of the learning support needed, each department appointing a person to assess, download and enable in-house seminars and meetings using them. Overall coordination will also need to be provided from a central source.

Figure 4.2 The LILLIPUT modules on learning cities and regions

Module	Title	Description
1	Introductory module – the learning city in action	Basic concepts of the learning city, why it is important in the 21st century, what it is and how it can be implemented.
2	The individual in a learning city/region	Strategies by which individuals can become active learning citizens within a learning city including the use of learning audits and personal learning plans and the concept of active citizenship.
3	Adult learning providers in a learning city/region	Materials to enable adult education colleges to understand the changes that lifelong learning brings to their internal organisation, and their roles and responsibilities in the growth of a learning city externally.
4	Understanding the community in the learning city/region, part 1	Changes that are taking place in the community and the need for more learning in order to cope. Attitudes to learning, and the 'learning community' and how local strengths can foster it through active citizenship and volunteering.
5	Implementing the community in the learning city/region, part 2	The future of communities and how they will evolve. Case studies of evolving learning communities, consultation methods and ways of involving citizens in the development of their own communities. Aspects of social inclusion and innovative ways of resourcing learning.
6	The politics of the learning city	Materials to educate elected representatives and others responsible for creating the learning city and what needs to be done to build it. Case studies and initiatives for celebrating, communicating, marketing, developing leadership and inspiring citizens among others. Charters.
7	The economics of the learning city	Drivers for change, wealth creation, employability, sustainability, technology, socio-economic strategies and the financial and other resource implications and strategies which politicians can adopt to help construct a learning city/region. Includes many case studies.

continued…

Figure 4.2 continued

Module	Title	Description
8 and 9	The workplace in the learning city/region	New workplace paradigms and learning organisations. Quality management, continuous improvement, corporate social responsibility, skills and competencies for a knowledge society, coaching and mentoring and the development of thinking skills in the workforce.
10 and 11	Administration in the learning city	Language learning in local authorities and public administration and law. How public administrations operate within legal frameworks and the importance of language learning together with concepts of how administrators can better learn languages.
12	The school in the learning city/region	Characteristics of a lifelong learning school and its role and responsibility in the construction of a learning city. School management, the role of partnerships, the effective use of technology, continuous improvement for teachers, learning styles, and recent research on how children learn.
13	The family in a learning city/region	Materials to allow an understanding of the importance of family in lifelong learning. Strategies and case studies for promoting family learning, and especially for satisfying the learning needs and demands of the pre-school and third age groups.
14	The university in a learning city/region	The centrality of university roles and responsibilities in the growth of a learning city. Case studies and exercises on the university as a learning organization, widening participation, quality and standards, flexibility and outreach, student and staff development

Summary

This chapter has provided a round-up of some of the tools available to cities and regions for isolating, measuring and monitoring their performance in their journey towards becoming learning cities and regions. Hopefully they, and the results shown, will prove to be useful for those at all stages of the voyage. However, they are not the only tools, as subsequent chapters demonstrate.

Suggestions for further work from this chapter

1 Download the TELS Learning Cities Audit Tool from tels.euproject.org and select the sections you think are appropriate for your city or region. Give them to different departments of the city able to respond or to a student who can do the research on your behalf. Use the results as indicators for further work.

2 Contact the owners of the Stakeholder Audits at Stirling University (www.ioe.stir.ac.uk/Indicators/). Work with it and the university (or your local HE establishment) to improve insights into learning municipalities in department heads and staff.

3 Educate your councillors/elected representatives. Download the Learning Materials for Elected Representatives from module 6 of LILLIPUT (www.appui.esc-toulouse.fr) (in French or English) or from the councillors section of www.longlearn.org.uk.

4 Look at Figure 4.1 in this chapter. Give two marks out of 5 to each action. The first on how relevant it would be to your authority to implement. The second on how far it is has been implemented. 5 = fully relevant/fully implemented; 0 = not relevant/not implemented. Give this exercise to several people in the administration and compare notes.

5 Look up the PASCAL site www.obs-pascal.com. Explore what is relevant to your authority. If you feel that it would be in your authority's interests, join the PASCAL group.

Chapter 5

Equipping, empowering, enriching

Tools and techniques for activating learning in learning cities and regions

We turn now to the tools that assist individual citizens to develop their own potential and ultimately enhance the prospects for cities and regions to create a culture of learning. But before addressing the available tools and techniques, it is important to know just how important individual development is in the growth of a learning city and region, and why and how underachievers, the disaffected and the disadvantaged, can and should be as much a part of the learning society as everyone else. As we have seen in other chapters, the movement towards implementing concepts of lifelong learning in cities and regions is primarily a response to the complexities of change, culture and civilisation in the modern world, and should be acknowledged in those terms. But, however much the conditions for supportive learning are made available, in the end it is the individual citizens who exercise the choice to learn or not to learn. The American journalist and futurologist, Alvin Toffler, is aware of this. In *The Third Wave* (1980) he, not surprisingly, sees education as the answer: 'The responsibility for change lies with us. We must begin with ourselves, teaching ourselves not to close our minds prematurely to the novel, the surprising, the seemingly radical'.

Gordon Dryden, another journalist turned educationist, speculates on the deeper purpose of school education.

> The main aim of the school is to prepare its students to become self-acting, self-learning, self-motivated 'inventors of their own future', global citizens competent and confident to analyse any problem based on the past, the present, the likely alternative options for the future. And, more importantly, to then reinvent an even better future.
>
> (Dryden and Vos 2005)

It is possible that many schools see their mission in these terms, but rarely do teaching methods, allied to centrally imposed examination systems, allow them to achieve anything near the desired results. One of the key ideas behind Naisbitt's ten *Megatrends*, first published as a trend forecasting service for multi-national corporations in the 1980s and repeated for the 1990s and the present decade, was 'The triumph of the individual'. By this he suggested that individuals have finally burst out of the corporate chains that bind them to a particular company, group, city or ideology, and are now in a position to make their own decisions about lifestyles, work styles and leisure styles.

The theme is evident in actions taken by international governmental organisations such as UNESCO. The 1972 Fauré Commission Report, considered by many to be one of the most important educational reform documents of the second half of the 20th century proposed, among many other things:

- the development of human skills and abilities as the primary objective of education at all levels;
- support for situation-specific learning in the context of everyday life and work so that individuals could understand, and be given the competency, creativity and confidence to cope with, the urgent tasks and changes arising throughout a lifetime;
- the creation of the sort of learning society in which independent learning is supported and provides an essential part of the continuum of learning as people move into, and out of, education during their lives.

Individualisation is indeed a most powerful movement, although in recent years the pendulum has begun to swing back towards values of community, society and responsibility for others. Indeed, Fauré's fourth dictum was:

- the involvement of the community in the learning process and the wider social role of education in understanding conflict, violence, peace, the environment and how to reconcile differences.

So here may be the first modern signs that learning is considered to be a holistic process in a holistic world. The curriculum seamlessness proposed in present-day educational philosophies is an attempt to reconcile the personal 'renaissance man' holism, in which self-analysis, self-reflection and self-understanding can be translated into learning action, and into the needs and demands of togetherness in the community at large. Individualist concepts of ownership of learning, the changing role of the teacher from enforcer to co-creator, personal learning styles, multiple intelligences and enhanced access, so central to the lifelong learning ethos, have to be balanced with the environmental, social cohesion and learning community imperatives that require all of us to understand each other and work together in rapidly changing conditions on a fragile planet.

Lifelong learning as wealth creator

Since the millennium the number of words, actions and initiatives for individual lifelong learning has seemed to proliferate geometrically. The European Union Lisbon Summit in March 2000 produced for Europe the strategic target of 'becoming the most competitive economy in the world capable of sustainable growth, with more and better jobs and greater social cohesion through the development and promotion of a comprehensive lifelong learning strategy'. As a result the Commission organised a number of policy input seminars, the results of which were published in a *Memorandum on Lifelong Learning for Active Citizenship in a Europe of Knowledge* in 2001. This seminal document boldly states:

> Lifelong learning is no longer just one aspect of education and training; it must become the guiding principle for provision and participation across the full continuum of learning contexts. The coming decade must see the implementation of this vision. All those living in Europe, without exception, should have equal opportunities to adjust to the demands of social and economic change and to participate actively in the shaping of Europe's future.
>
> (Commission of the EU 2001)

Again there is an emphasis on both individual responsibility and equal opportunity, but this imposes responsibilities on national, local and regional governments to activate this process by:

- *providing lifelong learning opportunities as close to learners as possible*, in their own communities and supported through ICT-based facilities wherever appropriate;
- *building an inclusive society which offers equal opportunities for access to quality learning throughout life to all people*, and in which education and training provision is based first and foremost on the needs and demands of individuals;
- *adjusting the ways in which education and training is provided, and how paid working life is organised, so that people can participate in learning throughout their lives* and can plan for themselves how they combine learning, working and family life;
- *achieving higher overall levels of education and qualification in all sectors*, to ensure high-quality provision of education and training, and at the same time ensuring that people's knowledge and skills match the changing demands of jobs and occupations, workplace organisation and working methods;
- *encouraging and equipping people to participate more actively* once more in all spheres of modern public life, especially in social and political life at all levels of the community, including at European level.

As *Lifelong Learning in Action* has noted: 'The learning field is alive with ideas and ideals, activities and actions, experiences and exemplars, advice and opinions. The emphasis is undoubtedly on the rights of the individual as a learner and the development of individual human potential. But there is an increasing movement to pose the question whether individuals can, by themselves, solve all the problems of learning.'

National and local plans now put an emphasis on the support structures which need to be put in place from the community in order to allow individual learning to flourish. 'Team learning' and 'organisational learning' now complement individual learning in the educational lexicon. The synergy between individual and community is rapidly becoming one of the driving forces of education at local level.

Energising local learning

It is therefore one of the learning city's and region's most important tasks to awaken the desire to learn, by convincing citizens of the benefits of learning not only as a means of creating wealth, stability and prosperity, but also as a means of developing their own potential and making a contribution to the development of the sort of community they would want to live in. Of course the new technologies will be at the leading edge of this, and we have already cited the experience of North America's 'smart cities', but the first priority has to be to win the hearts and minds of people, especially those who, for whatever reason, have adopted an anti-learning stance.

Despite the acres of print devoted to making an unanswerable case for lifelong learning, the essence of the debate still lies largely in the hands of a handful of committed educationists and politicians, who are, almost by definition, remote from the real chalk-face of learning as it is currently delivered. The message that lifelong is 'lifelong' (from cradle to grave), that learning is 'learning' (and learner-focused), and that it is for everybody, has not yet reached the vast majority of people targeted as the new generation of learners, especially those in large urban depressed areas. It has not even reached most of the teachers in the schools. Back in 1973 Martin and Norman identified one of the reasons for this in *The Computerised Society*. In describing the impact of new systems and approaches, they say:

> We need new laws, new education, new attitudes. The danger is that two cultures exist, those that know about, influence and are able to cope with, the implacable growth of computer interference in our lives, and those that ignore its implications. Most sociologists trail along some way behind, not quite knowing what is happening. Behind them come the majority of civil servants, lawyers, politicians, and last of all, teachers, who are preparing people to live in this new age. They belong to the other of the two cultures…

What goes for the application of computer technology to solve problems also, it seems, applies to the application of new concepts in education to do the same.

Few would argue about the need. In the UK Royal Society of Arts (RSA) sponsored project report *Learning Does Pay*, Sir Christopher Ball (1995) made the economic case for increased learning. He made the connection between learning and economic success, much in the same way that the UK Chancellor equates the acquisition of new skills to economic growth, and urged urgent government action to raise the standards, expectations, awareness and self-esteem of children leaving school. He said:

> The link between learning and earning, while apparently obvious, raises a question of causality. It is difficult to prove that education and training create wealth. The position may be analogous to the contribution of exercise and abstention from smoking to health. It took years to prove … but today, that is accepted alike by science and the public. In tomorrow's learning society the assertion that learning pays will also no longer be questioned.

He asserts that we have vastly underestimated the human capacity to learn and should invest more in ensuring that learning opportunities are provided for everyone.

The RSA's Campaign for Learning was born from this message. Supported by government, industry, education and the media, the campaign has set out to radically change the public perception of learning through a variety of high profile initiatives such as family learning week, learning local authorities, learning at work programmes and street surveys. It has made considerable progress in influencing attitudes and practices in education, but it is but one voice in the mad scramble for media attention. There is still a long road to travel before public attitudes to learning improve on a massive scale, a journey that is not eased by some of the antiquated curricula imposed upon schools and colleges. The campaign can be, and is, a valuable partner for local and regional authorities in their efforts to motivate the populace in the UK. Few other countries have an equivalent organisation so separated from government.

As *Lifelong Learning in Action* points out, one of the Campaign for Learning's first projects in 1994 was, with the UK's National Institute of Adult Continuing Education (NIACE), to develop a tool to encourage learning which it called a Personal Learning Action Plan. This is still in use today by public organisations. Its approach is forward-looking and person-centred. It advocates self-analysis before decision. It takes potential learners through a process of reflecting on their own learning successes and what had happened to make them so. It encourages them to consider different learning models – self-learning and classroom learning. It builds up a personal profile of learning needs and finally ends with a learning plan. It has provided a conceptual template for other tools to encourage learning, such as the ones described in fuller detail later in this chapter.

Tools for individual learning

These new perceptions of learning as a sharing, caring and everyday happening carried out by people, rather than as something taking place collectively in an educational institution, demonstrate a worldwide perception of new learning concepts. However, the real practicalities of creating a learning community lie in the tools that are created for the purpose. They are not over-abundant. However, some tools do exist, many, perhaps most, of them developed in industry rather than in the formal education systems, thus illustrating a greater urgency for personal development of the workforce propelled by commercial objectives. As was seen in Chapter 2, personal learning development has become part of the management system in a 'learning organisation'. It is much in vogue in the larger industries, particularly multi-nationals, where the requirement for self-development is often written into the management system.

While companies in general have an economic interest in fostering the habit of learning in their people in order to remain competitive in the marketplace, some go further than others in requiring employees to articulate their personal learning plans. Scottish Power is one of the most advanced. The company makes available a detailed employee 'Personal Development Plan' which, it claims, will help you 'think about your development at work as well as at home' and 'achieve your work and personal objectives. Personal development', it suggests, 'is not a one-off activity, it is a lifelong activity which grows and changes as you grow and change'. Its plan suggests that, 'Taking charge of your own development is all about knowing who you are, where you want to go and how you're going to get there'.

It sounds simple but more often than not, people don't know where to start. As a result personal development is often left to chance and nothing much is achieved. The Scottish Power programme takes the prospective learner through several processes. First, it gives information about the plan and how it can help. Second, it makes a personal exploration into learning needs, learning motivations and learning preferences. Third, it provides a guide to the production of a personal development plan, ending with the completed proposal, which is then incor-porated into the employee's self-management development programme. Interspersed in all of this is information about learning styles and available open learning centres, exhortations to the individual to identify personal strengths and weaknesses, short- and long-term career aspirations and objectives, and advice on how to monitor the plan.

Employees are asked to assess the importance of, among other things, location, job security, salary, contribution, family, status, being challenged, influencing people, working methods, career progression, creativity, quality, freedom from stress, and happiness to their own personal and working life. They follow a progression from guided self-analysis, through self-realisation to the elaboration of a personal learning commitment. The process of developing a plan encourages a personal SWOT (strengths, weaknesses, opportunities, threats) analysis. To complete the process they receive guidance on the many learning methods and opportunities available, and how they can stay committed and fulfilled through mentors and guides who help to overcome problems.

Scottish Power sees the benefit in improved attitudes to work and learning, and ultimately of course on the bottom line. But the use of the tools and tech-niques can also have beneficial effects on the full range of personal development, helping many people to come to terms with the extent of their own enormous potential. They are increasingly used in family and community environments as well as business and industry, as we shall see.

Typical of the support programmes to back up the plans would be:

- Job development programmes – courses, available to all, for improving the competence and performance of employees on the job.
- Skills development courses – courses to improve the personal skills of employees.
- A personal development grant – available annually to each employee to take a course in a subject which need have nothing to do with the business or performance at work. There are no restrictions – it can be pottery, cycle maintenance, learning a new language, playing the guitar, tennis coaching. Its purpose is to stimulate the habit of learning in people.
- Distance learning and Open University – all fees paid by the company for courses undertaken.
- Computer-based learning facilities on every site, including new self-teaching courses available via computer for those people who need, or want, to update their knowledge and competence.
- Coaching, counselling and mentoring – from counsellors who advise on content and learning opportunities to mentors who give friendly advice and monitor progress, to coaches who can help with the learning.
- Liaison with local organisations – encouragement to participate in local life, to become governors of schools or colleges, to offer services to clubs and societies, to organise fetes and festivals and to involve not only themselves but all their family in these.

While much of this may appear to extend beyond the everyday mission of manufacturing and service industries to make a profit, in reality it is an acknowledgement that learning is becoming the most important success factor in achieving this. In contrast with the public education systems, people are being made aware of the need for learning within an environment where learning is neither a threat nor a competition, and where its content and method is decided by the learners themselves. Naturally Scottish Power is not the only company using sophisticated employee development tools and techniques, and such tools need not of course be geared to business needs. Local and regional authorities can learn much from the example set, not only in respect of and for their own employees, but for their own citizens.

The Personal Learning Audit as a tool for stimulating learning

The concepts and tools we have discussed so far have given rise to the development of the Personal Learning Audit. In essence, this is a carefully worded questionnaire that allows people from any background or of any age to gain insights into their attitudes to, and the need for, learning, and to become motivated to improve their personal performance and commitment. One of the more sensitive and comprehensive of these was developed for the European Commission's SKILL EUROPE project in 1996, a project to discover the across-the-board learning needs and demands of all employees in five small enterprises in four countries and to acquaint senior management with the results. It differed from the standard 'training needs analysis' by addressing the needs and demands of *all* employees rather than just those with an obvious need to update their skills for company purposes. The intention was that the company should then cooperate with local information providers to help satisfy these needs in order to help develop a habit of learning that would be beneficial to both employee and company.

Personal Learning Audits are interactive in the sense that, like Stakeholder Audits for organisations, they contain questions, exercises and statements that provoke reflection upon past personal learning experiences, present personal learning issues and future personal learning needs. They are designed to foster awareness, bolster confidence and create the motivation in participants to take the next step and develop a personal learning plan. In order to maintain confidentiality, every participant in SKILL EUROPE approached the audit through a personal interview with an educator from a local learning provider, thus furnishing the provider with new knowledge on learning needs and demands, and hopefully the impetus to satisfy them.

The audit covered all aspects of an individual's learning life including career, family, leisure, and personal development skills. According to this author, who managed the project, 'the replies to the audit uncovered a vast reservoir of neglected learning needs among people who hitherto had not been suspected as having any at all. The very act of asking produced a torrent of responses'.

In the results, two key points would be of interest to employers and providers alike (and by association to managers in cities and regions):

- For as much as 60 per cent of the employees interviewed, this was the first time that they had been asked questions about learning and self-development since leaving school. They reveal a large, latent lifelong learning demand from a wide section of the population. Many, including those whom, it had been assumed, had no learning interest, responded enthusiastically to the audit. This produced a huge increase in opportunities for learning provision which the learning providers could not always satisfy.
- In general, learning providers present what they are prepared to offer in terms of learning – courses, seminars etc. A lifelong learning approach would first find out what people want to learn – for career, for life, for personal development, for leisure activities, for family etc. – and then provide the courses. The project highlighted the responsibility of all learning providers in cities and regions to carry out more research in this area.

Further development of learning audits

The lessons learned from the SKILL EUROPE Learning Audit became the template for a more ambitious attempt in the LILLIPUT project to widen the circle of participation by comparing the processes involved in a learning journey. Here will be described in more detail the processes and content of Personal Learning Audits, since local and regional authorities may find them useful in their own contexts.

The journey begins under the following rationale:

> The 21st century heralds a world in which both workplace demands and family and leisure habits are changing rapidly. The demand for new knowledge, new processes and new education is increasing, while the future remains more difficult than ever to predict. The global economy influences what happens at national level, and this in turn has its effect on local and family life. The new emphasis for everyone, irrespective of age, circumstance or background, is on learning throughout, and for, life, and on the development of individual strategies to cope with both the explosion of information and the changing nature of living and working.

One important part of the process in local and regional authorities will be to train a cadre of learning counsellors and mentors who become the personal keys unlocking the door of learning to people participating in the Personal Learning Audit. Such people would need to be well-trained and relatively numerous. The exact counsellor/participant ratio depends on many factors but a mix of professionals and volunteers might be a feasible way of meeting the demand.

Processes involved – exhortation to travel

The personal learning requirements journey starts with a message to the potential travellers explaining why they might want to travel along the learning highway thus:

A Route Map for Personal Learning – what is it about?

> Learning is the most natural human instinct. And in a rapidly changing world, each one of us needs to remain adaptable, flexible and versatile. Equally, each of us has a personal challenge to recognise our own greater potential and our ability to achieve it. This can only be done through motivating ourselves to learn continuously.
>
> There are new tools and new approaches to make learning more effective, more attractive and more pleasurable – throughout life, whether you are 5 or 95, whether you have found it difficult in the past or not, whether you are rich or poor. None of us is immune from the need, or the desire, to

learn more. We may want to enrich ourselves in our personal lives by developing new skills or improving old ones; we may want to improve our performance, and our salary, at work; we may want to give ourselves and our families a better quality of life.

Whatever our motive, we believe that Lifelong Learning is:

- for *everybody* throughout life, from cradle to grave, from hatch to despatch, from womb to tomb;
- about making *progress* at work, about more enjoyable *leisure* and a better *quality of life* – all those things which encourage you to live up to your own potential;
- about *continuously* acquiring *new* knowledge, skills and understanding;
- about learning in a variety of new ways and focused around *your own needs*, *your own circumstances* and your preferred *ways of learning*.

It's the natural human condition which sometimes many of us lose during formal education. What follows is a route map to help you achieve this – to take stock of your own learning needs and then to take action to do something about them. It is your own personal voyage to self-fulfilment through learning. On the voyage you will be asked many questions to help you understand yourself and your learning requirements and goals. At the end, you will complete an exercise to put these into a realistic perspective so that you can commit to meeting all your objectives confidently and creatively. It is not a process to be rushed. Journeys offering the greatest reward take time to plan.

We involve you in the journey planning all the time – this isn't an exercise in telling you what to think or what to do. We want your opinions, your thoughts, your dreams. Naturally, those with an already high commitment to learning will find it easier to embark on the trip and may wish to take a short cut by by-passing some of the questions. But this route planning process can be used by everyone – employed and unemployed, young and old, qualified and unqualified, rich and poor, those who have been inspired by past experiences of learning and those who have been damaged by it. You are about to become a Lifelong Learner, so that you and each individual in your family and your community will benefit. Your journey starts here.

Thus, as Figure 5.1 intimates, there are two parts to the learning journey, the first a preparation, a 'taking stock', and the second the journey itself. Learning counsellors would first discuss the whole process with the participants and establish a rapport. They would emphasise that the questions invite opinion, self-reflection and comments, and that the intention is not to pass any value judgements on past performance, behaviour or outlook but to increase self-awareness in all participants as to why they are where they are. In other words the primary purpose of the learning audit is as a tool for raising awareness and

Figure 5.1 An individual's lifelong learning journey

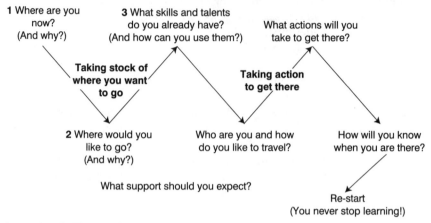

Source: LILLIPUT project materials.

helping people rather than a research exercise to gather data, though much data would indeed be gathered in the process.

Processes involved – the journey's starting point

One further piece of information and encouragement is given before the start of the questioning, as follows:

Where are you now (and why)?

You may have several reasons for setting out on the learning journey – an urge to improve your own personal skills or knowledge, a desire to earn more or to make progress in a career or to change careers, as a contribution to a better family life, or simply because there is deep hunger to learn for the improvement of the self and the mind. Whatever your reasons, whoever or wherever you are, whether or not you have high, low or no qualifications, the voyage to self-improvement is a worthwhile one for everyone.

At the same time your will to learn is influenced by many things – availability of time and opportunity, lack of money – and sometimes what happened in the past. You are where you are often because of the opportunities you have had, or not had, and the way in which you were, or were not, able to take advantage of them. And so, part 1 of this Personal Learning Audit allows you to explore your own personal educational experiences and opinions, and helps you to understand where you are now and to some extent why you are there. It should be completed together with a learning adviser or counsellor.

The questions recognise that your willingness and ability to take further education or training, whether for work or for fun, will be affected by your personal circumstances. It asks for general personal information such as age, nationality and name, as well as particular information about the learning you have (or have not) already done at school, after school, at work and in your leisure time. It also explores your attitudes to all of these at the time and whether or not you participated in out-of-school activities and gained any qualifications.

The purpose of this is to take stock of your past learning life, to obtain a profile of why you are where you are. This list of your existing skills, knowledge, values and experiences, will be invaluable to help prepare the next step on your learning journey – that is to examine where you may want to go to from here in your learning life.

The information will, of course, be kept confidential.

Then follow the first series of questions and exercises in part 1 of the personal learning audit designed to induce self-analysis and to produce the sorts of insights into each individual's own learning past which would develop an interest in present and future learning. There is of course little space to include all the questions and comments in this book, but a small selection is shown as an example in this chapter (see Figures 5.2 and 5.3), and the whole audit is contained in lessons in session 5 of the materials in the Longlearn website and module 2 of the LILLIPUT materials (see notes on websites in Annexe 1). Throughout the process participants are invited to feed back their own opinions and thoughts, and to use the questions as opportunities to help internalise their experiences.

What then follows this in part 1 is an exploration into any kind of formal learning taken after secondary school, whether for employment, sports, leisure or personal skills, so that, by the time the exercises in part 1 have been completed, participants should have some insight into their attitudes towards learning and the reasons for those. Hopefully, some will have decided to overcome any fear of learning they may have had in the past and proceed to the next section. Cities and regions and their stakeholders implementing Personal Learning Audits on

Figure 5.2 Sample feedback question (to be found after every part of the audit)

1.1.13 Do you wish to add any information about yourself which might affect your ability to learn. 1 = yes; 2 = no.
If yes please go ahead here
....
....
....
....
....
....

Figure 5.3 Sample questions from part 1.2

Part 1.2 THE PAST – here we ask some questions about yourself and about the education and training you have (or have not) received in the past.

1.2 YOUR SCHOOL EXPERIENCES *(this refers to your secondary education)*

Here we ask questions about how useful you think the education you received at school was for later life.

1.2.3 Which of these most closely describes your experience of school education?

  1 = I enjoyed most of it and worked hard at my studies   ....
  2 = I enjoyed most of it but didn't work very hard   ....
  3 = I did what I needed to do to satisfy my teachers and parents   ....
  4 = Some good bits but I wasn't really interested in schoolwork   ....
  5 = I dropped out   ....

1.2.4 How much influence do you think your schooldays had on:

  A. Your attitudes to learning   1 = a lot ... 2 = a little ... 3 = Not at all
  B. Your ability to learn throughout life   1 = a lot ... 2 = a little ... 3 = Not at all
  C. Your future career   1 = a lot ... 2 = a little ... 3 = Not at all

---

an organisational or community basis will have the opportunity to include more specific questions and exercises.

Processes involved – prospective destinations

Having dealt with past learning, and armed with new insights into personal motivation, at this point the Personal Learning Audit enters into a new phase – that of determining the participant's present needs. Here there is an augmentation of questions and exercises dealing with self-perceptions and personal preferences, and in the information that is given, as is evidenced both in the lead-up to section 2 and in the questions themselves. This is an essential difference between a research questionnaire and an audit. In the former the intention is to provide data for statistical analysis avoiding the variables which would taint the results. The audit has a different purpose – it has the welfare of the participants at heart, attempting to obtain *informed* answers by providing essential information and setting exercises and tasks.

Thus the prospective learning traveller is now confronted with an introduction explaining why the journey is really necessary.

Where would you like to go (and why)?

Having completed your learning Record to date, you will have become aware of the need to extend your journey into learning. Wherever or whoever you are at this point in your life you have talents, skills, values and knowledge you can use for your own self-improvement. So part 2 of your Personal learning Audit looks at your current location, where you may wish to visit in the future and what you may wish to do when you get there. At the same time it examines some of your opinions about learning and the world in general in order to bring you closer to the reasons why you are making the journey in the first place.

Once again, it takes the form of questions to stimulate your thinking about your present learning requirements. This may be to improve your personal skills for leisure, life and, if you are still working, for the workplace. It might be subject-based, a topic you have always wanted to know about but have never had the time to find out – the human condition is naturally hungry for new knowledge and understanding. It may be to help you take a more active part in the life of the community, to communicate more persuasively or to meditate more effectively.

Whatever your wish, this section also gives you some ideas on how you might want to proceed. Again it is best filled in together with your learning adviser. The purpose of this is to give you a better vision of the need for your journey, and some insights into your own ability to keep to the route you will map out for yourself in future modules.

Then follow the questions and exercises in section 2 of the Personal Learning Audit. Again only a small proportion of the questions and/or exercises is shown (Figure 5.4). Participants are asked why they may wish to take up learning and given a few suggestions to stimulate the mind. They are also asked to give a view about their own personal skills and their present attitudes to learning.

A certain amount of introspection and self-analysis is required. Experience shows that some find this uncomfortable and others difficult or challenging.

Figure 5.4 Sample questions from part 2.1

2.1.3 Which most closely represents your present attitude to learning?

| = I enjoy it and will always be a learner   ....
2 = I learn mostly to make myself more employable   ....
3 = I enjoy it but don't have time to learn continuously   ....
4 = It's necessary to get and keep a job but I don't really enjoy it ....
5 = I'm not interested in formal learning   ....

2.1.6 Have you ever discussed your learning with a 'Learning Counsellor or Adviser'?
(someone who could advise on how to develop your own personal learning
pathways)
| = Yes ... 2 = No...

Most find it useful as would people in cities and regions. Further, new concepts such as the possibility of support in the form of a learning adviser, the notion that learning can be fun and fulfilling and the idea that the participant has responsibility for designing his/her own self-improvement are introduced. There is also considerable scope for the addition of opinions, more personal information and comments. All of this in preparation for a section 3 which looks at the future in a more challenging way.

Processes involved – constantly changing routes, expanding the itinerary

The next sub-section of the Personal Learning Audit tries, through its questions and exercises, to reinforce the message of rapid change in today's society, and the need for learning to cope with it (Figure 5.5). It expands the scope of the journey from a single destination to the possibility of multiple stops.

In this section the debate has widened considerably. The participant is asked to make judgements about the future, responsibilities for learning, learning methodology preferences, family support and opinion, time available and is even given a few ideas about what may be of interest to learn. The participant has been led to an awareness not only of the importance of learning in the modern world but also to the notion that he/she is not alone and that there are support services available – not least in this case the participant's own learning counsellor. At this point the first part of the learning journey is almost complete. The passenger has been led to the ticket office with a reasonable idea that the journey is a worthwhile one. The opportunity is open for a second front in the form of designing a Personal Learning Action Plan and this is described below.

Profiting from Personal Learning Audits – developing Personal Learning Action Plans

We will continue the story of the learning journey later, but first let us examine Personal Learning Action Plans generally as instruments for increasing awareness. We have already mentioned their existence in the context of the UK Campaign for Learning. We have seen too that they are well used within the management systems of many companies. But these are just the tip of a very large and fast-growing iceberg. Personal Learning Action Plans, sometimes called individual learning plans or personal development plans, are now heavily used in the medical profession and in schools and professional teacher development as a way of handing ownership of learning over to the learner. A trawl of the internet will reveal many excellent examples, of which just a few are mentioned here. Naturally, most of them are specifically oriented towards the needs and objectives of the organisations and professions in which they are used, and most do not stray beyond career development, subject specificity or organisational obligation. There is, however, no reason why they cannot be generalised for use with communities in cities.

Figure 5.5 Sample exercise from part 3

3.1 THE (UNKNOWN) FUTURE

At this point you have said what you feel about your self and your present needs for learning. Here we are trying to relate this to the sort of world we may find in the future, and to find out your opinions and perceptions on a range of subjects influencing the way we will live.

3.1 These are statements which have been made in the press as a result of research carried out. Please let us know your opinion about the degree of truth of the statements on a scale from 1–5.

	1 = Strongly agree	2 = Agree	3 = Don't know	4 = Disagree	5 = Strongly disagree
3.1.1 Many skilled and semi-skilled jobs (more than 50%) will disappear in the future as a result of new technology					
3.1.2 The amount of work available is decreasing and there will never be a return to full employment					
3.1.3. Most people will need to have a much wider range of skills to remain employable					
3.1.4 Educational levels will need to increase for a country to remain competitive in the world					
3.1.5 Companies are becoming more international, more mergers with foreign companies are likely and language skills will be highly valued					
3.1.6 In the future people will have several jobs in a lifetime and will need to be trained and retrained many times					
3.1.7 The more people give to the learning of others the more they will learn themselves					
3.1.8 Everyone can be a learner. For me, learning is the key to achieving my full potential					

Personal Learning Action Plans for adults

Whereas the Personal Learning Audit encourages participants to enter into considerable personal analysis of their learning history, their needs, their opinions, their desires and their contribution, the Personal Learning Action Plan tries to encourage further learning participation in the future, culminating in the construction of a plan to identify mentors, and assess available time, locations, learning methods, styles, priorities and topics. Further, a good plan would cover a multitude of life activities including personal development, leisure-time, family, the community and work. The process of analysis is meant to activate the (re)commitment to learning and the achievement of the plan is a confirmation of the intention to honour that commitment.

Processes involved – preparing for the journey

As an example, in the LILLIPUT materials, the participants continued their journey into the development of Personal Learning Action Plans. Section 5 entails some revision of the lessons already learned and a more purposeful articulation and analysis of desires and experiences. Cities and regions and their stakeholders will find these useful in motivating people of all ages and enabling them to be more precise about their intentions, the support they would need and the results they would expect. The introduction starts thus:

What else do you need to learn in order to get where you want to go?

At this point you enter the action phase of preparing your learning journey. By the end of the process you will have a complete (but reasonably flexible) itinerary which maps out where, when, how and with whom you will travel with personal targets and achievement records. The Personal Learning Action Plan is a practical tool to help you realise your dreams and achieve your ambitions in life, in leisure and in work. It is best worked out with the help of a Learning Adviser.

But first you may need to understand why you are making this journey, and a little more about yourself and your own motivation for embarking upon it. If you are not habitually an introspective person who examines inner motivations this can often be a quite difficult process. But the rewards of such understanding will make it more likely that you both set out a realistic plan and that you complete it successfully.

In the stock-taking process, you have recorded your past journeys – your experiences and present requirements for learning. It helped you, and your learning adviser if you have one, understand the experiences that have shaped your attitudes to learning and your learning values. At the same time it hopefully helped you to realise the part that learning plays in allowing you to cope with the world as it is, whether you do it formally in a classroom or informally as a part of your everyday life. Truly lifelong learning is now a reality, and an essential, for many people. In this section you use these to re-examine yourself and your values, and to modify these to cope with a world of constant change.

It is the first part of your development of a Personal Learning Action Plan. In later parts you will:

- assemble your learning needs and desires – put your personal learning goals into words,
- make your own Personal Learning Action Plan,
- explore ideas to make sure it works.

Again this is not a process to be hurried. How long it takes is up to you. You may decide to let the exercises you go through incubate in your mind or choose to deal with them straight away. You might want to re-write what you have written several times. You may complete part 1 in a day or so, and you may want to take longer with the other parts so that you get it right. You can share your thoughts with other members of your family or use the help of someone who can stimulate you to keep up with your schedule (a mentor or Learning Adviser) – perhaps even several people. There are no prizes for finishing your plan quickly. But there are great prizes for making a commitment to carry it out, this year, next year, in the years to come.

As you work through the processes you will be encouraged to reflect upon your life, your work and your leisure, and consider any changes you may like to make. But remember, your Personal Learning Action Plan is not written in concrete to be slavishly adhered to. Other learning pathways – side-trips – may intervene or you may change your mind. But the only person who can make the decision to learn in the first place is yourself. And that is why you need to spend so much time examining your own motivations – and take into account potential obstacles as well as potential rewards.

The Learning voyage can, and should, be enjoyable. So enjoy it! It can certainly be profitable, whether you measure that in terms of finance or in the enrichment of you personally. It doesn't matter what age you are. Learning is something we can all do and something we can all benefit from. Module 5 comprises the first part of your Personal Learning Action Plan. Have a look at it and make your own assessment about yourself and your willingness to continue.

The Personal Learning Action Plan is thus duly activated. However, the (lack of) availability of space precludes attempts in this book to dissect the Personal Learning Action Plan in the same detail that it has portrayed the Personal Learning Audits. Most cities and regions are familiar with them and they and their stakeholders can obtain copies of existing plans from many sources, and materials for counsellors, educators and others exist on both the LILLIPUT and Longlearn websites. In brief the plan covers all aspects of an individual's life (and not just work and career) and the journey to plan development covers the following stages:

- What do I have to do? A few exercises to put the individual at ease, build up confidence and to recommend the use of a learning counsellor. For example, it recommends the taking of considerable time to get it right.
- Why do I need a Personal Learning Plan? Exercises to convince individuals of the advantages of having a Personal Learning Action Plan.
- Starting the process: a few exercises to encourage self-reflection on why the individual is making this journey.
- Recalling learning experiences: a few exercises to review an individual's past positive learning experiences.
- What makes me learn? Exercises to help the individual to understand how to get him/herself motivated to learn. Why he/she starts, keeps going and the influences of others.
- Actions to move forward: exercises to consolidate the decision to formulate a Personal Learning Action Plan.
- Making a personal learning record: exercises to make an inventory of the individual's existing skills, talents, knowledge and experiences in working and non-working life.
- Making a list of future learning desires: using a personal learning planner (see Figure 5.6) to list all the things the individual might want to learn in the next year and beyond.
- Analysing the list with others: friends, family, mentors, counsellors, educators etc. to make sure that the individual can achieve everything he/she wants to achieve. Including assigning priorities, identifying mentors, counsellors, coaches or guides, identifying type of learning (personal skill, knowledge, information etc.), length of time required, learning method (formal course, classroom, home study, computer-based, study group or circle, private tuition etc.), qualification (or not), cost, time available, obtaining further information, place and travel.
- Refining the list into a personal learning action plan: recording the results of the analysis.
- Keeping to the plan: assigning checkpoints and reviewing, contacting mentors and counsellors, informing family, friends etc., signing up for courses, modifying if necessary.

The final exercise would be the completion of the plan itself and this would include for each item:

- This is what I intend to start to learn/experience or join in the next 6 months.
- This is where I intend to learn it (home, work, college etc.).
- This is the person(s) who will help me.
- I plan to start it (date).

Figure 5.6 A personal learning planner

Category	Learning topic/skill	Type	Priority	Time?	How	Q?	M?	Where?
To enhance your family life	1.							
	2.							
	3.							
	4.							
	5.							
To improve work performance and prospects	1.							
	2.							
	3.							
	4.							
	5.							
For your own personal development	1.							
	2.							
	3.							
	4.							
	5.							

continued....

Figure 5.6 continued

Category	Learning topic/skill	Type	Priority	Time?	How	Q?	M?	Where?
To improve your sport, hobby or leisure interest	1.							
	2.							
	3.							
	4.							
	5.							
To help contribute to the community	1.							
	2.							
	3.							
	4.							
	5.							
To develop new experiences, attitudes and values	1.							
	2.							
	3.							
	4.							
	5.							

- I plan to finish it (date).
- I will devote x hours per week to this.
- I know I will have succeeded when (e.g. qualification type, job, feeling etc.).

Feedback

The Personal Learning Audit and Personal Learning Action Plan tools described above are more than instruments to stimulate individual learning, they are processes to be gone through by individuals, preferably with a knowledgeable and sympathetic learning counsellor or mentor and most certainly over a period of time. What has been shown is a complete set of processes used in one project. Not everyone will want, or need, to go through every stage. People already half-motivated will complete the tasks much more quickly, and omit large sections. But as tools, used flexibly, they can help make a difference to a great number of people, as the results below show. They are self-awareness and empowerment tools that can be used in workplaces, schools, colleges, city administrations, community centres and small and large communities to help break down learning barriers and inculcate a learning culture, and to help build a learning city or region. Several cities, for example Helsinki, Southampton, Derby and Ballarat, are now actively incorporating their own versions of them into the continuous improvement programmes of their staff. However, the examples shown above should not be used as shown, but as a template modified to suit the profile of the audience and the resources of the administrator.

Lessons for cities and regions and their stakeholders from projects that have implemented such plans include:

- In such sensitive person-to-person situations, effective learning counsellor training is crucial. Future projects should start in the early days with such training and experts should relate it to the project inputs.
- The overall impression of those who have been involved with it is that it is mostly exciting, occasionally frustrating, and certainly time-consuming, but with a huge potential to transform communities into learning communities.
- Tools must be tailored to the needs of the audience.
- The importance of communication, of ensuring that every person from project leader to participant is fully familiar with the background, rationale, tools and modus operandi of the project. Tools should be backed up by booklets and leaflets explaining the basics.

Results also show that:

- the tools give a new way of looking at life and learning;
- they broaden perceptions;
- they increase balance between work and leisure;
- they bring new vision into communities;

- they introduce new, previously untapped, resources into the community;
- they give learning counsellors a sense of purpose and empowerment;
- they change the mindset of those who participate;
- they afford opportunities to give as well as to take.

Other examples

LT Scotland's Assessment is for Learning project, active in many Scottish municipalities and regions, addresses the issue of learner demotivation in the face of poor test and examination results. It suggests that learners learn best when:

- they understand clearly what they are trying to learn, and what is expected of them;
- they are given feedback about the quality of their work, and what they can do to make it better;
- they are given advice about how to go about making improvements;
- they are fully involved in deciding what needs to be done next, and who can give them help if they need it.

Schools participating in the project use personal learning plans in order to develop formative assessment strategies in which peer and self-assessment figure large. Tests and examinations are seen as learning opportunities, rather than strategies to divide the sheep from the goats, with concomitant loss of face, drive and stimulus for learning. The Personal Learning Action Plan is indeed personal and the targets it sets for the individual pupil become owned by that pupil. A failure to adhere to them is then the responsibility of the individual and can be rectified by greater efforts in the future with proper encouragement and an enlightened use of personal psychology from the teacher. An additional advantage is that they improve home–school relationships and bring parents into the learning circle, a particular advantage in distressed urban areas. Perhaps surprisingly the majority of schools participating in this scheme are from the primary sector, and there is even a smattering of nursery schools.

Naturally there will need to be a sensitive and sensible application of the plan in order to alleviate feelings of anxiety among both children and parents. Social, cultural and psychological factors are not always taken into account when targets are set by teachers and governments anxious to advance league table positions and produce ever-improving results in SATs and other external examinations. But Personal Learning Action Plans, however narrowly defined and administered, are a laudable attempt to deal with deep-seated and long-established fault-lines in educational practice. In Burnfoot Community School, for example, a participant in the LT Scotland project, their use has led, in the opinion of teachers, to:

- both pupils and teachers remaining focused on learning targets;
- the production of a less threatening reporting document which has encouraged more focused discussion at parents' night;
- more regular information about children's learning being shared between home and school;
- the adoption of the PLP by the school as the annual report.

The Learning Ladder

As we have said, the use of such tools emphasises the value of personal learning. This author introduced the idea of the Learning Ladder in 'Learning Communities for a Learning Century', and again in *Lifelong Learning in Action*. It is shown in Figure 5.7.

Figure 5.7 The Learning Ladder

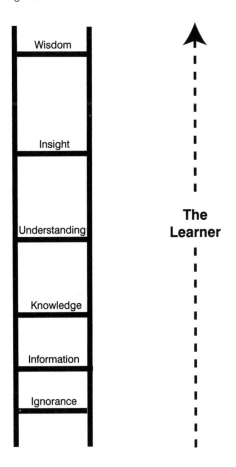

In this, the individual's journey towards wisdom is to climb a ladder on which the rungs become ever wider to reflect the greater difficulty of achieving higher levels of consciousness. The level at which most teaching takes place in the formal education institutions is little more than the passing of raw information for regurgitation back as raw information. If connections have been made, it may demonstrate that knowledge has been acquired, but not necessarily understanding. Only with the personal ownership of the learning can the higher rungs be reached.

Summary

In this chapter we have explained the rationale behind the individualisation of society during the 1980s and 1990s and the backlash towards community now happening during the 21st century. We have also described some of the tools and techniques for helping to create a learning culture in learning cities and regions, in their communities and in their stakeholder organisations – tools such as Personal Learning Audits and Personal Learning Action Plans. A close-knit community will find it relatively easy to implement the tools, but larger, more diffuse and more diverse communities in the cities and regions of most countries will find it far more difficult. Outreach strategies, and the sensitisation of stakeholder organisations to make themselves more receptive to modern methods of continuous improvement for their staff and students, will help but in the end, much comes down to the way in which community counsellors can galvanise, motivate, inspire and assist the aspirant, and the reluctant, learner. It is not always an easy task. The process of self-confrontation can be a tense one, particularly if one's self-esteem is not as high as it might be. As Fred Korthagen says, 'Reflecting on your own behaviour can be a rather confronting experience in which self-defence mechanisms play an important role. Counsellors therefore need to know the most important principles of human change processes'.

Nevertheless what has proved to be successful in industry often finds its way into other organisations. Apart from the examples we have cited in the chapter, Joan Richardson reports that:

> More and more districts are requiring teachers to develop individual learning plans. Such individual plans are crucial cogs in a system of staff development that links individual learning with school goals and schoolwide learning with district goals. Several districts that have received the U.S. Department of Education's Model Professional Development Awards – including Broward County (Fla.) Public Schools, Wichita (Kan.) Public Schools, and Carrollton Independent School District in Texas – have long required teachers to develop individual learning plans as part of their staff development programs.

Cities and regions elsewhere can take heart from this. Increased self-understanding within the parameters of rapid societal and community change, overcoming, in Ernest Bevan's phrase, the 'poverty of aspiration', is an essential prerequisite to active participation in the learning that takes people out of the trap they find themselves in. This chapter has tried to identify and describe some of the necessary tools and to emphasise how the use of counsellors, guides and mentors to administer those tools provides the crucial personal touch currently lacking in many cities and regions.

Suggestions for further work from this chapter

1   Download the sample Personal Learning Audit from www.longlearn.org.uk and use it while reading the relevant parts of this chapter. Modify it for use in your organisation/city/region.
2   Download the Personal Learning Plan lessons from LILLIPUT module 2 and apply the same principles. If they are not already doing so recommend to your schools and colleges that they assess/modify it for use there.
3   Use the Learning Ladder in Figure 5.7 to assess at what point you and others are in a variety of learning situations.
4   Establish a pilot project in one of the city neighbourhoods to administer the tools described in this chapter.

Chapter 6

Participating, partnering, profiting

Tools and techniques for involving stakeholders in learning cities and regions

Figure 6.1 is a schematic of stakeholder involvement in learning cities and regions.

It might seem to be complex at first glance but in reality it is deceptively simple to understand. The Anglo-Saxon model of a centralised education curriculum and assessment system with some (albeit decreasing) local authority management responsibility is used. Other systems may be different, but the general thrust of contribution by stakeholders remains valid and modifiable whatever the set-up.

The inner rectangle represents the city or regional administration and a breakdown of some of the coordinating tasks it undertakes in order to help create a learning city or region.

On the outside of the diagram are six boxes representing six types of learning stakeholder i.e.

- Schools, including primary, secondary and kindergarten.
- Business, industry and commerce, including small, medium and large enterprises situated in the city and region, each with their own learning needs and offerings.
- Adult vocational education colleges offering professional, trade and business education to students, usually, but not exclusively, at non-degree level. It would also include tertiary colleges and those organisations with learning centres, such as hospitals, police and firemen's colleges, non-university teacher training and management colleges etc. where vocational education is given.
- Universities and higher education centres offering a range of degree, post-degree and general interest courses for a wide range of students.
- Non-vocational adult education bodies and voluntary organisations offering community education either from specially built and staffed centres in community settings, or other premises such as church halls or any other location offering learning.
- Cultural learning centres in non-formal learning settings such as museums, libraries and galleries where the learning can be active or passive.

Figure 6.1 Learning cities, learning regions and their stakeholders working together

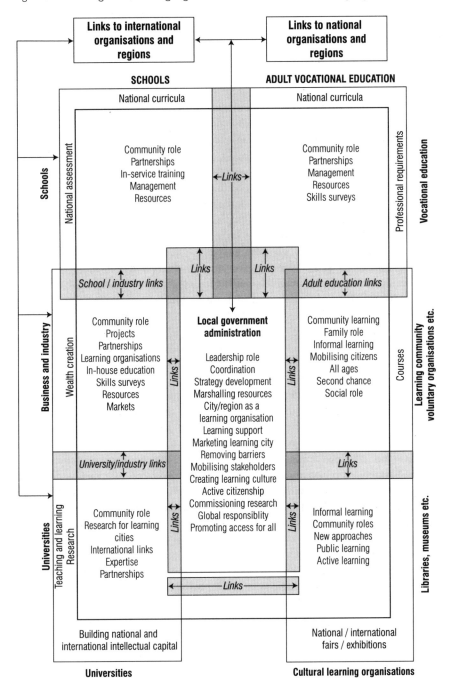

In the outer middle is a large rectangle which represents the boundary between the things that the city can normally influence and those over which it has little control. Everything within this is an opportunity, a contribution, a responsibility, an issue that can help in the construction of the learning city. Thus it will be noticed that cities and regions have little control over the national curriculum or the national assessment systems, but that there are also many aspects of school life that are community and city based. Equally business and industry has its own path to tread in its pursuit of wealth creation, but it also has a great deal to contribute to city and regional growth outside of the local taxes it pays. Universities similarly are outside of local control but, although their major *raison d'être* is the development of intellectual capital, it would be unwise to do this in an ivory tower vacuum, and they give and receive expertise, finance and human capital to cities and regions as a part of their normal operation.

Everywhere there are links, whether they be between the stakeholders themselves or between the city/region and the stakeholders. These links are a vital part of the bloodstream of the learning city, the haemoglobin that offers resources, talents, expertise, possibilities, opportunities, partnerships, knowledge and experience to whichever organisation or whoever needs it. There are of course many more links than it is possible to depict on a two-dimensional chart. Add to these the links with national and international cities, regions and organisations that create yet more trade, markets, knowledge, wealth creation, employment, finance, insights and prospects, and we have a workable schematic of the scope of the learning city or region as a holistic, interactive, inter-dependent and vibrant learning place for its citizens.

Such a complex organism needs a strong heart to pump the blood around the stakeholder arteries, and a keen intelligence at the centre of operations to energise the mindset that will comprehend and activate transformation, projects and progress. Lifelong learning extends so much further than the education departments of cities and regions. Some of them, as in Glasgow and Dublin, operate from the development agency, recognising the economic and social gains to be obtained from becoming a learning entity. In others, for example Stirling, the impetus emanates from the chief executive's office, and yet others, particularly in countries, such as Italy, France and Finland, where elected politicians take on responsibility for educational matters, obtain their vision from imaginative and creative councillors. Espoo, Livorno and Sannois provide examples. Whatever the origin of the thrust forward, it should transcend the present day obsession with education and training as a separate and compartmentalised part of city life.

There is of course much more to it than a diagram, and this chapter will put the flesh on the bones of stakeholder responsibility in the typical learning city and outline some of the tools that can be used to identify the contribution each can make to its construction.

Schools as stakeholders in learning cities and regions

For both the present and the future, schools are potentially the most powerful allies for local and regional governments in the creation of learning cities and regions. This is not only because today's schoolchildren are tomorrow's learning citizens, but also because they open up so many awareness doors to parents, teachers and to the community at large. The introduction to the schools stakeholder audit expresses it thus.

> What happens to individual children in schools will determine the learning values and attitudes of thousands of people as adults. And since a positive, lifelong, learning attitude is the basis of local and regional prosperity and stability, not to mention personal well-being, schools will need to involve themselves in its creation. Change is inevitable – in the way that schools are managed, in the way that teachers enable children to learn and in the way that they interact with the local community. Schools are now part of an active partnership with local government and other local and regional organisations to help create the sort of vibrant learning society that will deliver more skilful, sensitive and fulfilled people.

Although local administrations have little control over the content of curricula and the examination systems that drive them, schools are nevertheless essentially community organisations, and the symbiosis of interest between city and school can, if effectively managed, bring great benefits to both. Very few adults can remember what happened in classrooms, but they will recall without effort their participation in school journeys and camps, plays, musical events, sports, community contribution and of course the individual quirks of the teachers, a sobering reminder that life skills, rather than knowledge bytes, are more the real essence of schooling.

Governments are broadly in favour of this idea. The European national education systems organisation, Eurydice, reports that article 6 of the French speaking communities of Belgium proposed three outcomes from schools:

- the promotion of self-confidence and the personal development of each pupil;
- the acquisition of knowledge and skills by all pupils in such a way that they are capable of learning throughout life, and assuming an active role in economic, social and cultural life;
- preparing all pupils to become responsible citizens able to contribute to the development of a democratic pluralistic society which displays solidarity and is open to other cultures.

In the UK 'social and moral responsibility, community involvement and political literacy are three things which every child should have more than a glimmer about on leaving school', according to Sir Bernard Crick's advisory group on citizenship. Similar exhortations on the contribution of schools to the community, to political processes and to the development of a civic and social conscience are to be found from national, regional and local governments in all parts of the world. But very few are willing to provide additional resources to enable it to be done in a way that engages, involves and inspires. Citizenship or Civics as an academic classroom subject is hardly likely to stimulate young people to become lifelong contributors to a better society, or to empathise with the needs and demands of others less fortunate than themselves. The European Policy Paper on the local and regional dimension of lifelong learning (Commission of the European Union 2001) recognises this. 'Involvement is all', it says, 'community involvement implies more than just helping out in voluntary activities. It implies doing something about perceived injustices, and making a positive difference to the life of the city and the people who live there'. Crick too recommended learning by doing, by becoming active citizens in local life, by experiencing democracy in the classroom and by balancing rights with responsibilities.

And indeed there are many good examples of this in action. Forty-three of the TELS cities give courses in schools on civic rights and responsibilities to the community. In 38 of them, schools and classes have student councils with elected representatives and in 32 special courses are given to improve debating, public speaking, communications skills and self-esteem. The voice of the young campaign in Helsinki actively promotes the participation of young people in the management of schools, youth clubs and local communities. 'It is the right of children and the young to participate in the decisions concerning their life and to become capable of having their say in society', states *Helsinki, an Educating, Training and Learning City*.

Perhaps one of the regions of the world where school and community are most at one is South Australia. As a result of the PALLACE project, St Columba College, a joint Anglican/Catholic college near to Adelaide, published a list of its commitments to the community. Its mission statement begins as follows: 'We seek to be a Learning Centre of excellence for the community we serve. The days of the schools opening at 8.00am and finishing at 4.00pm are fast coming to an end'. It expounds its philosophy in eight statements and 'hopes':

1   We believe the facilities at St Columba offer the wider community opportunities to experience lifelong learning.
2   The courses that could be offered will be for a variety of age groups.
3   Our facilities will be available for Community use where appropriate.
4   We seek to nurture in the wider Community a lifelong love of learning.
5   We seek to build partnerships with Local Council, Further Education Providers, The Business Enterprise Centre, Service Providers and our local Parishes.

6   We seek to provide courses of training that are needed in the wider community.
7   We seek opportunities to be a 'Satellite' Centre for programs offered in other Regional Centres.
8   We see our Library/Resource Centre/Careers Centre/Recreational facilities as practical dimensions of a *St Columba Learning Centre*.

Our Hopes for the Wider Community

- Build the confidence and skills of the members.
- Enthuse members' love of Learning.
- Enable members to create new opportunities in their lives.
- To see St Columba as a vibrant part of their community life.
- Have opportunities to search and develop their spirituality.
- Use particularly our Entertainment Facilities to celebrate family and community functions.
- Build bridges between all cultures of the community and the various age groups.
- To have a positive self-belief in their ability to succeed and make a difference.

Here we see a refreshing willingness of a school to not only serve the community in every way it can find, but also to take active leadership in this process. It is not the only one in this part of the world. North of Adelaide, Mawson Lakes School, mentioned in other chapters as a centre of community partnership, incorporates every stakeholder organisation in the community into the delivery of its wider curriculum, and contributes to those stakeholders' activities in a two-way interaction. In order to do this every teacher in the school has a personal responsibility outside of the school. Classes can include mothers, fathers, grannies, big sisters and members of the public. *Lifelong Learning in Action* suggested that every school should employ a responsible person whose task it is to mobilise every resource available in the community – human, financial, physical, cultural and environmental – into the service of the school. Equally that same person, who could well be a volunteer or a leader of other volunteers reporting to the head, would look for opportunities that enable the pupils to make their own contribution to the world outside.

Twenty-first century schools are changing, and being changed by the world. As long ago as 1993, again in Australia, the Principal of Wesley College, David Loader, was saying that schools had 'had their day'! He argued for their transformation, at some point not far into the future, into neighbourhood learning centres addressing the learning needs of the whole population. He also asserted that learning 'at school' is not the only or best way to equip young people for their future lives. He raised two issues central to current educational debates and germane to the theme of this chapter. First, that we must all now embrace learning as a continuous process, rather than an event early in life which ends with the passage into adulthood and the world of work, a sentiment constantly repeated throughout this book. Second, he emphasised the social value of schooling and the importance of the nexus between schools and their communities

The death of schools as we know them is, like that of Mark Twain, probably greatly exaggerated. They have a great deal of mileage left in them, if only because of the effects of inertia and the lack of a suitable alternative, but they will need to change in order to bring them into line with the real needs of the 21st century. This is a huge area worthy of a book in itself (*Lifelong Learning in Action* would be a good starting point), and there is insufficient space to include all the implications behind that statement. Figure 6.2, taken from that book, shows some of them in brief.

It remains only to describe one of the tools available to local and regional authorities to enable them to stimulate schools to at least understand the parameters of change. The schools stakeholder audit, developed by the INDICATORS project, contains a number of indicators that will open the doors of perception. As the introduction states,

> The audit itself is not simply a questionnaire. It is a carefully-worded instrument to engage the school in debate with itself about its own future as a quality learning organisation, and its relationship to others in the city/ region and beyond. The lifelong learning rationale is embedded in each action element of the tool, in order to help school management and staff understand what a lifelong learning organisation within its sector will be like and how it can make that transformation.

By using the tool, schools become closely involved with the transformation process through questions soliciting opinions, information and comment, and exercises developing internal and external debate. There are therefore four objectives, all of which are connected with meeting these criteria in a learning region:

- it will enable schools to measure their performance as 'learning organisations' within a learning region;
- it will explore all the parameters which enable a modern school to address the vast number of changing needs and demands of all its own stakeholders – parents, governors, teachers, children and members of the community around it – in a 21st century lifelong learning society;
- it will examine the contribution the school might make to the construction of a learning region in which it can play a part and from which it can benefit;
- it will act as a basis for comparisons with schools in other regions.

Figure 6.2 Quality in a 21st century lifelong learning school

Education and training C20	Lifelong learning C21	Action for change
1. Sets narrow academic objectives and targets and works to achieve these in the present	Not only works to achieve present targets but also to impart future long-term values and attitudes to learning	More schools/life links and partnerships – with industry, community etc. construct a wider curriculum dealing with life skills
2. Rudimentary short-term business plan usually around academic matters. Little effort to keep every stakeholder informed and on-side	A full written organisational strategy, available to all, for developing the school into a lifelong learning organisation, and covering all aspects of the school's activity	Develop longer-term school business plan and make it available to all. Create proactive information strategies to bring all stakeholders on-side. Adopt external quality indicators like Investors in People
3. Some teachers go on educational courses according to need or desire. Occasional seminars in schools for teachers only	Every person in the school has a continuous improvement plan for academic and personal skill/ knowledge development embedded into the management system, and part related to the school development plan	Develop written continuous improvement plans for academic and personal development of pupils, teachers and administrative staff. Extend these to parents and community as desired
4. Teachers only human resource for curriculum delivery supplemented by helpers. Other resources supplied from local government and school events	School adds human resource by tapping into skills, talents and knowledge of governors, parents and everyone in the community and other resources by exploring funding and other sources in the community	Appoint someone to identify and use ALL the human and other resources in the community and beyond. Use innovative strategies to involve the community in school development
5. Curriculum based on discrete subjects, and assessed on memorisation of facts with pass–fail philosophy	Curriculum based on skills and knowledge, the enhancement of self-esteem and the acceptance of lifelong values. Examinations as stock-taking part of the personal learning process	Incorporate personal skills development into curriculum. Take the notion of failure out of the system and replace it with strategies for improving personal self-esteem

continued …

Figure 6.2 continued

Education and training C20	Lifelong learning C21	Action for change
6. In-school pastoral care systems staffed by overworked teachers. Sparse support services to identify and solve individual learning and social problems early	Guidance, support and counselling systems available for all learners and their families using all available resources. Rapid identification and solution of learning and social problems	Introduce individual learning guidance systems for all pupils and update frequently. Use resources in school and community – mentors etc. Involve the family. Initiate rapid response system
7. Focus on curriculum and examination success within the school. Social curriculum dealt with on an *ad hoc* basis. Some social and community programmes	Looks outward to the world, learning by contributing to the community in which it exists. Strong social curriculum to promote a sense of tolerance and understanding of different races, creeds and cultures	Introduce an active social curriculum in and out of school to enhance tolerance and understanding. Use internet networks in projects to link pupils to other pupils throughout the world
8. Teacher as a passer of information through didactic teaching methods using chalk, talk and paper exercises	Teacher as developer of learning skills using motivational power of ICT, multimedia, networks etc. in individualised active learning programmes	Train all teachers in the many uses of technology as learning tools. Invest heavily in ICT through innovative programmes with industry etc.
9. Parents invited to school to discuss child's progress once a term. Occasional public information meetings	Involves the family in the life of the school through increased home–school cooperation and active participation in school events	Write a family participation guide outlining all the things parents etc. can do for the school. Open an email line. Establish a contact point
10. In some schools a play or a show once a year. Out-of-school activities led by enthusiastic teachers. Annual School Fair and Presentation Days	Enhances confidence, creativity and the cultural vision of staff, parents, children and the community through a wide range of extra-curricular activities	Establish an impressive programme of school societies, out-of-school activities, cultural events etc. and involve the community where appropriate
11. (In some countries) Concentrates mainly on high academic achievers in order to enhance attractiveness to parents through position in league tables	Concentrates on academic and personal success of all pupils as a means of enhancing the school's reputation and satisfying society's need. Invites the public to share in it	Market the school strongly. Emphasise the positive learning opportunities for all children, staff and the community at large. Create own league table of all-round achievement

Source: Longworth (*Lifelong Learning in Action*)

This is a tool and not just a questionnaire – its purpose is to stimulate reflection, debate and action. Inevitably the full version is long. The transition to a learning organisation affects all parts of the institution, often in quite fundamental ways, and the change process takes months and years.

Learning cities and regions may contact the University of Stirling's Department of Education for fuller details, but as an indicator of some of the quotations and questions contained therein, the following gives a taste.

> The aim of the questions is to stimulate thinking about learning in your school, how it is fostered to produce people who will learn for life and what the school can contribute to the growth of your area, as a 'learning region'.
>
> As concepts such as 'region' and 'lifelong learning' mean different things to different people, we welcome thoughts and reflections on what they mean to you, and we have provided space for you to write these down.
>
> We appreciate that decisions made elsewhere, maybe at governmental level, affect actions in schools. However, the purpose is not to judge past and present procedures, ideas and practices but to prepare schools to prepare children for life in a 21st century future in which change is an ever-increasing feature, and in which they will have to have the skills that enable them to adapt quickly and easily.
>
> Administrators and teachers are urged to use the audit as a tool for questioning basic assumptions and determining future strategies and policies, and even to bring the pupils into this debate. They will learn much from doing so.

A small sample from section 3 illustrates the point (see Figure 6.3). Other sections of the audit include:

- school leadership and lifelong learning;
- the school as a learning organisation;
- management of lifelong learning in the school;
- standards and quality;
- the School's role in helping to build a learning city;
- partnerships for mutual benefit;
- bringing the world to the school;
- bringing the school to the world;
- extra-curricular activities and learning;
- removing the obstacles to learning;
- skills, values and the curriculum;
- school organisation and ownership of learning;
- learning support mechanisms in the school;
- individual learning styles;
- the assessment of learning;
- promoting the school to the outside world;

Figure 6.3 Extract from part of section 3 of the schools stakeholder audit

The school runs courses for the community on modern educational methods

The school invites members of the community to share their knowledge and experience in the classroom in support of the curriculum

The school invites members of the community into school clubs and societies

The school has a thriving community involvement

The school encourages members of the community to help out in school lessons

The school keeps the community informed through newsletters and magazines

The school invites the community to contribute to newsletters and magazines

Members of the community can sit in and learn on school classes

The school carries out a learning requirements audit in the community

The community is used as the source of information for surveys carried out by pupils

The school has governors from community associations

Members of the community act as learning mentors for pupils

There is a telephone hot-line for the community

The school suggestions box is open to the community

The school runs brain-storming sessions on its relationships with the community

There is a school email address which members of the community can contact

Members of the community participate in school plays

Members of the community with expertise coach sports teams, run school choirs, clubs and societies

The school reaches out to the community and does not wait for the community to volunteer

The school runs open days for the local community

Other (Please state)

- internal communication methods;
- continuous improvement of staff;
- technology and the school;
- sources of additional funding.

The audit is a very comprehensive one and can be used as a staff and/or parents and/or governors discussion and training exercise, as a means of delivering new insights to school management or as an aid towards a gradual modification of school strategies to fit 21st century needs. It is also liberally spattered with quotations for reflection from official documents such as these from the PALLACE report, the European Policy Paper on Lifelong Learning and other sources.

The South Australian experience highlights the importance of considering in a major way the sustainability of the initiatives started. Too many times they are driven by the enthusiasm of a single person, whether that be the

Principal or a key teacher, and cease to operate when that person leaves the school. The importance of embedding the initiative within the development plan and ongoing priorities of the school, and establishing a governance model for the management of the learning community that is valued and owned by the community stakeholders is crucial to its long-term continuity (Longworth and Allwinkle 2005b).

Such a definition implies that all sectors of a local community, including schools, are 'stakeholders' in the construction of a mutually advantageous and interactive learning city, town or region that will deliver prosperity, social stability and the personal well-being of its citizens (Longworth 2003a).

We recommend a more robust and hands-on approach with interactive materials, frequent visits to council chambers, school parliaments and active involvement with those less fortunate in the community, such as the aged, the handicapped and the dysfunctional (Crick 1998).

The methods used to promote a healthy sense of self-esteem, learning motivation and learning skills in young people's basic education are critical for the development of lifelong learning values and attitudes. Educational Institutions should encourage their students to learn beyond their organisation and analyse how that contributes to the whole spectrum of an individual's intellectual growth (Finnish National Lifelong Learning Strategy).

… to create a lifelong learning community where learning is available for everyone, at any time, and in any place. Educational services will become a catalyst and a conduit for the creation of a community that has a culture of continuous improvement, and where the school both contributes to and receives from the community of which it is a part (Mawson Lakes school vision statement).

Effectively operated lifelong learning partnerships with other organisations can create a win-win situation for all partners. They can help to identify new talent, enhance awareness of the importance of lifelong learning and increase the physical and human resources available to each partner by sharing equipment, and the skills and knowledge of people and organisations. (NewTELS Education Survey)

Universities as stakeholders in the development of learning cities and regions

Although universities in most countries are outside the jurisdiction of local and regional government their potential involvement in the building of a lifelong learning culture in cities and regions is also the subject of a large number of reports, papers, documents and books. The UNESCO Commission on Higher Education predicates a Universal University which 'makes its intellectual resources and independence of thought available to increase debate about, and consciousness of, the many social issues arising in the community, nationally and globally'. *Making Lifelong Learning Work* suggests:

> The mission of the university as a place which adopts a leadership role in the local community, serving it and involving its citizens in the research it carries out, would see the community as a huge learning research laboratory. It would act as a conduit to the rest of the world through its national and international dimensions and contacts, importing and exporting new knowledge and ideas from and to it. By involving the people it would disseminate valuable knowledge, understanding and insights to the whole community.

'Education must move rapidly to a customer-orientation', says Professor Michael Thorne, Vice-Chancellor of the University of East London, and later,

> If the UK is to be able to compete globally than strategic partnerships will need to be formed between Further Education, Higher Education and the private sector to ensure that economies of scale are achieved, networks and infrastructures developed and constructed thus facilitating learning for the learner at a time and place that meets their needs and demands.

This world-view from a respected member of the council of the European Lifelong Learning Initiative (ELLI) recognises four things that may come as a surprise to traditionalists:

- that universities have a key part to play in the economic development of a city, a region or a nation;
- that students are customers and need to be treated as such in the way that learning is provided;
- that universities will need to supplement the income they receive from the public purse through strategic partnerships with industry and the community;
- that universities can no longer work alone independently of other providers in the tertiary sector.

The community theme is expanded by Bruce Muirhead, Director of the Ipswich Community Service and Research Centre of the University of Queensland. 'The university's ability to innovate in a radically changing society will become critical to its ongoing relevance to communities in the 21st century', he says. 'The traditional boundaries of disciplines, research, teaching, learning and community engagement are blurring. Universities are being challenged to re-invent themselves', and, in support of the objectives of the organisation he runs, he asks 'Can universities function as community problem-solving civic resources? Is the energy of the university a key to solving some of the economic and development concerns of our communities?'

Many of these questions are already being asked in countries where universities have a great deal of autonomy and where change is at its most evident. They are in tune with, but not driven by, lifelong learning ideas and principles at this level, and they will entail changes internally and in the way in which universities see their privileged place in the world. But the key indicator lies in the way that they fulfil their new role. Will they adopt a position of leadership in the development of lifelong learning in their own community or will they stand on one side, playing their part but not re-orienting their mission in order to accept the new challenges it throws up? The *Community Action for Lifelong Learning* booklet produced from the ELLI conference in Rome is in no doubt about the importance of the position of higher education: 'The University lies at the hub of local life in all sectors of activity ... It is a natural place to initiate, develop and maintain Lifelong Learning programmes within its geographical area while also maintaining links with national and international projects and activities.'

The new lifelong learning university

But what does this mean? How does the university's mission and operation change to accommodate its new role? Figure 6.4, an updated version of the chart produced in *Lifelong Learning: New Visions, New Implications, New Roles*, outlines some of the changes currently taking place in many universities in order to fulfil their changing role locally and to come to terms with the community demands of the 21st century.

As we have seen in previous chapters the purpose of learning cities and regions is to open up new opportunities and new horizons, empower people and expand ideas, concepts and actions in the field of learning. If we accept that the pathway to a learning society lies in the creation of a learning culture as the final E in Figure 6.4 indicates, then higher education is indeed a key part of that scenario. It will need wise leadership and, in the words of Professor Philip Candy, now of the University of Ballarat, 'helicopter vision', the ability to see the big picture and one's place in it. But also, every part of the community has a stake in developing the capability of people and organisations to participate. It is a holistic mission which no single stakeholder can fulfil, but which imposes a greater responsibility on those organisations more able to achieve it. Here is one area where there is an opportunity for dynamic leadership as advocated in the V in Figure 6.4, activating those actions and approaches that will lead the university itself into the future – willingness to change and the ability to manage it, vision to discern opportunity, dynamism to act on conviction, determination to succeed

Figure 6.4 The new lifelong learning university – at the heart of the community

U	**U**nlock the doors to higher learning for more sections of the population through universal university strategies that widen participation
N	**N**etwork with other universities globally to import and export new knowledge, experiences and research on learning cities and regions
I	**I**nitiate innovative strategies for learning city development by tapping into the pool of creativity existing within all universities
V	**V**olunteer dynamic leadership to the community within which it resides by developing and providing expertise, knowledge and action
E	**E**nergise learning city/region development through commissioned research, development and consultation activities that include the whole community, and improve decision-making by keeping both management and people informed of progress and results
R	**R**elease their resources and the energy of their students and staff in the service of learning city development
S	**S**atisfy the needs and demands of people by delivering courses wherever, whenever and however people want them and providing a continuous updating service for graduates and local workplaces
I	**I**nclude themselves in creative and fruitful partnerships with local government, schools, industry and other stakeholders to help build learning communities, cities and regions
T	**T**ransform themselves into true learning organisations through continuous improvement and quality management programmes for all students and staff
I	**I**ncrease the employability of graduates and others through modular courses that include the obligatory development of language, entrepreneurial, management and personal skills
E	**E**nliven learning city development through the development and application of tools and techniques that create a culture of learning
S	**S**timulate the message of learning city and regional development by becoming involved in celebration events such as learning festivals, fairs, open days etc. and representing the city in projects, missions and other events nationally and overseas

and humility to learn – all pointing to the UNESCO vision of the 'universal university'.

The University of Queensland is one example of good practice. Its community service and research centre based in the township of Ipswich, near Brisbane, is an integral part of the University's Community Engagement Strategy. The centre's main purpose is to develop genuinely democratic, mutually beneficial partnerships between the university and the community with the aim to build a 'sustainable, inclusive and socially just community in the township'. The centre sees itself as a loosely-coupled entrepreneurial organisation and strategic alliance/ network. It brokers distributive teams of academics and community leaders focusing on social enterprise and development, by systemically integrating research, teaching, and service in response to community issues. The centre is also considered a hub for the generation of innovative ideas for economic and community development programmes, collaborative research projects, consultancy services, inter-professional courses and training programmes, and the placement of faculty students with skills and interests that match community needs. Denise Regenzhani, formerly a senior lecturer at the centre, observes, 'we see this work as the heart of everything the university should be in the community – understanding and solving problems, energising people to work for each other, creating a community that is alive and dynamic whatever its make-up or circumstances'.

Such perceptions treat the community as a vast socially inclusive research laboratory, incorporating citizens into the design, collection, analysis and dissemination procedures and processes. It is the university equivalent of corporate social responsibility as a *raison d'être* rather than a handout when profits allow. *Lifelong Learning* expands this into opportunity.

> The practical implications of this privileged position are far-reaching and would drastically change the university's role, purpose and modus operandi. At the same time it would considerably enhance its status in the community by adding a wide range of additional functions to the research and teaching which are presently its raison d'être. It would remain as a depository and developer of intellectual capital, a storehouse of basic facts and information from which new knowledge emerges and is disseminated, but its enlarged role would provide learning and enlightenment for a far wider constituency of people and concepts.

University and city/region opportunities

But this is not all give with little take. There are opportunities for commissioned research and development everywhere in the field, as Figure 6.5 elaborates.

There is something here for all faculties and a vast range of staff and students. The value of the learning materials on language and law developed by Palacky University for the LILLIPUT project are a good example of university/local authority cooperation. Already many universities contribute informally to learning city and region development without counting the scale of the effort. There are many formal and informal personal relationships at all levels and from most faculties. The development of centres of expertise in learning city and region matters, such as those already existing in the University of Stirling, Glasgow Caledonian and Napier in Scotland and Toulouse, Newcastle, Akershus (Norway), Catania, Limerick, RMIT (Melbourne) and Palacky (Olomouc, Czech Republic) elsewhere, would help formalise some of that into income-generating

Figure 6.5 University opportunities in the learning city and region

1	Carrying out commissioned research, surveys and studies into all aspects of learning in cities and regions in order to give a deeper insight into needs and strategies
2	Designing and delivering tailored courses, conferences, seminars and workshops for people in all walks of city and regional life in order to increase the lifelong learning leadership base
3	Managing and/or evaluating local, national, European and international projects in the field of learning cities/regions
4	Developing case studies of good practice and writing them up
5	Carrying out learning needs audits and identifying new resources for cities and regions
6	Developing personal learning action plans for administrators and citizens to use, and acting as mentors/counsellors
7	Advising on the effective use of electronic networks and the internet for lifelong learning in cities and regions
8	Developing indicators for lifelong learning development in local institutions and measuring and monitoring their progress
9	Developing booklets, leaflets and brochures for the city
10	Including the city or region in international projects with other cities
11	Providing facilities for city people to study
12	Developing/delivering degree courses in lifelong learning city matters
13	Encouraging post-graduate research and study in the subject

opportunities. At the same time the establishment of linked centres on a European and global scale, as for example in the INDICATORS, LILLIPUT and PALLACE projects, would expand the availability of a specific range of expertises to cities and regions badly in need of them. The PASCAL Observatory project is another example of the synergy between town and gown. This provides a worldwide technology delivered service for cities and regions on place management, social capital and lifelong learning. Commenced with an OECD grant at the Royal Melbourne Institute of Technology and operating from the University of Stirling in Europe it is rapidly expanding into a global information facility for cities and regions.

At the same time universities need to be aware of the Argyris dilemma – a quotation from Botkin explains this:

the Argyris dilemma, first articulated by Harvard professor Chris Argyris. ... The dilemma is the difficulty of teaching smart people to learn. Many intelligent people have never had to learn by failure because they have never failed. They have become quite convinced that they know the right answers. The smarter someone is, the more convinced he or she is that they are above criticism. They become less open to alternative viewpoints. Highly intelligent people can easily become arrogant about their learning and fall into a monopolistic thought process that they know all the answers. This occurs in government, education, and other institutions as well – which generates popular backlashes against so-called experts.

The universities stakeholder audit

An example of the output of one of these expertise clusters comes once more from the INDICATORS project. Like the audit developed for the schools described above, the universities stakeholder audit is a comprehensive tool that will enable both universities and their clients in cities and regions to focus in on joint needs and possibilities. 'Institutions become closely involved with the transformation process through questions soliciting opinions, information and comment, and exercises developing internal and external debate' it says in the opening blurb.

> The 'stakeholder audit' tool we have created for universities … has four purposes, all of which are connected with meeting these criteria in a learning region:
>
> - It will enable universities to measure their performance as 'learning organisations' within a learning region.
> - It will explore all the parameters which enable a modern university to address the vast number of changing needs and demands of a 21st century lifelong learning society.
> - It will examine the role of the university in the construction of a learning region to which it can contribute and from which it can benefit.
> - It will act as a basis for comparisons with universities in other regions.

The university audit is divided into sections dealing with different aspects of the institution's operations in order to make it both more flexible and useful. It is a tool and not just a questionnaire – its purpose is to stimulate thinking, debate and action. Figure 6.6 gives a very short taste of one part of section 3.

However, the audit is a much richer document than this. It covers the following sections:

- existing lifelong learning strategy;
- institutional structure of lifelong learning at your university;
- membership of lifelong learning organisations and European projects;
- the university as learning organisation;

Figure 6.6 Example from the university audit

Does your Strategic Plan outline a commitment to work with the local community?
Does your Strategic Plan outline a commitment to work with the local authority?
If yes to either, do you have a senior officer charged with this responsibility?
If yes, does that person report to senior management?

Is there a lifelong learning partnership in the city or region?
If yes, is the university represented upon it?
Has the city launched itself as a 'Learning City'?
If yes, has the university played a role in this?
If no, has your university ever considered the creation of the learning city in collaboration with the civic authorities?
Has the university ever been involved in any of the following types of cooperation with the local authority?

Assisting its development of a lifelong learning strategy
Taking leadership in the development of a lifelong learning city strategy
Encouraging staff to participate in city lifelong learning activities
Developing and delivering courses in lifelong learning for city staff
Getting involved with joint lifelong learning projects with the city
Carrying out lifelong learning research studies for the city
Representing the city at conferences and seminars
Running a conference or seminar on lifelong learning on behalf of the city
Offering accredited lifelong learning courses for city employees
Delivering courses in community centres
Involvement in city regeneration projects
Offering its premises and facilities for local authority organisations
Creating a Lifelong Learning Centre at the university for use by all

- incentives/reward systems;
- quality and standards;
- working with the local community;
- the university and lifelong learning in the community;
- partnerships between the university, the city/region and stakeholders;
- research, development and delivery in lifelong learning for the city/region and stakeholders;
- courses and literature;
- your yniversity and wider participation in higher education;
- support for non-traditional students;
- credit systems and assessment;
- accreditation of prior experiential learning;

- flexibility and access (wherever, whenever, however, whatever, from whoever);
- information and communication – internal/external;
- key learning messages;
- student and staff support and development for lifelong learning;
- distance learning, multimedia technology and electronic networks for learning;
- e-learning, the internet and international networks;
- employment/employability/skills/wealth creation;
- resources for lifelong learning;
- learning celebration, recognition and family learning;
- lifelong learning values for environment, democracy and citizenship.

As in the schools stakeholder audit the university version is liberally sprinkled with quotations from official documents, papers and books to add authority and spice and to promote reflection. For example:

The universality of higher education implies the use of varied forms of intervention in order to meet the educational needs of all at all stages of life. The facilities they can provide include modifying its approach to individual needs – part-time courses, linked work and training, distance learning, modular courses, virtual delivery methods and the decentralisation of training groups. If Universities exist to serve individuals, they have to be prepared to take risks, try out new systems and processes, and make full use of the potential of new technology and distance learning (UNESCO Higher Education Panel).

Education is a service supplied to students, society and business. Like any service, its quality should be constantly evaluated and updated. Continuous quality improvement of education should be a standard part of educational planning at every institute, in all levels of education (Korhonen: Challenges of Higher Education in Finland).

Universities can make their intellectual resources and independence of thought available to increase debate about, and consciousness of, the many social issues arising in the community, nationally and globally. Paramount among these are those which affect the future of society and are most likely to build a better and more sustainable development (UNESCO Commission on Higher Education).

The way in which the image of learning is presented internally and externally as an attractive and pleasurable activity can make the difference to the success of both the University and the student. Modern, innovative strategies for attracting students, keeping them informed, involving them in their studies and providing facilities for two-way communication need to be utilised. Similarly, a lifelong learning world demands that the needs and demands of every student and member of staff are addressed, including the ability to give and receive learning in the community wherever, whenever, however and from whoever it is required (*Making Lifelong Learning Work*).

Private sector organisations as stakeholders in the development of learning cities and regions

The role of business, industry and commerce in the development of learning cities and regions is a crucial one. It provides the dynamic, the awareness of needs, the innovative purpose and often the funding not just for wealth creation activities but also for social and community projects that make cities and regions better places to live. Small and large companies have a vital interest in fostering learning. Botkin expresses it thus:

> Learning isn't what we do only in school; learning is what we do for our entire work lives. The most innovative thinking and action in lifelong learning today is occurring in the workplace. And by workplace, I include every workplace, whether that place is located in business, foundations, universities, in religious communities, at home, in politics or even the military. Your work life is where your learning takes place. Any workplace that doesn't strive to value, use, promote, enhance, celebrate and develop learning is going to lose out.

The European Round Table of Industrialists, representing the continent's 42 largest employers, agrees. 'Companies are beginning to realise that one of their main problems is how quickly the competence of their workforce becomes outdated', they say; 'the competitiveness of European industry now depends on meeting two contradictory demands: a short-term focus to enable companies to adapt quickly to the immediate business environment and a long-term view to develop the strategic capabilities to compete in the future'.

Industry is moving into the educational marketplace in a big way. Botkin again:

> In the U.S., the number of corporate universities will soon surpass the number of traditional universities. No new traditional university has been built in the U.S. since 1963. Meanwhile, 10,000 new corporate universities have been built since that time. For some people, this trend may be a threat. But it reflects the new appreciation of learning in the workplace. Naturally, the corporate universities don't have the same curriculum as traditional universities, but students can learn more about values, personal behaviour, and leadership in a corporate university than they can at the Harvard Business

School or at Harvard University. Corporate universities offer an alternative avenue for learning. They teach more about leadership, ethics, and trust than can be taught in formal, traditional schools struggling to keep church and state separate.

Michael Thorne echoes those sentiments and gives some examples:

> In the USA the public and private sector work together to compete in the North American education market. Sylvan Learning Systems has 48 sites in shopping malls and business centres. The Jones education company wants to get the cost of real estate out of education. Michigan Virtual automotive college has 115 courses, 27 providers and 95 subject areas. CASO internet university has 2440 courses and Global Network Academy 250 providers, 770 programmes and 10000 online courses. If Europe is to compete globally then strategic partnerships will need to be made between Industry and the Higher and Further Education Sectors to ensure economies of scale.

These give a measure of the importance of learning within industry and business as a function of survival, but at the same time there is an equivalent realisation that it has a part to play in creating a community of learners in cities and towns. Corporate social responsibility gestures by companies are not usually entirely based on altruism and good works. They are more often founded on enlightened self-interest since, like cities, regions and nations, they have come to realise that the foundations of prosperity rest upon social stability and cohesion, and the incidence of learning in the community. This is why so many US corporations support the highly popular and fruitful adopt-a-school programmes; why, as the *Observer* newspaper reports, TESCO in the UK devotes a proportion of its profits to providing computers for schools; why the *Sun* newspaper does a similar thing with books; why the Royal Bank of Scotland funds courses on responsible finance for schoolchildren; and why IBM and a host of other companies encourage their employees and retirees to involve themselves in community matters. Corporate active citizenship is not only big business but also provides big returns in the form of customer feel-good factors and the bottom line.

Some go further and profess a genuine concern for aspects of community living such as the environment. Anita Roddick, founder of the Body Shop, expresses her philosophy in this way:

> Open up a typical management book and you will find it hard to avoid words like leadership, team-building, company culture and customer service – but you will be lucky to find words like community, social justice, human rights, dignity, love or spirituality – the emerging language of business. 11 years ago the idea of an environmental audit was popularly regarded as the province of a lunatic fringe.

Now the principle has been universally adopted, largely due to the shift in public opinion. 'If all of us in business and leadership roles committed ourselves to social responsibility, big things would indeed happen.'

The Body Shop goes further than this. It links with Amnesty International to run the world's largest citizens movement for human rights and encourages its customers to 'make a mark'. As a result twelve million Body Shop customers did so, and another three million 'thumbprint pledges' were added from 34 countries. Susan Simpson (1994) puts a business school spin on this, 'The holistic view of what managing needs to be about puts leadership at the heart of the matter, where the primary need will be for flexible free-thinking minds capable of not only doing things right but of doing the right thing'. Business schools particularly and other higher education establishments will have to re-evaluate how they tackle the subject of corporate responsibility. Because, far from being a satellite module of a typical business management course, corporate responsibility and accountability is fast taking up a centre stage location and will be used to inform all the skills and competencies that are needed to run a company in the 21st century.

Public–private ventures at local and regional authority level are proliferating at an exponential rate. In Australia Delfin-Lendlease involves itself with local, regional and state authorities to create model learning communities. As well as architects, planners and builders, it employs educationists to advise on the learning aspects of estate planning and to liaise with local and regional educational organisations. In new developments near to Brisbane, Melbourne and Adelaide, learning opportunities for both adults and children are a powerful attraction to prospective house buyers. Stan Salagaras, who works in this capacity on the Mawson Lakes development near Adelaide, is totally immersed in the concept of lifelong learning there. In his final report to the PALLACE project (2004) he suggests several outcomes that will be of interest to local and regional authorities.

> Collectively, the South Australian PALLACE project initiatives signal a number of key roles for schools in building their surrounding region and environment as a learning community:
>
> - Infusing the community with a range of integrated learning services, programs and activities that can be brokered through a range of public and private educational providers.
> - Incorporating partnerships and alliances with other institutions and the private sector to increase the potential for on-going activity and the sharing of resources.
> - Creating a collaborative and sharing environment, conducive to joint development and innovation and one which has an outward focus.
> - Developing linkages between education and training, and research and development to sustain the economic growth of the community – education and industry are mutually supportive.

- Broadening the range of educational services offered through more flexible management and administrative arrangements.

These themes are considered fundamental to the success, sustainability and affordability of the development of an integrated learning community.

But of course not all public/private collaboration is around green field sites. And not all is a rosy story. What happens when companies are scaling down their operations as many have done in the past 20 years? Certainly it is the local and regional authorities which pick up the pieces in terms of lost employment, greater poverty and finding the measures to recreate lost hopes and dreams. They are entitled to assistance in this and there are some good examples in which business and industry have provided it. The European Round Table of Industrialists again:

> If a company stops production at a local plant and does nothing more than pay the local social costs before moving out of the community, it can feel the negative effects for years afterwards: failure to obtain public procurement contracts, diminished customer satisfaction. Restructuring can be used to renew a community. Job-creating SMEs can thrive on sites abandoned by large companies. This takes constructive thinking, a lot of planning and some hard work. Regeneration need not cost more than paying redundancies. The main obstacle is not money but negative thinking.

Examples abound. This story is told in the European Round Table's stimulus to job creation.

> In 1992 Philips Italy had been operating a lighting factory in the Italian mountain village of Alpignano for 65 years. But the pressure of competition was forcing Philips to rationalise its European manufacturing sites. It therefore decided to move the Alpignano production line equipment over to Hungary by the end of 1994. Philips and the local people were faced with a large problem. 400 redundant employees, for whom the hope of finding another job locally was minimal, 30,000 square metres of building space and 15 hectares of land, not all of it fully developed. It took just two years of hard work and plenty of entrepreneurial flair to find the solution. A cooperation between company and regional authority provided the training and finance to transform the site into a series of small businesses. Alpignano today is a site transformed. In place of one standard and tubular lighting factory there is a multifunctional condominium occupied by a number of SMEs, all of them thriving. This business park is surrounded by spare land that is still being developed. The place is humming with productive activity. Local citizens are delighted with the renewal of their community and the opportunities it represents for their future.

Similar stories are told of the steel industry. In the 1970s, steel in Europe was an industry plagued by obsolescence, and with capacity far exceeding demand. The stark choice facing steel companies was either to make drastic cut-backs or to die a lingering death. For generations it had been a mass employer, providing jobs for life for whole communities. Then it embarked upon a gigantic restructuring that would entail the loss of some 180,000 jobs at 19 sites. But, while British Steel slashed the old jobs, it accepted responsibility for creating new jobs. Over the following two decades the company has helped to create more than 100,000 job opportunities situated around its former sites. It is still working hard today to increase that figure. Vernon Smith, Managing Director of British Steel, shares his advice:

> Get local authorities on the bandwagon right from the start. Their cooperation is immensely important for achieving successful economic regeneration. That is why you need a dedicated team to bring in all available support from national and local government and from any other source of assistance. You cannot do it on your own. The success rate for SMEs helped by BS is 80 per cent, which is 30 per cent higher than the overall average in the European Union.

While these are both examples of turning adversity into opportunity in local communities, the Territorial Employment Pacts developed by the European Commission were more a future planning exercise to stimulate cooperation between local and regional authorities, business and industry, learning providers and the voluntary and community sectors. Again they are examples of the key role played by business and industry in local affairs. An example comes from Ireland. The atrocities committed by the IRA on the city provoked the development of the Armagh City Peace and Reconciliation programme. The committee comprised one-third elected representatives, one-third voluntary and community organisations and one-third people from businesses. Recognising that one part of the problem was a high unemployment rate in the area, its objective became to contribute to peace and reconciliation through integrated social and economic actions targeting those most marginalised from social and economic life, and in particular those most affected by violence and suffering. Its mission was to promote reconciliation by creating an inclusive society characterised by a high level of self-esteem and mutual respect. With the help of structural funds provided by the Commission, it has been successful in providing employment for a great number of people in small businesses.

Of course most local and regional authorities can relate similar ventures and they are aware that learning is a vital component of all of them. The business and industry sector becomes the crucial stakeholder in all of local and regional development, not just at organisational level but also in the mobilisation of employees to make their own contribution. For some companies, for example

IBM, this is a powerful way of engendering employee satisfaction. Guinness Ireland distributes an attractive learning information sheet entitled *Learning and Growing* to all its employees. In it employees are encouraged to develop new skills, whether for the job or not, past learning success is celebrated and some of the opportunities to learn and grow are described. 'Open your mind', it suggests, 'and your eyes and ears and your senses, and we will support and encourage you to expand your knowledge in work, contribution and personal development'. Figure 6.7 shows how the 21st century workplace is different from that which preceded it. It will be recognised by the perceptive reader that all of them relate to ideas portrayed in this book, and especially the P, the C, the K and the E have resonances with local and regional authority objectives.

The small business stakeholder audit

Much of what we have so far described affects large companies, but the SME sector also has a strategic part to play in building learning authorities. And so we come to the tools that may help stimulate that role. The fourth Stakeholder Audit developed by the INDICATORS project was aimed at small and medium sized enterprises with the objective of reinforcing their commitment to becoming learning organisations and stimulating their contribution to local and regional matters. On the front page it announces itself as, 'A tool to enable small companies to analyse and respond to a changing world in which continuous and lifelong learning is the key to business success, and cities and regions are in the process of becoming "Learning Cities" and "Learning Regions" '. The introduction contains these words:

> For small businesses this has important implications and benefits. They are the present and future growth sector of the city and the region. The prosperity so desired depends upon the ability of industry to create wealth. And the basic wealth-creating fuel of a knowledge society is learning. And since a positive, lifelong, learning attitude is the basis of local and regional prosperity and stability, not to mention personal well-being, small businesses will need to involve themselves in its development. Small businesses have much to contribute and much to gain from an active partnership with local government and other local and regional organisations to help create the sort of vibrant learning society that will deliver more skilful, productive and fulfilled people.

Once again the audit is long, although a shorter version exists, and the processes it recommends will take place over a period of months and years, but its purpose is to sensitise and encourage those SMEs less familiar with the principles it espouses to implement them in their strategies. Figure 6.8 shows one very small part of the audit.

Figure 6.7 Ten indicators for 21st century workplaces

		Fostering the symbiosis between customer, employee, supplier, stakeholder and community
W	Willingness to change	Welcome the challenge of change by empowering greater decision-making among employees
O	Organisational objectives and culture	Offer a set of open, outward looking organisational objectives and beliefs to employees and customers and encourage contribution to them
R	Recognition and reward	Refresh *all* employees constantly through individual continuous improvement and recognition programmes
K	Knowledge and learning	Kindle, through innovative programmes, the habit of lifelong learning in all employees and encourage them to spread this into family life
P	Profitable partnerships	Participate actively in mutually beneficial partnerships sharing resources and expertise with education
L	Learning organisations	Learn and re-learn constantly in order to remain innovative, inventive and invigorating
A	Audits for learning	Analyse the learning requirements of all employees and discuss with learning providers how these can be satisfied
C	Community involvement	Create, contribute to, and cooperate with, projects in the community in which they operate and encourage employees to participate
E	Environment	Encourage employees, customers and suppliers to care for the environment in which they live and work
S	Strategies	Share their vision of tomorrow with all employees and stimulate them to challenge, change and contribute to the strategies which fuel it

Figure 6.8 Example from the SME Stakeholder Audit

Does your company help the local or regional authority in any of the following ways?

Is represented on local lifelong learning committees

Takes in students for work tasting from schools

Takes in students for work experience from local colleges

Works with local colleges to develop and deliver courses for its employees

Works with universities to develop and deliver courses for its employees

Works with the local authority on learning matters

Encourages its employees to make their talents, skills, knowledge and expertise available in the local community

Encourages mentoring between employees and local students in schools or colleges

Encourages family learning among its employees

Gets involved with national lifelong learning campaigns (e.g. learning at work days etc.)

Shares its resources with other local educational organisations

Runs open days for the local community

Participates in learning fairs and learning festivals organised by the city

Sponsors local events for charity

Regards itself as a good active corporate citizen in the community in which it operates

Has a published environmental policy

Works on joint research projects with local universities

Supports local voluntary organisations

Other sections of the audit deal with:

- your company as a learning organisation;
- standards, quality and recruitment;
- the company's relationship with the learning city and region;
- the company's role and activities in helping its city/region become a learning region;
- partnerships for mutual benefit;
- external company lifelong learning activities;
- the company and the learning habit – why, who, where, when and how;
- expectations and requirements for education received from external sources;
- personal learning support structures;
- financial and other incentives to learning;
- recruitment policy.

As in the other stakeholder audits there is an abundant selection of quotations from official reports etc. to stimulate thinking and lend authority. They include the following:

> The knowledge society of the 21st century will discover that learning is the source of wealth, welfare and competitive advantage. We are experiencing a paradigm shift. The evidence suggests that the development of learning organisations is not merely desirable, but essential to the survival of companies in the 21st century (Ball and Stewart 1995).

> Large companies can help by offering or sharing their own training facilities with SME suppliers; forecasting skills required for future labour markets and helping SMEs and local education facilities to adapt to new requirements; transferring know-how from large companies to small using company managers and retired executives speak.ing at courses and seminars (European Round Table of Industrialists 1996).

> In a company context a 'Total Learning Environment' means that the company itself becomes the learning environment. Learning is seen as a key element of the integrated strategic plan to achieve organisational and business goals. The continuous self-learning ability and level of over-all competence of the workforce, which go together to make up the total learning organisation, is recognised as the means to being able to undertake organisational and technological changes in order to meet business needs (Nyhan 1991).

> Education is a continuous investment; whenever the organisation reaches a certain level of expertise or performance, there is always another level to aim for. Companies should not only enable people to respond quickly to the new technologies, but also try to commit them to the goal of anticipating new technologies (European Round Table of Industrialists 1996).

> Today managers serve primarily as facilitators, coaches, mentors and motivators empowering the real experts who are the associates (members of the workforce). Managers and employees all work together as a potent force for continuous improvement in both quality and productivity (European Round Table of Industrialists 1996).

Other stakeholder organisations

There are of course many other stakeholder organisations in learning cities and regions and the following provides a brief summary.

Adult vocational colleges and other adult education organisations

The advent of lifelong learning is putting a great deal of pressure on adult education. It can be seen from the results of the SKILL EUROPE project reported in Chapter 5, and from the increased use of Personal Learning Audits in companies (and eventually in the community at large), that the demand for adult learning will rise exponentially over the coming years. It will also be obvious that current provision and classroom methods of learning delivery will be inadequate to satisfy the demand. Cities and regions will have to resort to the fusion of broadcasting, information and communications technologies, much as the smart cities in North America are already doing. Equally the number of private adult learning organisations is expected to grow in the future. A trawl in the telephone book of the education companies marketing educational services will confirm that this trend is already well under way. There will need to be some sort of external quality control to avoid abuses. Again this trend has been highlighted earlier in this chapter, and while they provide competition to the existing institutions, the high demand should be able to accommodate the increased provision.

At the same time adult education colleges have their own unique contribution to make to the development of learning cities and regions. They are, after all, more than the universities, likely to contain staff and students from the local communities. A focused tool exists. The Stakeholder Audit for Adult Vocational Colleges mirrors that of the schools and the universities in helping to identify their role in community affairs and ultimately of mobilising the considerable contribution they can make to the city and region in which they reside.

Voluntary, community and social service organisations

The Dublin City Development Board's lifelong learning development strategy suggests that:

> Today, people increasingly belong to a greater number of communities, both geographic and based on shared interests (job, social, ethnic origin, sexual orientation, age, sport, school, etc.). Community participation, notably through volunteering, is essential:
>
> • For people to learn skills of co-operation and a sense of solidarity,
> • For the construction and maintenance of a 'voice' around communities of interest,
> • As a generator of ideas and experimentation for democracy,
> • To give a sense of belonging, pride and security to citizens.

Voluntary and community organisations also play a key role in the development and implementation of the learning city concept. Places of worship, special interest groups, uniformed organisations such as scouts and guides, community centres, sports and leisure clubs, advice bureaus, retirement homes, associations of all kinds all have their part to play in transmitting the learning city message and encouraging participation. Often they are closest to the real problems of social exclusion and can identify an informal learning need where it exists. They can also profit greatly from the volunteering ethos of those learning cities and regions, such as Brisbane, Dublin and Birmingham, where a ready source of assistance to help them foster the community spirit exists. In Dublin, the 2,000 plus organisations in the community and voluntary sector play a key role in ensuring quality of life in local communities. In the words of its learning city strategy document:

> Many of today's organisations began as support or networking groups who came together around specific issues, for example, residents groups, disability or sports groups. Today, these organisations are providing essential services funded by the state. Irish Central Government suggests that a key role of the Community and Voluntary Sector is to form channels of communication through which citizens can be involved.

Chapter 7 expands on the theme of active citizenship through voluntary contribution.

Cultural services organisations

Similarly museums, libraries, galleries and theatres have a central role in the building of the learning city and region. Here is where there is great scope for innovative approaches, both to the marketing and execution of learning city concepts. Chapter 8 relates the story of the PALLACE project in Espoo where a display about the city as a learning city was designed and set up in museums and libraries, inviting the feedback of the public on what their priorities would be. Elsewhere, for example in Manchester and Norwich, UK, modern libraries have provided a focus for active learning and the propagation of the learning message. In Norwich, the library is situated in the Forum, an attractive, modern, accessible facility that also includes a tourist information centre, a Learning Shop, a computer training room for adult education programmes and a coffee shop. The new Norwich BBC broadcast station will also be located in the vicinity. According to Pam Breckenridge,

> The library has become a learning centre that is attractive and accessible for a wide range of users beyond its traditional client group. With 100 computers that are linked to printers and the internet located throughout the library, the public has free and unlimited access to ICT. Currently, there are no time limits on use of the internet although the heavy use of this facility may see these introduced. There is no censure on young people playing computer

games and there is demonstrated an increased number of young people using other library facilities as well as the computers.

The Hume Global Village in Western Melbourne, described in fuller detail in Chapter 8, provides similar services but has a wider function to provide a focal point for all cultural and educational associations to meet under the umbrella of the learning city partnership. All of these creative approaches act as a beacon for others to follow.

People as stakeholders – local and regional elected representatives

In all of this we must not forget that cities and regions ultimately exist not for their institutions but for their citizens. The introduction to the LILLIPUT learning materials for local councillors starts thus.

> Ever-changing and developing learning cities and regions are no place for ideological dogma or single-issue politics. Local and regional politicians have as much, if not more, responsibility for creating the conditions under which future citizens can live in peace, prosperity and harmony with each other as they have with their present constituents. Current problems, which are always many and ongoing, need to be solved without prejudicing the progress of the city towards a learning future.
>
> Local elected representatives need vision as well as commitment, imagination as well as action, a long-term, as well as a short-term view, creativity as well as practical solutions, an open rather than a closed mind-set. Because they are key people to a city's healthy improvement, they have a heavy burden of responsibility to continuously educate themselves in the economic, social, environmental, cultural and ultimately political realities that affect city and regional development. Further, as representatives of the people they bear the responsibility to keep their constituents informed about these realities, a task for which they will need the assistance of professionals.

Cities and regions cannot grow under intolerant, populist or minimalist regimes. Politicians as decision-makers will work with professionals, administrators and advisers to arrive at the best conclusions in the interests of present and future citizens, and to explain why these conclusions have been reached in terms that citizens can understand. In a society founded on increasingly irrelevant adversarial politics and party caucuses, intelligent pragmatism is not an easy stance to take but it is an essential one. As always, learning is the answer. The materials by which passionate commitment can be transformed into informed decision-making already exist in several places, including those same LILLIPUT topics written for elected representatives. Equally it is incumbent on the professionals and administrators to offer advice and encouragement and to make it possible, and of course to go through the same processes themselves so that all parties know what they are aiming for.

Sometimes the route to the learning city is fashioned by the politicians themselves, especially in countries where they play a paid active role in the development of the region. This was so in Espoo, a city of 250,000 people within the Finnish Helsinki complex, where Liisa Tommila, the Deputy Mayor, became an ardent advocate of the learning city concept. The many initiatives, some examples of which have been related in this book, generated under her leadership in the late 1990s and early 2000s put Espoo onto the world map of advanced learning cities.

Local and regional authority managers, professionals and administrators

Chapter 4 has expanded upon the theme of the role and responsibilities of local and regional authorities. The emphasis is on the fostering of strong and vibrant local communities through partnerships, active citizenship, consultation, leadership and lifelong learning. A high proportion of the leadership element will come from people in local and regional government as committed representatives of the city and region to its citizens. However, the managers, professionals and administrators who work there will each have their own view of the meaning of the learning city and their relationship to it. For those totally immersed in fulfilling the requirements of their job it will have only a passing interest until they become convinced of the part it can play in creating a better future for them and their families. Others with a wider vision will want to contribute what they can to making it happen from within the opportunities afforded by their function in the administration. Yet others will play their part both as staff at work and citizens outside work. In countries like Japan where the lifelong learning ethos is strong, people in all local authority departments meet twice annually to discuss how their unit can contribute to the improvement of community life in the city and region. It will be evident that continuous improvement programmes for local and regional authority staff should include some ingredient that entails both learning about the city as a learning organisation and an active component that makes it a reality.

Educators

Educators are another key group of stakeholders with leadership roles and a vested interest in the creation of learning cities and regions. As influencers, and occasionally inspirers, of children and adults they have the capacity and the skills to fire imaginations and stir souls. However, as was discussed in Chapter 5, few educators are aware of the principles of lifelong learning, and even less the concept of learning cities and regions, and there is a large learning curve to be managed before action will result.

Citizens and their families

Last, but certainly not least, we come to the individual citizens and their families, the ultimate stakeholders of the learning city. No matter how much leadership proclaims the virtues of prosperity, stability and the fulfilment of human potential, they are the people who will decide whether or not the game is worth the candle, the ones who will or will not deliver their talents in the service of others and the city. But in order to at least give them the opportunity to make an informed judgement on that, they need to know the facts and the benefits, and therein lies the learning challenge.

The same goes for family learning. In those societies centring around family life, it is easier to imagine the existence of a learning culture, both formal and informal. In Japanese families many people keep their own learning diary, including details of significant learning events and achievements during the year. It is celebrated annually in the learner's own family, usually on birthdays. The acceptability of that process in other cultures may be questionable, but the principle is one that can be adapted. Certainly the incidence of home-schooling by parents in Western societies is on the increase. But many families here are dispersed, disrupted or dysfunctional. The distractions afforded in cities and regions are many and various – sophisticated television 'can't miss' soap operas, pubs and clubs, parties, homework, sports, the street corner – all mitigating against the idea of learning as a family. And yet a number of family learning initiatives have been started, not least the UK Campaign for Learning's family learning week. This is supported by the effective use of the media.

As *Lifelong Learning in Action* reports:

> Newspapers, television and radio all broadcast the concept in special programmes, and celebrities well known to the public play a key part in marketing ideas and actions. Football clubs, museums, galleries and libraries also participate. In 2001 more than half a million people took part in activities ranging from helping garden birds and family singing and dancing to puppet-making and family storytelling and writing. At the Arsenal football club, a much sought after venue for many, children were given the chance to teach the skills of computing and the internet to dads, mums, aunts and uncles, followed by a guided tour, five-a-side football and a picnic in the stands. By contrast the Corinium Museum in Cirencester persuaded families to create a Roman Newspaper. Such activities are not only educational, they provide the support which learners need and a means to celebrate it.

The LILLIPUT materials contain the suggested poster for families shown in Figure 6.9.

Figure 6.9 A family learning poster

```
                          THIS FAMILY

  ENCOURAGES THE HABIT OF LEARNING

  LEARNS FROM EACH OTHER

  LEARNS FROM OTHERS

  VALUES EACH INDIVIDUAL MEMBER

  CONTRIBUTES TO THE LEARNING OF OTHER FAMILIES

  CONTRIBUTES TO THE COMMUNITY IN WHICH IT LIVES

  FREQUENTLY CELEBRATES THE FUN OF LEARNING

  DEVELOPS THE FULL FAMILY POTENTIAL

  HAS A LEARNING PLAN FOR EACH MEMBER OF THE FAMILY

  CHERISHES THE ENVIRONMENT IN WHICH IT LIVES


  THE FAMILY THAT LEARNS TOGETHER STAYS TOGETHER
```

Summary

In this chapter we have explored the importance of stakeholders in the development of learning cities and regions. It has transpired that every organisation and every citizen is a stakeholder and a potential contributor to both the community in which it resides and the wider world outside it. Some, by their very function, are more capable of bringing the world to the city and the region, but the power of the internet has vastly increased that possibility within individuals and families. We have also looked at a number of tools for certain stakeholder organisations. These will not only encourage them to become knowledgeable learning organisations in their own right but also to contribute to the growth and development of the learning city or region in which they reside.

But above all else we have learned that the concept is very much in the cradle. As the European Policy Paper suggests, 'no city is more than 20% along the way and most are in single figures' (Commission of the European Union 2001). Some have not yet even started. The principal challenge is a learning one – making administrators, professionals, teachers, students, families, parents and all citizens aware of the benefits, the imperatives, the social stability and the fun that learning cities and regions confer upon their populations. It is a long, but worthy, task.

Suggestions for further work from this chapter

1   Ensure that the Stakeholder Audits are used by schools, adult colleges, universities and small companies to develop strategies that will convert them into learning organisations and contributors to city and regional life.

2   Input learning city/region learning awareness courses into continuous improvement programmes for all local and regional authority staff and educators in the city. Use the LILLIPUT or the Longlearn materials or tailor them to your own requirements.

3   Take the model in Figure 6.1 and ask a number of people to localise the stakeholder organisations to which it refers in your area. For each organisation assess the contribution it makes to the development of the city or region as a learning city or region.

4   Ensure that every school in your city/region has a copy of the section on schools. Ask each one to measure itself against the St Columba school activities with the community. Ask what they understand by the lifelong learning organisation characteristics in Figure 6.2. How far has each satisfied each requirement? Which of them are in the school's strategy document?

5   Ask the adult education colleges in your area to list an inventory of the contribution it now makes to the establishment of a learning city or region. Ask each one to set up a series of brainstorming committees of staff, administrators and students to examine what contribution it could make in the future.

6   Develop learning city/region courses for elected representatives. Use the LILLIPUT or Longlearn courses and tailor them to local learning needs and examples.

Consulting, convincing, contributing

Tools and techniques for citizen participation in learning cities and regions

One of the exercises in the LILLIPUT project materials, adapted from the Dublin city consultation process, asks participants to rate the following as typical of your region or city:

- falling levels of participation in local organisations and projects;
- low election turnouts;
- general apathy about politics;
- feelings of isolation in the majority of citizens from local government concerns;
- a lack of active consultation processes that are worthwhile, meaningful and consistent;
- need to improve the capacity of local communities to strategically tackle local problems;
- need to rationalise participation and partnership structures;
- a greater need for the transparency and accountability of statutory agencies.

City and regional managers in many countries will certainly recognise the truth in the majority of these and are actively pondering how to address the problem. This chapter therefore provides some information about the issues, and the tools used in certain areas to improve the ways by which the public can not only receive and digest further information but also how it can play its part in decision-making.

The Dublin City Development Board articulates the message thus:

Effective governance of the City relies on an empowered local government and strong avenues for participation by stakeholders such as citizens, businesses and communities. The strengthening of participation in the governance of a city relies on the strengthening of direct citizen and community involvement in decision-making channels. A truly participative society must design its channels of participation to include all citizens. Too often older people, people with disabilities, ethnic minorities, young people and children, to name a few are excluded from decision-making processes.

David Crockett, President of the Chattanooga Institute, asks us to

> Imagine a world where citizens and decision makers have access to visual displays of geographic information on their personal computers that help them see the impact of different policy choices on the place where they live. Imagine a world where 3-D graphic representations of neighborhoods could simulate different choices and show you different futures. Imagine a world where you could easily find information on the fiscal impact of different alternatives … The tools that allow you to do all those things, and more already exist.

That is indeed probably true but before the world of instant access to sophisticated information tools by a majority of citizens can be realised in a responsible way, there must first be a revolution in hearts, minds and brains.

> Effective community decision making starts with good public dialogue. Dialogue goes beyond facts and information; it also draws heavily on feelings and values. Effective public dialogue is about creating safe spaces for community members to share their perspectives and concerns. It is about building trust and relationships that can guide shared solutions.

So says the excellent monograph prepared by the Alliance for Regional Stewardship, and here again the value of public consultation and social learning is cogently argued in a series of examples from the USA. It describes its monograph as a 'user's guide to tools for community decision making'. 'In the final analysis', it says, 'both an effective process and useful tools are essential for civic engagement to work'.

Most reports and documents from whatever source describe community consultation as no longer an option, but an imperative in the 21st century. This is no less true for the establishment of learning cities and regions than it is for planning applications or regeneration projects. Indeed, in the former case it is an opportunity to engage citizens in the social, cultural and environmental improvement processes that will be of direct benefit to present and future generations in their own families. But the manner in which it is done is a huge challenge. Concept change requires mindset change, a difficult task at the best of times, and many minds react badly to anything that takes them out of their comfort zone. 'Consultation is not for the faint-hearted', says Dick (1997). 'No matter how well you design and implement consultation, you may finish up with all stakeholders disappointed. Even when everyone is better off than if you hadn't set up the consultation, they may still blame you for their disappointments'.

'How much civic engagement is possible in regional governance today?' asks the Alliance for Regional Stewardship ,

> Scale and speed challenges, combined with residents' lack of trust in ineffective institutions, discourage participation in regional governance. On

the other hand, without civic engagement, regional governance will not be responsive to residents' needs…. As a result, one of the imperative needs of democracy is to improve citizens' capacities to engage intelligently in political life.

And in the word 'intelligently' lies the challenge. Gilles Paquet looks at social learning as a way forward.

> In times of change, organisations can only govern themselves by becoming capable of learning both what their goals are and the means to reach them as they proceed. This is done by tapping the knowledge and information that active citizens possess and getting them to invent ways out of the predicaments they are in. Thus, to democratise the planning process requires that we look to an open, adaptive model of social learning.

Scott Bernstein looks to a more long-term solution of how social learning is approached:

> Many of our institutions, including our schools, government structures, and business organisations, operate on the traditional, linear model of learning. This model may be appropriate for hierarchical, bureaucratic, and authority-driven institutions, but it is less appropriate for learning in distributed networked governance … An alternative model is the 'ecological' approach to learning that emphasises self-organised, webbed interactions that are adaptive and nonlinear.

And it is of course the type of learning that we advocate for learning cities and regions throughout this book. Closing the gap between the experts and the citizens can only happen with an informed population willing to keep an open mind, to anticipate the future with intelligence, and to learn. Consultation is not a viable process if mind-sets rotate around 'I know what I think, please don't confuse me with the information', or 'nimby' (not in my backyard), though of course they too have the right to their say. The UK DFEE's 1998 *Guide to Assessing Practice and Progress in Learning Cities* recognises this:

> It is difficult for consultation to be effective if those being consulted are not aware of the options. Clear information about possible areas for action and awareness raising may need to precede consultation processes.

The state of Victoria in Australia is very enthusiastic about consultation, not surprisingly since it probably contains the highest percentage of learning cities, regions and towns in the world within its boundaries and has supported their growth with financial resource. The consultation guidelines booklet published by the State Governance Association, *Best Value Victoria*, is a document containing much excellent advice. 'Quality consultation and engagement are building blocks for good governance. Local governments that inform, consult and listen to their local communities, and communities which are engaged and participate in their governance, make for healthy democracies and involved citizens', says its President, Cr Julie Hansen, in the foreword.

It suggests the following focus principles to underlie all good consultation practice:

- Everyone should be clear on why consultation is being undertaken. Every significant project, policy development and strategy should have a consultation plan as part of the overall project plan.
- There must be a statement as to what the purpose of the consultation is. It should then be clear to all involved as to why the consultation is happening and this will help to ensure that appropriate methods are used and the consultation is properly targeted.
- In particular, it is important to identify and clarify whether the consultation is 'closed' (that is, do you agree or disagree with proposition X?) or 'open' (what do you think the issues are in dealing with situation or problem X?).
- It is also desirable to identify the start and finish of the consultation process. It is helpful when participants are aware of when consultation is finished and decision-making is to take place.

Using IT tools and techniques for consultation

The feedback classrooms of the 1960s were primitive instruments using five buttons to respond to multichoice questions. The educator had an immediate feedback of the level of knowledge of the class on any particular topic, and could, in theory, know where revision was needed and when it was wise to continue imparting new knowledge. Unfortunately they proved highly unpopular when educators were confronted with low levels of comprehension by students. Similar tools were used during this author's visit to Epcot in Florida where the possibilities of feedback allowed the audience to express its opinion on a series of environmental and political matters. As I recall at the time, the only way to solve the menace of the Russians, according to that particular audience on that particular day, was to nuke the country, while efforts to clean up environmental degradation was a red plot to break down capitalist society. Such are some of the perils of the indiscriminate use of what has become known as hyper-democracy.

High tech computer technology has of course improved greatly since that time and can greatly aid in the process of data and opinion-gathering, as well as that of delivering the information that improves the chances of that data being more informed. The Strategic Alliance describes the example of Washington DC:

Early in his term, the District of Columbia Mayor, Anthony Williams, searched for a way to keep his campaign promise to revitalize city management and make local government accountable to citizens. He turned to technology, partnerships, and two mass citizen summits to engage residents in city planning through a neighborhood action initiative. The mayor launched the initiative with a one-day 'citizen summit', using wireless polling keypad technology and networked laptop computers. To ensure that the summit reflected the diversity of the Washington community, the neighborhood action partnered with hundreds of non-governmental partners including private-sector organisations, nonprofits, faith-based and advocacy groups, and advisory neighborhood commissions. At the summit, 3,000 residents gathered around tables in groups of 10 to12 with a trained facilitator. Once tables reached consensus on issues, they could immediately use their laptops to send in their vote. Polling keypads allowed the mayor and the summit's moderator to poll citizens throughout the process on questions ranging from demographics to policy priorities. Poll results were instantly flashed on large screens at the front of the room. As a result of this real-time use of technology, 94 percent of all participants polled said they had the opportunity to fully participate.

Large events such as this may or may not be affordable, or even considered desirable, by cities and regions elsewhere, but many are now turning to their websites to open up the debate to citizens. Dublin's progress towards becoming an e-city is an example:

In 2012, Dublin will be a city where communities, agencies, businesses, citizens and decision-makers will have easy access to manageable information and have the means and ability to communicate with each other. Dublin will be a city that harnesses the power of communications technology to connect and inform people, create opportunities and tackle social exclusion. Creating a Connected and Informed City requires connecting people to one another ... These connections are the bedrock upon which individuals engage meaningfully in family, community, career and civil society.

(Dublin City Mission Statement)

Among Dublin's 'connected and informed city' strategies are:

- developing its website, www.dublin.ie, as a focal point for directing people to existing information, providing relevant neighbourhood information, facilitating the community and voluntary sector to use the web/digital media etc.;
- developing a comprehensive database of community and voluntary activity through www.dublin.ie so that people who wish to join groups in the city can keep in touch with their network or find voluntary work in their neighbourhood;

- making free web space and email services available to groups on www.dublin.ie for consultations, protected chat rooms for service providers working on shared caseloads and a learning marketplace where people can plan their learning journeys for life;
- developing theme 'marketplaces' which allow all stakeholders to shape and share information, agree policy, build statistical data, participate in decisions, and 'trade' in goods, opportunities and services.

Dublin is not alone in using technology for a wide variety of purposes including consultation. Most Nordic cities of Europe have similar plans, and, as we saw in Chapter 2, so have many North American cities and regions.

The opinions of the young and the old are especially courted in consultation. The city of Espoo has established youth councils and elderly people's councils as an adjunct to city decision-making. Espoo City Youth Council is an elected body under the city board with 30 members aged from 13–20 years. The objectives are to increase the influence of young people in city decision-making, and to look for new ways of activating initiatives and ideas which allow them to play a fuller part in city life. Next door in Helsinki, the voice of the young campaign has a similar objective. 'It is the right of children and the young to participate in the decisions concerning their life', says the city's information booklet (2002), 'We are building a grassroots participation system for under 18-year-olds in city life while at the same time developing democratic structures for the young to participate in school, youth club, and local community management'. A million Finnmarks has been set aside from the city budget to ensure that it will happen.

The LILLIPUT materials contain a planning tool, shown in Figure 7.1 for those in learning cities and regions setting out on the consultation journey.

A Dublin case study

Such a pre-planning exercise is useful to clarify the why, what, where, when, who, how and how much questions that inevitably arise. But it is only the beginning. In order to explore the processes involved we will examine the Dublin experience, an exercise in taking the pulse of a city and the region around it. 'In 2012 Dublin will be a vibrant city with an array of communities of interest that reflect the true diversity and interests of our citizens, thus contributing to a more participative democracy', says its vision statement for a yen year plan starting in 2002, and the starting point was a two year consultation process that was a thorough as any taken anywhere in the world.

The Dublin process worked within a vision framework of city development strategies comprising:

- A 'heart theme' – *City of Neighbourhoods* – creating and sustaining self-sufficient neighbourhoods within the city that develop 'local identity,

Figure 7.1 A pre-consultation planning exercise

1	<u>What?</u> Identify the issue, project or policy about which consultation is to occur
2	<u>Why?</u> Clearly identify the goal of the consultation process. Write it down
3	<u>Why?</u> Develop a consultation plan? The best way to achieve the result required or is a statutory requirement. Why is this?
4	<u>How?</u> Examine the consultation method options
5	How difficult – complexity of the issue
6	<u>Who</u> are the target groups (affected parties)
7	<u>How easy?</u> Whether the target groups are easy to access or not and how you will achieve this
8	<u>When?</u> How much time and what level of resourcing is available
9	<u>Who</u> is managing the consultation process and who will be doing the work?
10	<u>How</u> will you go about making the information available?
11	<u>How</u> will you ensure understanding?
12	<u>How</u> will you ensure a response?
13	<u>Where</u> will you obtain the response?
14	<u>What form</u> will the response take?
15	<u>How</u> will the results be analysed?
16	<u>Who</u> will make the decision to act on the results?
17	<u>How</u> will the results be acted upon?
18	<u>How and when</u> will you give feedback to the participants?
19	<u>What</u> support do you have?
20	<u>How</u> can you make this an interesting experience for the participants?
21	Are there any other comments you may wish to make?
22	<u>How much</u> will all this cost?

vibrancy and spirit', deliver integrated services and develop bottom-up participative structures.

• Four 'enabling themes':

– *A Diverse and Inclusive City* – recognising and celebrating diversity and difference within the city and its neighbourhoods, while ensuring at the same time that everyone regardless of circumstance, belief, ethnic origin, or economic status is supported.

– *A Connected and Informed City* – acknowledging that information is the key to empowerment and promoting the use of the city's web portal www.dublin.ie as a single focal point for integration of service delivery, consultation, information exchange and research.

- *An Integrated City* – encouraging collaborative action at neighbourhood, city and regional levels and strengthening the linkages between local government and agencies.
- *A Democratic and Participative City* – enhancing democratic accountability in the city through effective consultation procedures and participative structures enabling fully informed citizens and communities to share in decision-making.

- And ten 'outcome themes':

  - *A Safe City* – tackling crime at neighbourhood level in an integrated and community-based manner through prevention, detection and rehabilitation.
  - *A Greener City* – exploring sustainable ways of putting the environment at the centre of the city's, and the people's, agenda.
  - *A Family-Friendly City* – recognising the value of family in all its forms and seeking effective and integrated ways to support it.
  - *A Healthy and Active City* – creating a culture of health and fitness in the city and providing accessible sports and recreational facilities and supports.
  - *A Cultural and Enjoyable City* – integrating culture and the arts into the social and economic priorities of the city.
  - *A City of Homes* – ensuring that everyone has access to a home, facilitated through effective governance of the housing sector.
  - *A Learning City* – increasing co-ordination and partnership amongst learning providers and users, ensuring that all types of learning experiences and intelligence are recognised and equally valued, and promoting the concept of lifelong learning.
  - *An Enterprising City* – supporting a co-ordinated approach to sustainable economic development and developing Dublin city as a world-class centre of excellence, entrepreneurship and corporate social and environmental responsibility.
  - *A Community-Friendly City* – promoting and developing a comprehensive and sustainable range of community facilities and supports as channels for participation and social cohesion.
  - *A Moving and Accessible City* – encouraging debate about sustainable and accessible transport and seeking to reduce the negative environmental impacts of transport.

It will be seen that none of the above exists in its own compartmentalised vacuum. Each is related to the other in a synergetic relationship that contributes to the overall development of the city. Equally several of the themes act as co-ordinating themes for many others in their own right. Learning, for example, is self-evidently a component of every other theme as are the environment, the primacy of communication, sustainability and the need to obtain the consent of the people through consultation. Figure 2.5 in Chapter 2 puts learning at the centre of the strategy and this works equally well as a template for the construction of the learning city.

Consultation phases

However, devising a consultation process to satisfy Dublin's key principles of good governance – openness, participation, accountability, effectiveness and coherence – within such a large and eclectic set of strategies was evidently a labour of considerable importance and complexity. It meant reinventing the systems, structures and level of governance in the city and expanding its remit to account for all services delivered to the citizens and local communities.

The process of ensuring that everybody had the opportunity to participate in the development of the strategic vision started in 2000. As the Dublin City Development Board says,

> Participation in the early stages of strategy development is desirable, as it is often the outcome of decisions made at this stage that have the greatest effect on people's needs and chances to benefit. It provides the greatest opportunity to develop a sense of ownership and opportunity to make a difference.

The first phase involved 90 individuals and organisations from key stake-holders in developing the strategy working papers under the title 'Capital Vision', and making them available in hard copy and through the web (www.dublin.ie).

Phase two saw the process of informing and gathering feedback from citizens and organisations, and included:

- advertisements in local and national newspapers, a free-phone information number, articles in newspapers, journals, newsletters and on websites, information on television, radio interviews and a video;
- using the Dublin web-portal www.dublin.ie – encouraging people to provide feedback via the online feedback form;
- a consultation brochure sent to over 70,000 households, businesses, schools, libraries, organisations and agencies around the city;
- a consultation pack including a video presentation for use at focus group meetings for specific interest groups such as the city council, FÁS, health boards, third level institutions (students), ethnic minority groups, economic focus groups etc.;
- civic fora – involving city councillors, public servants, community organisations, local business and residents invited randomly from the electoral register from within each of the areas of the city;
- consultation seminars on city integration, participation and social inclusion for voluntary groups, businesses, statutory organisations and citizens' panels

- a concentration on the participation of schools and youth – including a video highlighting the key issues distributed along with copies of brochures to secondary schools in Dublin.

The modified draft strategy resulting from these processes then underwent a further consultation round of exhibitions in public places, radio and TV interviews, brochures, press articles and advertisements, and stakeholder meetings (23), while the *Irish Times* published a full supplement describing the strategy in order to also attract a wider audience in the surrounding region.

Peter Finnegan and his team at the Dublin City Development Board included a number of further innovative approaches in the draft strategy for the learning region, including:

- consulting local community organisations directly about its learning region policies;
- consulting individual citizens directly about learning region policies;
- including representatives of community groups on a lifelong committee or board;
- consulting local SMEs about their learning needs;
- including local schools in the learning region consultation process;
- creating new channels of participation at neighbourhood and city level;
- carrying out a region-wide neighbourhood mapping exercise to determine new neighbourhood participative structures;
- ensuring greater accountability of service providers in the city to the communities they serve;
- ensuring the inclusion of all groups in decision-making processes, especially older people, people with disabilities and young people;
- establishing a good urban governance audit and excellence mark;
- promoting examples of national and international best practice of good participation;
- providing an on-line directory of community and voluntary organisations active in the city;
- increasing the number of community bulletin boards;
- supporting the development of a community TV channel for the region;
- facilitating the development of a support secretariat for each neighbourhood.

The above demonstrates a determined attempt by the Dublin City Development Board to involve as many of Dublin's citizens as possible in the planning of its strategy for the next ten years. Further, there is an equally serious intention to maintain the consultation and empowerment process as the strategy develops through the effective use of the web portal for accessible information giving and receiving, a continuing social research commitment, community media, sustainability proofing and the development of an infrastructure focused entirely on the strengthening of the human bonds and connections that make civic society work. Although Dublin does not describe the complete set of strategies as a formal learning city policy development, that is exactly what it has done within the wider understandings of the term contained within this book.

A consultation hierarchy

What it also shows is a hierarchy of consultation processes, which might be expressed as a staircase, as shown in Figure 7.2.

In the figure:

The *Information Provision* process is the basic act of letting citizens know about an event or a development and asking them to accept it. From the local and regional administration viewpoint, citizens are *subscribers* (or not) to the decisions made by the city or regional council and its professionals.

The *Discussion* process sets up a dialogue between cities and regions and their citizens. In this citizens are *confidants*, whose opinion may or may not be taken into account at final decision time, but at least they have been asked.

The *Engagement* process goes one step further by requesting the input of citizens into the decision-making process. They become *partners* with the decision-makers by providing feedback that will be taken into account in the final decision.

The *Motivation* process is still a part of consultation but also the beginning of the action phase. Citizens become *learners* in an effort to raise understanding and awareness of the needs of the city and the region in the future. This step is a big, but important, one to take as shown in the diagram.

The *Participation* process is a combination of consultation and action. It negotiates with the public before the decision is taken, and also assumes that citizens will act as *implementers* of the solution in partnership with the administrators.

The *Empowerment* process hands over decision-making to the citizens themselves. They become both decision-makers and *managers* of the consequences of those decisions. The city and the region are now in real learning organisation mode. The achievement of step four becomes crucial to the success of the strategy.

Such an ascent up the staircase can be seen in the Dublin example above. It takes sensitive and sensible management to bring to fruition.

Figure 7.2 The consultation staircase: from information-giving to citizen power

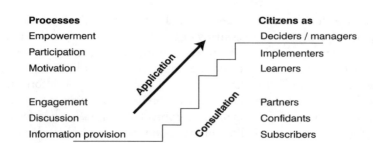

Active citizenship in the learning city

A successfully implemented consultation system should inspire citizens to do more than just deliver an opinion. As has been consistently advocated throughout this book one of the most important indicators of successful learning cities and regions is the extent to which their citizens participate in active citizenship programmes that enhance community living, learning and social cohesion. Bill Williamson describes it as a 'framework of values and institutions which evolve, adapt and enable people collectively to seek creative solutions to the problems they continue to encounter'. The TELS Learning Cities Audit asked its 80 cities if it had plans to formally identify talents, skills, knowledge etc. to encourage contributions made by citizens to the development of a learning city. 'Yes' was the answer given by two cities, but for the rest the activity in this area was generally very low. At the most, six cities said that they have a database of the skills, talents, knowledge etc. available from members of the community to assist in its educational organisations, but none have a formal plan to use them and only three offered rewards and incentives for doing so. If one measure of a learning city is the extent to which it is able to stimulate participation among its citizens, then these statistics show a mountain of work ahead.

Three of the recommendations in the European Commission's *Memorandum on Lifelong Learning* (2001) are:

- to build an inclusive society which offers equal opportunities for access to quality learning throughout life to all people, and in which education and training provision is based first and foremost on the needs and demands of individuals;
- to adjust the ways in which education and training is provided, and how paid working life is organized, so that people can participate in learning throughout their lives and can plan for themselves how they combine learning, working and family life;
- to encourage and equip people to participate more actively once more in all spheres of modern public life, especially in social and political life at all levels of the community, including at European level.

The International Association for Volunteer Effort (IAVE) adds its voice to the clamour. 'We recognize and celebrate the right and responsibility of all people to voluntarily contribute their time, talent, and energy to address pressing human, social, economic and environmental problems and to build healthy communities', it says, and proposes a universal declaration on volunteering thus:

Volunteering is a fundamental building block of civil society. It brings to life the noblest aspirations of humankind – the pursuit of peace, freedom, opportunity, safety, and justice for all people. In this era of globalisation and continuous change, the world is becoming smaller, more interdependent, and more complex. Volunteering – either through individual or group action – is a way in which:

- human values of community, caring, and serving can be sustained and strengthened;
- individuals can exercise their rights and responsibilities as members of communities, while learning and growing throughout their lives, realising their full human potential; and,
- connections can be made across differences that push us apart so that we can live together in healthy, sustainable communities, working together to provide innovative solutions to our shared challenges and to shape our collective destinies.

At the dawn of the new millennium, volunteering is an essential element of all societies. It turns into practical, effective action the declaration of the United Nations that 'We, the Peoples' have the power to change the world.

IAVE sees the advantages of volunteering as:

- it elicits the involvement of the entire community in identifying and addressing its problems;
- it encourages and enables youth to make leadership through service a continuing part of their lives;
- it provides a voice for those who cannot speak for themselves;
- it enables others to participate as volunteers;
- it complements but does not substitute for responsible action by other sectors and the efforts of paid workers;
- it enables people to acquire new knowledge and skills and to fully develop their personal potential, self-reliance and creativity;
- it promotes family, community, national and global solidarity.

And it has a message for local and regional authorities who should:

- create environments in which volunteers have meaningful work that helps to achieve agreed upon results;
- define the criteria for volunteer participation, including the conditions under which the organisation and the volunteer may end their commitment, and develop policies to guide volunteer activity;
- provide appropriate protections against risks for volunteers and those they serve;
- provide volunteers with appropriate training, regular evaluation, and recognition;
- ensure access for all by removing physical, economic, social, and cultural barriers to their participation.

Such noble sentiments have in fact already been put into place in many parts of the world. Volunteering Queensland, for example, offers a state-wide referral service which links people who wish to volunteer their time and effort to community organisations in their local area. Its sophisticated website addresses potential member organisations thus.

> As a member you can take advantage of our services and tap into the latest thinking on volunteering issues. Volunteering is the basis on which healthy communities are built and the means through which individuals can become involved and actively participate in their own environments and communities. This can be through sporting or leisure activities, social action or environmental groups, health and community welfare, education, emergency services to name a few. VQ has thousands of voluntary jobs listed within its member organisations. Last year VQ made over 7,500 referrals to member organisations.

It is run as a business and provides the detailed tools by which member organisations can match the demand to the skills and resources available. In addition to its referral service, it offers training courses for both volunteers and member organisations, distributes newsletters, markets the concept to Queenslanders, organises events such as National Volunteer Week and International Volunteer Days, provides help with insurance matters, designs volunteering forms and administers community grants and awards. An organisation choosing to take advantage of VQ's offerings can choose from several levels of membership depending on how much it wishes to pay and which services it chooses to use. The following excerpt from a press report in the *Brisbane Advertiser* gives an idea of the scale of the operation.

BRISBANE LAUNCHES IYV WITH THE BIGGEST CELEBRATION OF VOLUNTEERING THE STATE HAS SEEN

Sunday December 3rd, 2000 will long be remembered as a red letter day in the history of volunteering in Queensland. It was without doubt the biggest and most impressive showcase of volunteer effort this state has seen. Stretching over a six kilometre route from Kurilpa Point to the City Botanic Gardens, it took the 6000 participants in the parade one and half hours to pass through city streets.

With everything from mounted police to fire trucks, belly dancers and performers on stilts, dogs and balloons along with bands of all kinds, it had all the colour and sound of one the city's major public events. There were groups from a huge range of sectors; from the arts, heritage, sport, emergency services, aged care, child & youth care, environmental, health, disability, education, multicultural, social justice, advocacy and community welfare.

The launch was without a doubt a 'for volunteers, by volunteers' event. In all, more than 100 volunteers contributed to the success of the Parade & Festival in roles such as Parade Marshals, Festival Guides, Performer Supporters, Promotions, Parade Assembly and staffing the Event Hotline.

The primary goals for the Brisbane launch were met with amazing success. The Volunteers Parade & Festival allowed Brisbane to:

- showcase the strength and diversity of volunteering,
- recognise the huge contributions of volunteers across all sectors, and
- bring the community together to celebrate those involved in volunteering.

Teenage volunteer armies

The UK has similar plans to mobilise people into community work, particularly young people. *The Times* newspaper of 17 March 2005 reports,

> A teenage army of one million young volunteers is to be recruited under plans for Britain's first National Community Service Corps. Borrowing heavily from the *AmeriCorps* scheme in the United States, which enables volunteers to work on community service projects for a year in return for a modest education and living allowance, the UK Chancellor said he would consider paying full-time gap year volunteers around £75 a week.

The scheme would 'match the idealism and willingness of young people to serve with the needs of communities across our country and internationally'. The proposals also include opportunities for young volunteers to try out volunteering though short-term or part-time 'taster' schemes working in health, heritage, culture, community, safety, conservation, education and sport. Up to £150 million will be invested in a new volunteer framework – £100 million coming from government and the remainder from private enterprise. The aim of the initiative is 'to ensure that young people, whatever their background, can afford to take part in types of community work that have traditionally been the preserve of better-off middle-class youngsters'.

Industry and business to the rescue

Active citizenship in the community can also be energised through industry and commerce. Most large companies operate programmes that encourage their employees to involve themselves with the community within which the company resides. One example is IBM in the UK. Among the several initiatives in its 'on-demand community' programme, all employees and retirees are urged to work with the schools of their choice in supporting the donation of free equipment and software. The management and communications skills built up in the company are also valuable for community groups. The story of

Christopher Bowers is but one example. On his retirement he established a foster carer's association in Kingston, UK, with a grant from the company, created a website offering training courses, practical advice and a forum for foster parents and linked this into the borough's website. The company also runs several other social programmes, including the 'Reinventing Education' project to share best practice methodologies between schools, which won a national lifelong learning award, and 'Book Buzz' which encourages Nottinghamshire children to post a review of a recommended book they have read on a local website.

Science camps for girls take place in IBM locations to help them choose maths and science as a career, and a mentoring service offering guidance and study support is available to those students who want it. Seven per cent of the IBM UK workforce participate in grant-aided support schemes in the community, which, together with programmes for retirees who tend to have a little more time, amounts to 1,200 people participating in active citizenship projects. Add this to the thousands of other actual and potential activities by business and industry, such as *The Guardian* newspaper's and Hewlett Packard's science mentorship programmes, and learning cities and regions have a substantial additional resource on their hands that can, with proper management, be augmented and channelled.

Service learning

Schools too can contribute much to the development of active citizenship. In Canada, service learning is a way of doing this. According to Kate McPherson (1991), 'Service Learning is a method of teaching through which students apply their academic skills and knowledge to address real-life needs in their own communities'. It is a way of relating concepts, content and skills from the academic disciplines to the challenges of community involvement. An essential part of the assessment process is to enhance student learning and to document and evaluate how well students have met content and skills standards. Students engage in service tasks that have clear goals, meet genuine needs in the school or community and have significant consequences for themselves and others. A number of skills are developed in students through communication and interaction with the community including sensitivity to the needs of others, self-reflection, and critical thinking.'

Some examples of typical second grade projects in another Canadian programme 'Giraffe' related by Wheeler and Bernier (2002) are: weed and plant a garden, build a bird house, visit nursing homes, collect clothes for the homeless, pick up trash on the roadside, raise money for charity via bake sales, and many more. One boy collected school supplies from his classmates which he packaged and sent all the way to Haiti. To explain the dire situation in schools of Haiti, he invited a family friend to show her slides taken while on a mission trip to this small country. Views of children walking miles and miles to school, which only lasts a few hours a day, made the need very clear to second graders. They generously gave a large quantity of basic school supplies to children who had few pencils and crayons. Such stories are commonplace in Canada where, in the Ontario Service Learning programme, all schoolchildren are required to deliver 40 hours of active service to the community. Equally, in schools embracing the International Baccalaureate worldwide, students will complete 50 hours of community service, paving the way for a lifetime of active citizenship.

Service credit

If service learning has a great deal to contribute to the growth of learning cities and regions, service credit is an entirely different animal. It is for those who are uncomfortable about giving their talents and skills away for nothing, or where they wish to have some tangible reward. It creates a social currency based upon time and so is sometimes known as time dollars in the USA or time banking elsewhere. The principle is simple. If someone spends an hour on a charitable cause, he/she earns a time dollar. It is deposited into a time bank and spendable in a variety of ways – perhaps an hour of another volunteer's time or a service. Participants receive regular statements from the time bank. Some companies in the USA have agreed that time dollars can be exchanged for goods and credit accounts, whereby people do voluntary work to qualify for help when they become infirm, and they can also be used as a form of old-age insurance. Time dollars can also be traded for such services as meals-on-wheels, house cleaning, nursing care, neighbourhood security patrols and computer training work. In Chicago, teenagers who agree to mentor younger pupils can 'cash in' their dollars on computer software.

Time dollars are in use in more than 100 communities in 30 states and three countries (the United States, Great Britain and Japan). These are a couple of snapshots of the most innovative practices:

Brooklyn: Seniors insured through Elderplan, a social health maintenance organisation, can cash in time dollars for a 25 per cent discount on their health insurance by helping other seniors to remain self-sufficient. Seniors provide their own informal support system, including pain management seminars, telephone bingo, home repairs, shopping, rides, and peer counselling. Elderplan now offers a time dollar redemption catalog so members can cash in their time dollars for health and beauty equipment, taxi vouchers, and social events.

Washington, DC: A Time Dollar Youth Court brings first offenders before a jury of their peers. Jurors earn time dollars as they hear cases and impose sentences that may include community service, restitution, an apology, writing an essay, and jury duty. They redeem the time dollars for computers recycled by other youths at three high schools. In those public housing complexes where a jury pool has been formed, a new peer culture enables one youngster to hold another accountable for their actions.

Whether alternative social currencies catch on in other cultures is debatable but it is undoubtedly an innovative idea with a future.

A tool for catching the potential contributor

But how do local communities harvest the potential in their midst? One answer is to include a section in the Personal Learning Audit for the purpose. Part 4 of the Longlearn audit is intended to give participants an opportunity to feed something back into the system:

What skills and talents can you already contribute?

> So far you have made a record of your past learning journeys and connected this to the itinerary you may want to make now and in the future. But we have constantly emphasised how each of us has talents, skills, knowledge, values and experiences which could be valuable to others on their own learning voyages. They range from subject knowledge to interpersonal communication skills, to coaching and guiding talents for which one does not necessarily have to be a trained teacher. So this last item in the stock-taking phase is to find out what your own talents and skills are, and then to explore how you might apply them in the service of yourself and others. Sometimes people, especially those who are coming back to learning after a lay-off, need no more than a guide to ask them how they are faring and to supply moral encouragement if things are getting difficult. Others may require a little bit more, such as a weekly or monthly meeting or telephone call to review how they are making progress – a sort of conductor to take the fares. Yet others would benefit from a subject specialist who can spare a few minutes to act as a personal support tutor to help understand difficult concepts – an assistant driver to keep them on track. Every learner has different needs and requirements. And equally there are different ways of satisfying these.
>
> You may be a little shy of doing this, especially if you have not done it before. And of course it is not obligatory to become a full learning adviser before you yourself have sorted out your own learning plans. You may wish to concentrate on mapping your own learning destination before embarking on offering help to others. And this is perfectly acceptable. But it is a well-known maxim that helping others to learn also helps you to learn, and the act of putting your name onto a register of learning helpers or potential learning helpers will provide a powerful system of learning support within the community.

Figure 7.3 shows the opening exercises in this section of the personal learning audit. It goes on to suggest a number of roles that people might want to play in the learning of others

Section 4 – Your contribution to the Learning of Others

Everyone has talents, skills, knowledge and experience to offer to others. In communities many people already work for and with each other on a variety of projects and this is a great strength. Modern technology makes it easier to communicate in new ways to do this. Here we ask a few questions about your potential contribution to the learning of others in your community.

Cities and regions carrying out similar exercises may wish to learn from organisations like Volunteering Queensland or to use other agencies to gather such data.

Guides and mentors

The general principles of active citizenship and volunteering as tools for motivating people and regenerating creative formal and informal learning have

Figure 7.3 Sample exercises from section 4

4.1 Your talents, skills, experience and knowledge –

4.1.1 Knowledge and Experience – please list which subject areas you have a working knowledge of, which might be useful for others studying these topics, e.g. mathematics, engineering, language, accountancy, banking, plumbing, psychology etc. – the list need not be confined to work.

....

....

....

4.1.2 Talents and Skills – please list your practical skills, e.g. tennis, public speaking, meditating, teaching, piano-playing. Think carefully – you have many more than come to mind at first.

....

....

....

been mentioned above. Here we concentrate on the particular issues concerning the deployment of guides and mentors. Many schemes for using and training guides and mentors in the community now exist as result of the recent emphasis on lifelong learning. In several senses their use has become an additional tool for promoting self-awareness and empowering people. In another sense the possibility that volunteers, friends, family and members of the community can all be mentors makes us all into potential teachers now, especially at the community level, and this poses interesting questions about how the talents, knowledge, experiences, skills and empathy inherent in any community can be mobilised for the good of all. In TELS, 60 of the 80 cities did not actively encourage the use of learning mentors or coaches in any of their own organisations. In a paper by this author in the *JOLLI* magazine,

> The key to implementing successful ideas, strategies, programmes and dreams in a learning community lies with people, and in particular those people with the insight and the energy to take the leadership role. The whole concept of leadership is of major importance in the effectiveness of learning.

The European Round Table of Industrialists suggests that, 'Everybody can help to facilitate and encourage and so make it happen. Spontaneity, innovation, experiment, diversity and decentralisation are the key words'.

There are already many mentoring schemes in the community. As *Making Lifelong Learning Work* reports,

> In the UK, the strategy of the city of Southampton's learning outreach project is to develop and train a team of community mentors who will support the learning needs of all people in a neighbourhood. The aim is to raise levels of self-esteem and motivation amongst 'harder to reach learners' in the city in order to both encourage them to return to learning and to provide on-going mentoring support to help them fulfil their potential. Outreach workers come from learning institutions, from other agencies in the city which have day to day contact with local people and from volunteers who are keen to encourage and support people in their local community to return to learning. They are trained and accredited to work at basic, intermediate or advanced level, and work through housing associations, further education colleges, community schools, careers services, the workers educational service, parents associations, employment offices – any organisation which can help them to make contact with people and spread the message of learning. They act as a support mechanism, assessing learning needs and opportunities and, most importantly, as mentors to those who most need encouragement to continue in learning. Other neighbourhood support facilities in Southampton are provided from the community centres, which run, for example, programmes for new mothers (the first babies group), parents of young schoolchildren

(parents as teachers) and voices (a project to give disadvantaged people the confidence to negotiate with city offices).

Mentoring can take many forms. As a shoulder to lean on in case of difficulty, as a guide through the minefield of educational provision, or as a coach in particular subjects, as a counsellor expanding the horizons of what is possible. It doesn't need to be related to educational study. *Making Lifelong Learning Work* reports on a scheme in Brixton to provide responsible and respected adult mentors for children with behavioural or learning difficulties, and, as we have seen, the USA adopt-a-school programme contains many examples of managers and workers mentoring young people in schools in many different ways. Indeed, North America is the spiritual home of mentoring, and especially telementoring, in universities, research establishments, companies, churches, colleges and schools. Even film and sports stars get themselves involved in supporting single parent families. *The Scotsman* newspaper reports that the 'big brother and sister' scheme, in which respected mentors spend two to four hours with children at risk, found that children with a mentor were 46 per cent less likely to abuse drugs, 57 per cent less likely to play truant and 32 per cent less likely to be violent.

Mentoring is not an easy task nor is it one to be taken lightly. Each organisation or community adopts its own rules and regulations, publishes guidelines and runs courses for potential mentors. And of course there must, unfortunately in today's world, always be safeguards against those who would abuse both the system and the person. But a properly run mentorship programme can mean the difference between success and failure for some thousands of at-risk children, particularly in large urban depressed areas.

Telementoring is another model. In the Hewlett-Packard company's email mentoring programme new technology is employed in innovative ways to provide help to needy students. Its aims, like those of the IBM scheme mentioned above, are to improve mathematics and science achievement in secondary level education, to increase particularly the number of women and minorities in mathematics and science, and to help motivation in children at school. Students and Hewlett-Packard employee mentors collaborate on classroom activities such as science projects and mathematics lessons, under the direction of a supervising classroom teacher. Teachers are an integral part of the project. They submit a lesson plan for the student and mentor to work on together (and on which the student will receive a grade), and supervise the mentor–student interaction. Mentors communicate with the student at least two to three times per week and agree to be a positive role model. From 14 countries 2,900 mentors have helped operate the programme in the United States, Canada, Australia, and France. Teachers have noted increases in student attendance, better use of technology, more motivation at school, and greater self-confidence. There are hundreds of possibilities and opportunities for good mentoring programmes in the development of a learning city and region. They have a proven track record and the coming years will see a large increase in their number as the lifelong learning philosophy becomes more accepted.

Leadership in learning cities and regions

Embryo learning cities and regions will depend heavily on the commitment of leaders within the city and the communities they serve. They broadcast the message of lifelong learning and facilitate its acceptance in the community. Any strategy to engender progress must therefore inform and engage the decision-makers, opinion-formers and community leaders and expand their number as quickly and innovatively as possible. As *Lifelong Learning in Action* suggests,

> The process of renewal and regeneration of the learning city, and participation by large numbers of stakeholders, becomes self-sustaining over time. But such a happy state lies a long way ahead in most cities. In the primary stages of the development of any new project or system, ideas, solutions and procedures are imparted by the few with the insight and the energy to take the leadership role, to the many. The sensitivity and innovation with which this leadership is exercised can be the difference between success and failure in these circumstances. It is a process of empowering as many people as possible to play a responsible role in learning city development, in a cascade model of growth, so that the city itself becomes a learning organisation.

One of the first steps a city can take is to organise courses and seminars to develop the learning leaders who can help achieve common goals. The LILLIPUT and Longlearn materials would fuel these. Leaders should not always be the obvious candidates of teachers, social workers, managers and councillors. Leaders can, and should come from anywhere in the community, from any background – from industry, voluntary organisations, education, perhaps even from the ranks of the unemployed. They need to be given the vision of a learning city and invited to participate in its development, inserting their own ideas and practical advice. This is the learning city as a learning organisation, an exercise in participation and commitment with the aim of eventually involving everyone in the city in the common objective.

Finally, a lament from the author, taken from *Lifelong Learning in Action*:

> I live in a particularly beautiful area of Southern France. My village of some 300 souls is one of those villages perchés and one of the 100 most beautiful villages in France. The view from my office opens out across the valley onto the Canigou, a 9000 foot mountain, snow-capped for 10 months of the year. In the foreground are peach, apricot, almond, cherry and nectarine trees which, during blossom time, form a rich carpet of pink, white and green on which, it seems, one could float into El Dorado. Prades, the nearest town, comprises about 7000 inhabitants. Its secondary school and college

are fed by the families of the town and the many villages around. On its curriculum at all levels are languages, including English and German, Biology, Music, Geography, Mathematics, as well as a host of other subjects.

I am not the only British resident of this paradise. Among our small community of 100 people are a much-travelled world-class biologist who was secretary to the Prince of Wales environmental trust, a former teacher trainer in geography, a mathematics teacher who has taken early retirement, 3 English as a foreign language teachers, 2 former Opera singers also trained in music teaching, a former dietician and a former professor of German. These are just the skills I know about.

The application of logic seems to point to the marriage of these talents with the schoolchildren who might benefit from them, enriching their learning world with the stories, adventures and experiences of those who have personal immersion in the subject, and from time to time giving the teachers a rest from the stress of the school-day. And if asked, all of those people would be happy to devote a few hours a week, a month or a year to making their knowledge and assistance available.

But of course we are not seen as the answer to the school's prayers, bringing enrichment, assistance and enlightenment to the dull grind of everyday school life. We are in fact a threat, to the established order of the school and to the dominance and status of the teachers there. I am not aware of any school, with the exception perhaps of a few in Australia and Finland, which has begun to explore the wealth of human talent and expertise in its own community with a view to making education a living, breathing and pleasurable experience for our future citizens.

True learning cities and regions would not allow that to happen.

Suggestions for further work from this chapter

1   Ask one or more of your administration departments to make an inventory of the human skills, experiences, talents and knowledge from all its members. Then ask for a list of the places where they could be used (whether or not there is an intention to do so). Circulate this around all departments and ask for comments and ideas in the context of a learning city.
2   Ask another department to brainstorm the things they would recommend if an unlimited supply of volunteering resource were available. This can be a personal brainstorm by each individual followed by a general one.
3   Match the results from 1 and 2.
4   Give someone the task of putting together a group to devise a volunteering service for your city or region, to report back in three months time.
5   Identify and make a list of the people in your community who are leaders. Make it as long as you can and do not use only the obvious candidates. Devise a series of seminars on innovative active citizenship for these leaders

using the LILLIPUT modules 3 and 4 or the Longlearn materials. Make this a cascade process so that each participant runs a similar seminar for ten other people and so on.

6   List the pros and cons of mentoring programmes for schools and colleges. Use the lament at the end of this chapter to stimulate ideas.

Chapter 8

Imagining, internationalising, interconnecting

Global roles, global opportunities for learning cities and regions

Some causes of poverty are controlled by the person involved, but most are not. These include the person's surroundings, the family they were born into, the amount of education they have, the way they are treated by others, and their luck. Also, poverty and hunger are definitely connected to population growth, because when there are more people, there has to be more resources. The problem is that the Earth may not have enough resources, or the resources it does have may be inaccessible to those who need them.

(8th grade Canadian student, after participating in a Facing the Future global issues activity)

So far we have explored the purely local impact of establishing learning cities and regions as introspective entities looking inwards at themselves in order to enhance the economic and social life of their citizens. There is no dispute that the primary short- and medium-term objective of local and regional authorities is to build up local social and industrial capital, and to improve the physical infrastructure of the city through regeneration and maintenance projects. But, strong and urgent though this may be, there is another, more international, more extrovert, dimension to the learning city concept, notwithstanding ratepayers and other minimalist pressure groups to restrict its responsibilities to local issues. There is a sense in which cities and regions can play a much larger part on the national and global stage, often to their own medium and long-term advantage. The unprecedented emotional and financial response to the Boxing Day 2004 tsunami crisis by people of all ages, incomes and political persuasions is but one demonstration of the extent to which people have advanced in their perception of this planet as a global village, an integrated and holistic unity. The interest shown by participants in global projects such as PALLACE, and the vast maturity gain resulting from them, is another.

The willingness to interact with, and help provide for, others less fortunate than oneself is sometimes an on–off affair, difficult to argue against adherents of the 'charity begins at home' lobbies so prevalent in every city. But as the 21st century progresses, the more participative components of lifelong learning concepts to develop and mobilise intellectual and human capital are gradually opening additional doors of perception in a larger number of citizens, while the technologies of email and the internet are breaking down the barriers to international understanding still further.

Cities and regions as mini-states

John M. Eger, former adviser to US Presidents, suggests that cities and regions may be on the verge of becoming new city and region-states to rival in potential power the likes of Venice and Athens in their heyday, and many regions of Northern Germany before unification. And certainly government policies in many countries encourage more autonomy in the regions, a movement that can only increase as the concept of learning cities and regions advances. In Europe, many emerging regions transcend the physical and linguistic boundaries of nation states. Transmanche covers the area of Kent in the UK and the Pas de Calais in France; Oresund links the Copenhagen area of Denmark with South Scania in Sweden; and the links between Alsace-Lorraine and the Black Forest areas of Germany have resulted in a flourishing region around the city of Strasbourg. They are well on the way to becoming new region-states, powerful in their influence on global trade and comparatively rich. The momentum is certainly gathering for a more expanded role.

In many ways the exhortation to wider international participation is inescapable. The Eurydice report on National Education Systems quotes for Austria,

> Young people have to be able to develop independent judgement and understanding of and responsibility for social relations, sensitivity to the political and philosophical views of others, and the ability to contribute to the economic and cultural life of the country, Europe and the world. Humanity, tolerance, solidarity, peace, justice and ecological awareness are values that stimulate action in our society and interact with economic issues.

Fine words indeed, not always visible in the real world, but nonetheless in keeping with the times.

Environmental pollution created in one region respects no geographical boundaries. As with disease, it is visited upon others by wind, sea and plane. Chaos theory predicates that the fluttering of a butterfly's wings in Japan has an effect on people in North America. And though that image may be a difficult one to grasp, it acts as a metaphor for a planet rendered conceptually smaller and more intimate by the power of modern communication methods. Nightly, citizens see on their screens the misery and happiness, poverty and wealth, terror and beauty, profit and loss of human existence throughout the planet. Unscrupulous politicians, religious fundamentalists and sensation-hungry mediamen present the outside world as an evil place, preying on ignorance and prejudice, and using the weak, the insecure and defenceless – asylum seekers and travellers, nonconformists, gay people, bohemians – as symbols of alien cultures, fecklessness and an end to secure civilisation. That outside world impinges, whether we see it as a place of fear or of opportunity, on all our consciousnesses.

Learning Cities for a Learning Century argued that,

> The steep increase in the standard of education required to produce a learning city able to cope with 21st century work patterns; the enhanced under-standing of the technological tools which will come into common usage in many households; the environmental imperative to safeguard and sustain an ecologically sound and stable environment in the city; the threat to democracy caused by a loss of interest and informed thought on issues affecting the livelihood of millions; these will not be addressed without the stimulus of a new learning environment accessible to, and comprehensible by, all people.

Such environments are now becoming more and more common in many cities and regions, and where they exist, they are expanding horizons in the adult population, as well as the young.

And many of them are now international. Almost every South Australian school has links with schools in other countries in South East Asia, North America and Europe. It is a key part of the educational experience for their young people. 'Seniornets', linking pensioners in New Zealand, Canada, USA and the UK, have been operating for many years. There can be little doubt in this digital age that the internet is compressing the planet and changing radically the way that people see the wider world. 'A Learning Region is an inclusive and democratic region. It will inform its citizens about the need for the journey and engage them in it not just as passengers but as activators and drivers', says the local authorities Stakeholder Audit developed in the European Commission's INDICATORS project.

Cities and regions, whether their citizens like it or not, are now an essential part of the global economy. The concept of the Ideopolis, introduced in Chapter 1 as a city capable of attracting new employment and other opportunities through its attractiveness to potential inward investment from wherever in the world, reinforces that. Further, the changing economic, social, environmental, political and cultural landscape in every city of the developed, and increasingly the developing, world, makes international investment a desirable priority.

Many other examples of global linking abound. Multinational companies have their own sophisticated networks between countries and locations worldwide. Much of their business, although carried out locally, is conducted on the basis of a global manufacturing, production, training and marketing system. In Europe a large number of towns and cities are twinned with each other in bilateral, and sometimes multilateral, partnerships. They were an essential element of the post-

Second World War rapprochement, though most do not extend beyond the occasional cultural visit of civic dignitaries. Again in Europe there exists a number of inter-city and inter-regional organisations such as Eurocities, the Committee of the Regions, Educating Cities and so on, each with their own centre of operations and each addressing issues of concern to themselves as municipalities. In education, the associated schools project organised by UNESCO has developed year on year a great number of collaborative projects between schools worldwide, concentrating mainly on international themes connected with the environment, tolerance, peace and other subjects that one would expect a charitable international non-governmental organisation to concern itself with.

Learning city-rings

What does not exist, and what there is a great need for, is a global network of learning cities that extends beyond an annual conference get-together, and instead mobilises its members to address political, social, cultural, educational, religious and environmental issues resulting from the need for human beings to live together in harmony on this planet. The idea has been around for many years. It could be a simple educational twinning or mentoring arrangement between two similar or dissimilar cities along the lines of the sister cities model, or it could be something much more ambitious. The European Commission's PALLACE project, described below, provides a model for learning cooperation between cities and regions. It did not establish a large worldwide network of cities and towns, but rather a smaller, much more manageable, group of seven or eight into a 'city-ring', each partner carrying out a project on behalf of the others. This idea could be replicated in other city-ring networks, each learning from the other, each contributing to the other and each mobilising its stakeholders to communicate meaningfully with and across stakeholders in the other cities. A similar possibility of 'twinning' cities between global regions was again mooted by UNESCO immediately after the terrible tsunami disaster of December 2004 as a way of personalising the aid effort, though little came of the idea at the time.

Certainly the creation of a system of linked learning cities and regions around the globe, each one using the power of modern information and communication tools to make meaningful and productive contact with the other, is one which is eminently possible, relatively easily implemented and has attracted far-seeing men and women for many years. It has the advantage of providing a focal point for horizon-broadening experiences for all ages and types of people in all cities and regions.

Why should a city or region, beset as it is by local problems and answerable to local residents and ratepayers' organisations, become involved in international activities of this sort? Where is the benefit for its citizens? How far should it go to play its part on the larger global stage? How relevant is it to the city's mission? There are no easy answers to these questions but where they do exist they lie in the scope of their vision, the extent to which they are planning for their future in a multilateral world, the depth of understanding of their leaders, and the quality of their humanity. There are also, as we shall see, measurable advantages. Previous chapters have referenced the rapid rate of change, the link between the local and the global in creating prosperity and social stability, the need for more global awareness and the benefits of learning from others. Many cities are already multiracial, multiethnic, multilingual and multifaceted. The tide of history is propelling them, sometimes reluctantly, towards greater understanding of, and cooperation with, other regions and other races, religions, creeds and customs.

Stakeholder cooperation

International links between cities can offer multiple advantages to their stakeholders as shown in Figure 8.1.

The possibilities are endless and the results of such collaboration would be invaluable as intellectual stimulators to a large number of citizens. The technology is in place to render such links relatively simple. What is missing is the vision, training and of course finance to help bring it to reality.

Where is it happening?

We can find the beginnings of such a movement in the European Commission's PALLACE project (Promoting Active Lifelong Learning in Australasia, Canada, China and Europe). Between 2002 and 2005, this pioneering project established multilateral links between cities, regions and countries in four continents to help facilitate the building of a new learning and understanding culture.

PALLACE linked the city's stakeholders, schools, adult education colleges, cultural services departments, elected representatives and community builders, in:

* the Adelaide and Brisbane regions of Australia;
* the Auckland region of New Zealand;
* the city of Beijing in China;
* the city of Edmonton in Canada;
* the city of Espoo in Finland;
* the city of Edinburgh in Scotland;
* the township of Sannois in France.

Its objective was to stimulate these stakeholders to develop greater knowledge, experience and practice in helping themselves, and each other, to understand the nature of the learning city and their own role in helping it to grow. Activities within and between partners occurred at many levels of the learning city, challenging the stakeholders to engage in collaborative pilot activities whereby insights and action would result from the exchange of ideas and experiences. Each partner managed a separate sub-project, concentrating on the domains shown on Figure 8.2.

Figure 8.1 Linking stakeholders in learning cities globally

Stakeholders	Activities/advantages
School to school	To open up the minds and understanding of young people, to break down stereotypes, to learn collaboratively from and with others, to involve them in creative mutual discussions about how pupils, parents and teachers can contribute to the growth of their cities as learning cities and how it is done elsewhere, to increase tolerance, understanding and awareness levels of the young people who will lead the next generation
University to university	In joint research and teaching to help communities grow, to exchange people, knowledge and ideas, to discuss creatively what their contribution might be to the construction of their city as a learning city, to develop new knowledge from which city managers can develop their strategies
Adult education college to adult education college	To allow adults of all ages to make contact with each other, to act as telementors, to share courses, knowledge and experiences, to expand horizons, to exchange students and staff, to discuss how they can contribute to the growth of their city as a learning city
Business to business	To develop trade and commerce, to open up new possibilities for wealth creation and employment, to share training experiences and ideas, to exchange management knowledge and expertise and to create new markets
City administration to city administration	To share ideas on procedures, governance, finance, social, educational and environmental issues and how to create a learning city, to exchange officers, police, firemen and other personnel, to develop charters, to help each other out in times of crisis
Museum to museum, gallery to gallery	To exchange knowledge, artefacts, paintings and displays, to develop joint exhibitions and greater understanding of other cultures, to understand more about their roles in the creation of a learning city
Library to library	To share knowledge on procedures and methods, to make electronic information more available, to jointly develop displays about the learning city and what citizens can do to help create it
Hospital to hospital	To exchange knowledge, techniques and people in and out of times of crisis
Community centre to community centre	To put people in touch with each other and link whole communities
People to people	To break down the stereotypes and build an awareness of other cultures, creeds and customs and their role in the building of a learning city

Figure 8.2   Linking stakeholders in learning cities and regions globally: the PALLACE partners and their contribution

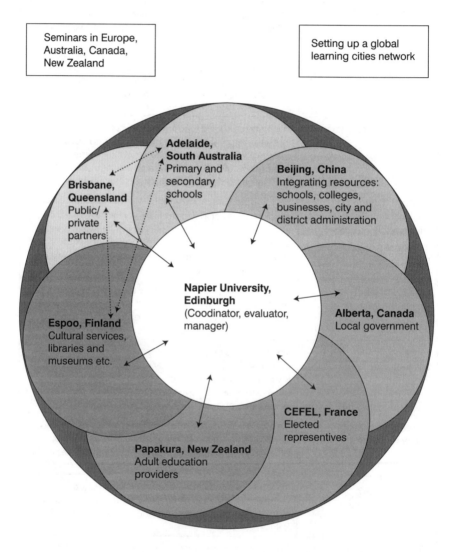

The PALLACE sub-projects

As the illustration shows, each partner concentrated on a different type of stakeholder in its own sub-project, and the results show an interesting range of outcomes.

South Australia and Finland: schools – their role and contribution to the building of a learning city

Gordon Dryden's fourth transformation suggests the development of a global curriculum in schools. 'Of course all students should emerge from school able to read, write, spell and count', he says, 'But more important, I suggest, is to encourage students to become global citizens, ready to produce a better and self-sustaining global civilisation'. Certainly the global schools networks that might help to achieve this are not new, but the network which South Australia put together was the first to involve children, teachers and parents in focused debate about the learning community and what schools can do to help create it. There is an important add-on value to this concept in that it not only creates heightened awareness of what a learning city can be but also potentially mobilises hundreds of people to contribute to it, not least those future citizens who will eventually inherit its administration.

In South Australia, 17 schools became enthusiastically associated with the PALLACE project from across the state – metropolitan and country, all ages and all levels of ability, pre-schools, kindergarten, primary, junior, secondary, single sex schools, co-educational, adult re-entry, specialist focus schools and Aboriginal schools. Initial organisation was from the state's Centre for Lifelong Learning and Development based at Flinders University under the leadership of Professor Denis Ralph. When this organisation was disbanded in June 2003, the regional administration took over local project management. All of the school principals attended initial workshops to explain the PALLACE project and, more importantly, were challenged to consider the roles schools play in building learning communities, cities and regions. Participation in the sub-project was voluntary, but also seen as a token of the school's willingness to develop its values, attitudes and working methods towards a much more inclusive community model. Students, teachers, parents and members of the local community all participated in this process. Further links were established with schools from Finland in order to internationalise the experiences. The sub-project outcomes, taken from the PALLACE report and shown below, demonstrate the extent to which the project has contributed to a much more mature outlook in the way that schools approach the outside community both as a resource and a focus for activity.

HIGHLIGHTS OF THE SCHOOLS PROJECT

Enthusiasm in South Australian schools was extremely high. The project manager, Stan Salagaras , reports:

- The stimulation of significant interest in the learning community concept amongst a broad spectrum and diversity of South Australian schools at all levels of schooling.

- Reinforcement of a fundamental component of their educative function, that schools are in fact, as a result of the nature of their role, involved on an ongoing basis in the development of links with their surrounding communities to enhance learning outcomes for all.
- The enabling of individual schools to benchmark themselves with learning communities elsewhere. The very nature of a learning community means that it should be open to review and analysis.
- The involvement of children, teachers and parents as well as tertiary education providers, business and community organisations in a debate about what schools can do to help create a learning community. There is significant add-on value to this in that it not only created heightened awareness of what a learning community can be, but also mobilised many people to contribute to it and to the school's development.
- The stimulation of case studies of a diversity of learning community initiatives. For example, *Mawson Lakes School* and *St Columba College* compiled comprehensive reports and distributed them to councillors, parents and other local stakeholders. The case studies also supported an understanding of school and system policy and operational matters that facilitated the building of communities and the development of lifelong learning.
- The creation of international links between schools in South Australia and Finland that will continue to grow and develop in the future. Although this proved to be a more difficult exercise than anticipated, despite initial enthusiasm on both sides of the world, the project became a catalyst for some schools to incorporate international links as a core component of their learning programs. *Mawson Lakes School*, for example, also initiated an 'e-pal' project with a school in Texas, USA and a Japanese overseas language and cultural program.
- New Insights into the 21st century learning process. As we think of learning as a pervasive, continuing element in the personal, social and economic life of any community rather than a preparatory activity to be completed in special places, with special people and at set times, then the places of learning become more dispersed to home, work and public places, less specialised and more 'fine grained'.

Outcomes like this are the honey that complements the bread and butter issues of everyday school life in every community. Although the international component was not developed as much as it might have been during the lifetime of the project, it has added a new dimension into the work of children, teachers and parents since project end, and will continue to become increasingly important as they explore new concepts, new cultures and new ideas for further developing learning communities. Indeed Darryl Dymock, former Deputy Director of the Centre for Lifelong Learning, believes that the very fact of participating in a project originating on the other side of the world and with the participation of eight countries added a spice and a motivation that would otherwise be missing.

INSIGHTS INTO SCHOOL/COMMUNITY RELATIONSHIPS

As an example, three schools offered the following as their major educational outcomes from the project:

(a) McLaren Vale Primary School

- increasing interaction with the community, both in amount and depth.
- linking with a range of schools across Australia and the world;
- increasing understanding by students and parents that learning needs to be directed by the learner;
- increasing links between the theory of learning and the value of practical activities;
- increasing links with community members, including elderly citizens.

(b) Mawson Lakes School

- reconceptualising the nature of learning;
- re-constructing the ways curriculum and teaching and learning are conceived;
- challenging traditional organisational frameworks;
- increasing accessibility and flexibility of educational programmes;
- developing a one-stop shop educational advisory and brokerage service.
- increasing school retention rates in Northern Adelaide;
- increasing employment opportunities in the north;
- creating stronger industry–education–community links.

(c) St Columba College

- beginning of a second energy audit programme totally decided and owned by the community and the use of train-the-trainer process;
- willingness of community members to go to meetings to find out about community gardens, community capacity and community programmes;
- running of a regional workshop on how we together can grow our young people and the involvement of community agencies;
- community ownership of a recycling computer programme – the project manager is long-term unemployed person from the community;
- moving of the school from provider to facilitator process in programme delivery;
- evolution of a process of engagement of the community in learning programmes – community consultation which leads to community ownership;
- ensuring that community members have fun in learning programmes, while at the same time developing self-esteem and confidence.

Collectively, the South Australian PALLACE project initiatives signal a number of key roles for schools in building their surrounding region and environment as a learning community, including, among others, new partnerships and alliances, a sharing environment, active participation in research, new management practices, new insights in staff and pupils and productive uses of ICT. Many of these themes echo and exemplify those made in previous chapters. More importantly, unlike many projects after the funding dries up, PALLACE has changed the outlooks and behaviours of the participating schools such that they would not even contemplate reverting to type. Stan Salagaras, the last South Australia project manager, reports:

> Results are outstanding especially in view of the small subvention available to the state. All involved are to be congratulated on the high degree of professionalism, enthusiasm and achievement. It is to be hoped that cooperation of this kind between Australia, Europe, Asia and North America will continue and the European Commission is thanked for making it possible in the first instance.

The Auckland region and France: adult education organisations and their contribution to building a learning city and region

PALLACE also provided the scenario for an adult education project led by Vicky Adin and Ron McDowell of the Papakura Lifelong Learning Trust in New Zealand. Its purpose was to encourage greater knowledge of the learning city/ region concept in New Zealand adult education by designing and developing courses, tools, a conference and a website, and by sharing this with the city of Sannois in the Ile de France region, which tested the tool in the context of the French adult education culture. The national CEFEL (Centre pour la Formation des Elus) organisation, which exists to spread these concepts to cities and regions in France, oversaw the project in France. The PALLACE final report (Adin and McDowel) provides the following insights into the experiences of this sub-project.

The learning city concept was relatively new to New Zealand, although some preliminary work had been done to introduce lifelong learning into the general educational culture there. This has proved to be a daunting task in a system where, as in France, education is a highly formalised, centrally directed and accreditation-focused service with specific rules, regulations, curricula and methodologies, and with little scope for introducing new ideas into national educational organisations. Nevertheless, the project managers did manage to make some breakthroughs.

- They used the international input from the PALLACE partners to design, develop and run a highly successful national conference in Auckland on the key concepts and characteristics of lifelong learning, learning cities and regions. This was attended by most of the movers and shakers in New Zealand education, including the Minister herself, and visiting speakers from the UK, France, China, Finland, Canada, the USA and the Pacific islands.

*   This provided the impetus to encourage some of the more innovative people on the New Zealand educational scene to incorporate some of these ideas into their courses. Indeed, a new masters course was developed at the University of Auckland's Faculty of Education which now includes as key topics such things as learning society, lifelong learning, lifelong education, adult education (and its various synonyms), learning organisations, social and human capital, globalisation, civil society (including service learning) and learning societies, regions and cities.

A distance education version is also now being developed post-project, stimulated by the experiences in PALLACE. In addition a short tool on the vision of and commitment to lifelong learning held by institutions, similar to the Stakeholder Audit described in Chapter 6, was developed and sent to one university, one college of education and the adult and community education sector in the Auckland region. Although only the Auckland College of Education completed the audit (the others refused on the grounds that 'it did not fit their profile'), the results provide a snapshot of the state of knowledge in the region. The tool was also sent to the adult college in Sannois, France, from which a partial comparison could be made where the questions fitted the organisation. The New Zealand partner also developed the PALLACE website www.pallace.net as an interactive forum to link students and staff in adult education colleges in debate about what such an institution and its people can do to help transform their own city into a learning city. It received 20,000 hits in its first month.

The French spin-off is in the form of a paper on adult education and the learning city, again inspired by participation in PALLACE and included in the PALLACE report. 'Les élus locaux et l'éducation des adultes' was written by Alain Bournazel, the President of CEFEL, to French local authorities and national government, one of the first on this subject in the country. The table of contents ends with this rallying cry to all local politicians, 'Conclusion: ouvrir la cité sur le monde' (conclusion – open up cities to the world). Its contents are:

*   Chaque collectivité territoriale doit évidemment adapter ses inter-ventions en faveur de l'éducation des adultes en fonction des besoins propres de ses habitants [Each city and region should evidently adopt strategies for adult education in order to satisfy the needs of their inhabitants].
*   Mais chaque collectivité sera mieux préparée pour cette mission si elle a connaissance des expériences qui se sont déroulées ailleurs [But each city and region would be better prepared for this mission if it had a knowledge of what is happening elsewhere in the world].

- Pour l'éducation des adultes, les communes doivent communiquer et se former les unes les autres par l'échange mutuel. Le réseau des cités d'apprentissage des savoirs constitue le moyen privilégié pour échanger les bonnes pratiques et stimuler les innovations [In adult education, communes should communicate with and educate each other through mutually beneficial exchanges. Learning city networks provide an excellent way of exchanging good practice and stimulating innovation].
- Mais les cités d'apprentissage des savoirs ne sauraient se limiter à cette communication de nature institutionnelle. Elles doivent également faciliter les échanges entre les apprenants, leur propre cité et les apprenants des autres cités [But learning cities should not limit themselves to dialogue at institutional level. They should equally facilitate exchanges between learners in their own city and in other cities].
- L'éducation des adultes, c'est aussi donner aux citoyens, quel que soit le lieu où il réside, une ouverture sur le monde. Cette ouverture qui permet souvent de mieux apprécier les valeurs de sa propre ville, de son propre pays [The objective of adult education is also to open up citizens, wherever they live, to the rest of the world. In so doing it allows them to appreciate their own city and world better].

Such sentiments from the leader of a national councillors' training organisation, prompted as they are from participation in PALLACE, will echo in the chambers of the conseils regionaux and municipaux of France. They demonstrate the power of international projects to initiate change at regional level.

Despite working from a knowledge-meagre base, coping with structural difficulties and financial problems, PALLACE has proved to be the catalyst for advances in the application of learning city principles in the Auckland region, and has increased the knowledge of teachers in training and administrators throughout the country. Here too, however, so much more could be accomplished with a well-funded continuation of the work it has started. Professor Ron McDowell comments in the final report (Adin and McDowell):

> We have enjoyed our participation in the Pallace Project and appreciate and value the connections we have made with our fellow participating countries. As a result the Trust is determined to continue its work in New Zealand to foster the lifelong learning philosophy. The difficulties encountered during the last two years as a result of being considered 'amateurs' in a field of 'professionals' has resulted in the Trust changing its target audience. Instead of targeting the teaching fraternity and government policy directly, we are now focussing our efforts on local government and community well-being. Thank you for the opportunity to be involved in this project.

France and Australia: learning city leadership – the role and contribution of elected representatives

As was discussed in Chapter 7, a learning city needs leadership and that was the theme of CEFEL's project for elected representatives. To quote from the PALLACE report,

> Local politicians are some of the most important groups of people in the foundation of the city as a Learning City. Contrary to popular opinion, most councillors are extremely hard-working people who give up a great deal of their time in order to be of service to their own community. Certainly there are differences of political emphasis but, in general, politicians work well with the professional administrators who have to maintain the continuity of city life.

Equally, responsible politicians have the well-being both of the city and its citizens at heart, and this includes the future as well as the present. This means, as in every other walk of life, that they must stay updated with the changes that are taking place with ever-increasing rapidity in the governance of the city and in the environment in which that governance has to take place. It means too a degree of flexibility and adaptability in order to make decisions that will be in the best interests of the city's present and future prosperity, its stability and the personal aspirations of its citisens.

CEFEL, the French organisation for training elected representatives throughout the country, was particularly concerned to bring the concept of the Learning City to the notice of councillors in a country where it is not widely known or practised. Its exemplar township was the municipality of Sannois in the Ile de France, well-known for its innovative policies in educational matters, and particularly for creating links between stakeholders in the city. Here most of the sub-project's activity was focused. The international dimension was provided through contact with the city of Marion in the Adelaide region, the same city that managed the learning festivals described in Chapter 3. As Alain Bournazel affirms in the PALLACE report,

> the task was to lead the design and development for elected representatives learning materials that would sensitise them to the nature, importance and opportunities to be gained from creating learning cities and regions. Sannois and Marion acted as testbeds for the materials.

PROJECT OUTCOMES

The learning materials for local councillors (conseillers municipaux) and regional councillors (conseillers regionaux), developed in both French and English, cover a variety of topics related to learning cities and regions. Like the LILLIPUT materials, from which they get their methodological provenance, they comprise toolboxes of exercises and recommendations based on the concept of the learner's ownership of learning.

The lessons provide an introduction to the concept of the learning city for city councillors, those with whom they have to work and others who may be interested in the field. The opening lesson explores the role and responsibility of the local politician, while the rest examine the different pressures on municipalities and regions in the 21st century and the rationale for the transformation of cities, towns and regions into learning communities. In total they present the crucial need for councillors to understand why administrations need to respond to rapid and wide-ranging change in most aspects of local, national and global economics, politics, social structures and cultures. They use interactive exercises to highlight how this change is affecting individuals and families as well as cities, regions and nations, and produce insights into the connection between past, present and future work and lifestyles. These lessons were tested in Sannois and, with some exceptions based mainly upon frustration with the highly centralised French educational system over which local councillors have little control, favourably received by the councillor-learners. In the PALLACE report, Dymock describes three actions taken to initiate this strand of the project in the Marion township of Adelaide:

a) A very successful workshop involving senior executive staff of the City of Marion as well as a meeting with the Mayor of the City was held with Professor Norman Longworth, the project manager, on 10 February 2003. The objectives of the workshop were to:

- Acquire information regarding national and international trends/ examples of local government involvement in the development of learning communities;
- Gain a better understanding of the role of the Marion Council in developing a learning community; and
- Identify potential strategies for realising the opportunities identified in point 2 above.

b) The Local Government Authority of South Australia worked to identify changes that need to be made to policy and program settings in order to facilitate local governments playing a significant role in building learning cities and communities.

c) More councillors became involved with the 3rd Marion Learning Festival, which is held in the heart of the largest shopping and enter- tainment mall complex in the southern hemisphere.

Once again, although no formal links were established between councillors in France and Australia, a deficit that may be amended post-project, the international dimension of PALLACE provided the impetus for the acquisition of new knowledge on learning cities and regions by local decision-makers.

Beijing: planning and building a cross-sectoral lifelong learning facility to kick-start lifelong learning in the city

In China the government published its modernisation plans to establish a lifelong learning system, develop learning communities and promote the overall development of its population in 2002. Indeed, to 'establish a lifelong learning system and develop a learning community' is one of the four concrete objectives of the *'Xiaokang'* (relatively better-off) society, which has as its aim to catch up with or exceed the mid-developed countries. At present, more than 60 cities have a clear objective to become learning cities. They include Beijing, Shanghai, Nanjing, Changzhou, Dalian, Qingdao, Zhuhai, Xi'an, Chengdu and others.

Professor Shi Long, Vice President of the Beijing Academy of Educational Sciences, reported in his address to the Canadian PALLACE Seminar in Edmonton,

> As the capital of China, Beijing's goal is to become the largest learning city in the world by 2008. It will do this
>
> - by initiating educational modernisation through a lifelong learning system which promotes social holistic development through learning,
> - by establishing a modern civilised community in residence blocks and sub-districts,
> - by fully utilising educational resources, and
> - by integrating various social sectors to promote the interactive holistic development of community and school.
>
> A management system and the operational mechanism of a learning community has already been put in place, information technology for community education has been strengthened, and a series of learning networks based on the interaction between school, community, family, enterprise and individual has been formed. Activities such as *'Citizens' Learning Week'* and a family learning competition are up and running.

The Beijing Academy of Educational Sciences is the operational arm of Beijing's journey into lifelong learning. It covers many aspects of educational research and development in the city. Its major project is the establishment of Beijing as one of the world's foremost learning cities, and it is in pursuit of that end that it joined PALLACE at the invitation of the European Commission and the project manager. Its intention was to explore further creative and innovative ways of bringing together the different sectors such as schools, adult education, business and industry, community organisations, the city and district administrations into one huge cross-sectoral lifelong learning facility that promotes and delivers lifelong learning in Xicheng, one of the central suburbs of the city, serving 800,000 people.

This is no easy task. Xicheng district boasts 77 primary schools, 52 middle schools, and 214 various adult schools and institutions, with a total of over 12,500 teaching staff. It comprises a total of ten sub-districts and 223 urban residents' committees each covering 100–700 households. Professor Shi Long outlines the following measures being adopted for Xicheng:

- Establishing and implementing a learning community through consultation with sub-district and urban residents' committees in a three-layer administrative system. For this it will need to foster top-down local and national government support and attention from city leaders in order to release finance and, at the same time, a bottom-up strategy of harnessing the enthusiasm of the public.
- Establishing learning organisations in companies, learning providers and even in streets and households. A series of pilot projects will be established to raise knowledge levels of the concept.
- Opening up education resources into a more community oriented model. For example, lessons in primary and middle schools become open to the public's participation, free daily public access to sports grounds, school playgrounds, auditoriums, computer rooms etc., the initiation of new sports competitions, cultural activities, computer and foreign language classes.
- Introducing and organising a 'Citizens' Learning Week' – classes, forums, competitions, events, performances, and visits for all ages. This will entail large events such as the training of local backbone art and literature teams, big class lectures for citizens and mass art and literature teams, and small ones, e.g. organising choirs from all parts of the community, drama etc.
- Undertaking research and development activities on learning city matters.
- Communicating: creating publications that encourage citizens to participate in learning activities and establishing a website for use by all Beijing as part of the Xicheng District Community Education Network.

In all the synergy of ideas and experiences that take place at conferences and in projects such as PALLACE it is difficult to know what idea or activity originated where, but this is the benefit of such interaction. Beijing has contributed as much to PALLACE thinking as it has gained from it, as would other cities in the same position. It has also adapted the ideas to its own unique Chinese environment and culture. Professor Shi Long again:

Everyone is a scholar, everywhere there are schools, and different groups of people have different schools as different forms of activities have also different effects. Each activity is based on requirement, and each activity has its series, knowledge, recreation, pertinence and effectiveness, forming therefore regional resource sharing and common understanding on community-education with synergy. All sub-projects can learn from, and contribute to, this ambitious programme (PALLACE), which should reveal much about how people can be persuaded to become active lifelong learning citisens. We can also learn much about language and culture differences.

Other PALLACE projects

It will have become obvious that the internationality of the PALLACE project has had an enlightening and activating effect on the participating partners. The full report to the European Commission comprises more than 300 pages of experiences, recommendations, plans, activities, ideas, results and outcomes. It remains only to briefly describe what is different among the remaining projects. This is not because less happened in these three, simply that constraints of space prevent a more detailed description.

QUEENSLAND – BUILDING LIFELONG LEARNING INTO THE ENVIRONMENTAL AND SOCIAL FABRIC OF A COMMUNITY THROUGH PUBLIC–PRIVATE COOPERATION

The Queensland project was of a different nature. South and West of Brisbane, a 'Learning Corridor' was, and still is, being created – a scheme to encourage greater community involvement in lifelong learning and community activities. The four suburbs involved are different from each other in social composition, age, existing facilities and income, but they have the promotion and improvement of community life through active citizenship as a common aim. The University of Queensland has helped this process in the older communities as a part of its PALLACE commitment, and has contributed a great deal to the common understanding. It also assisted a private company, Delfin/Lend-Lease Ltd, to build new communities in which lifelong learning concepts are embedded from their inception, an activity also endemic in many parts of Australia.

One excellent example of such public/private cooperation is at Springfield just south of the city. Here architects and planners from the private sector become educationists in order to develop true 'Learning Communities' from scratch. 'There is the need to integrate Lifelong Learning with Community development', says architect Laurence Taylor (2005), who personally visited other PALLACE partners to consolidate his ideas; 'the Australian Centre for Life Long Learning will recognise, foster and promote the fundamental role of learning in the wealth, prosperity and happiness of the community'. Springfield has already persuaded the University of Southern Queensland to establish a lifelong learning campus there and it will combine with vocational education training providers, industry, schools and private research organisations to create a unique 'Education City', open to the whole community. In the region as a whole, Denise Reghenzani, then a university project officer also working with PALLACE, organised well-attended and successful seminars for academics, and local and state authorities to encourage an international, inter-sectoral exchange of knowledge and practice. Certainly the rest of the world can take notice of the extremely vibrant and well-organised volunteering culture that has been created in Brisbane as a result, and which is described in more detail in Chapter 7.

ESPOO (FINLAND) MUSEUMS: LIBRARIES, GALLERIES, THEATRES AND OTHER CULTURAL SERVICE PROVIDERS – HOW THEY CAN STIMULATE THE BUILDING OF A LEARNING CITY

A similar outcome was written into the cultural services project led by the city of Espoo, one of the world's foremost learning cities. Here the objective was to engage museums, libraries and galleries in debate about their own contribution to the development of a learning city, and how they can inform citizens about, and engage them in, its development. The result is an attractively presented portable display which any city can use to explain what a learning city is, the place of the arts and education in it, and what the citizen can do to further it.

ALBERTA (CANADA): ENCOURAGING LEARNING COMMUNITY DEVELOPMENT

Finally, Sylvia Lee, President of KMI, the Albertan partner, used her knowledge of learning community development, built up in the developing North of Alberta and elsewhere, to create new materials for use in smaller learning communities within learning cities. They are now in use in Edmonton and the surrounding townships. She also organised a successful Canadian PALLACE seminar, at which partners brought and shared their knowledge with local people and organisations, organised a webcast on learning cities, and worked with the city of Victoria on its learning day. As President of the World Initiative on Lifelong Learning, Sylvia is in an excellent position to spread the PALLACE philosophy more widely around the world.

What's in it for us?

PALLACE has been used as an exemplar of the ways in which cities and regions can learn from each other, mobilise their communities, contribute to learning city development and add an extra international dimension to the work of both individuals and organisations. The seven sub-projects have pushed back the frontiers of what we know about, and how we build, learning cities, learning regions and learning communities using the technology that is available to us. As the project manager says in his report to the European Commission,

> The insights and perceptions gained by schoolchildren, parents, educators, administrators and ordinary citizens from running, interacting and

participating in these projects have been many and various. But the real challenge will come when city and regional administrations realise how useful they can be to their own development plans and to community stability, and engage many more members of the community – seniors, families, community leaders, citizens – in the debate.

One remarkable thing about the project, which may not be sustainable in the future, is that the funding of €50,000 covered only office expenses and travel. The resources for paying people came entirely from the partners' own resources. The project manager and those participants who were not employed by local authorities did this work without payment because they believed passionately in what the project was trying to achieve and prove.

There are of course many other international projects and networks with which cities, and stakeholders within cities, become involved. Universities, companies and cities habitually work with others in research, enterprise and trade. Schools and college networks are proliferating. Sometimes projects are carried out from city and stakeholder resources, and at other times the interactions may be instruments of national government policy. For example, in 2003, Hume, a suburb of Western Melbourne with a highly multicultural community, began the creation of the 'Hume Global Learning Village', an innovative new partnership linking organisations connected with learning from around the city and beyond. The 200 members of the village are dedicated to achieving the vision of Hume as a learning city, and have already embarked on some key strategies, one of which is to use the vast range of cultures and journeys of its residents from 97 different regions of the world as a focus for creating learning opportunities. Although the initiative is primarily a way of fostering a vibrant community spirit within the city itself, Vanessa Little, the Global Village manager, is also looking outwards to Australia and beyond to open up the city to the world and the world to the city. She reports, 'Even at this early stage, Hume has become a focus for other communities seeking to learn and build on Hume's experience and strategies. Australian and overseas interest in Hume's initiative is growing'.

Advantages of global interaction between cities and regions

There is whole new dimension to the debate when we discuss the global role of cities and regions for the future. Whatever model is adopted – city-ring, city mentoring, city-twinning, city networking – an even greater challenge occurs when we can include into these plans cities and regions from the less-favoured countries of this planet. Here is where the nexus of the case centres. City and regional management may be wary of becoming involved in such projects. And yet there are some very tangible global and local benefits to be obtained from such practical idealism. Six of them are shown below:

1   It is a preventative measure
    The giant leap in mutual understanding and transformation of mindset that
    takes place when people and organisations in cities and regions worldwide
    communicate with each other and learn together. Through such
    understanding social behaviour improves, racism and ethnic hatred
    diminishes and cities and regions no longer bear the costs of picking up the
    pieces. Of course such significantly desirable outcomes should not be
    expected to happen overnight, or even within one or two years. Other factors
    are involved, and several thousands of years of historical mindset cannot be
    overturned in a short period. But the fact is that the possibility exists and
    only through a change of outlook and practice at city and institutional level
    can the transformation be implemented.

2   It makes economic sense
    The profitable economic, trade and technical development that can result
    through increased contact between small and large companies in different
    countries, leading to increased employment and greater prosperity. Here is
    an attractive economic justification for greater learning city/region
    cooperation. Of course many cities have already trodden that path. Long-
    term trade links are already in place between many Chinese cities and those
    in Europe, North America and Australia. The ports of the Baltic have their
    COPERNICUS links. Most major industrial cities send trade delegations
    to other industrial cities with which they wish to do business. But very little
    of this is in the context of learning. Lucrative and fruitful possibilities open
    up when groups of cities and regions open up their learning establishments
    as well as their companies to each other, including universities, vocational
    education institutions, business and management colleges, in the context of
    trade and training.

3   It is incremental
    The transformation of mindsets, attitudes and behaviours that occurs when
    thousands more people and organisations are contributing to the solution
    of social, cultural, environmental, political and economic problems
    throughout the world right across the age groups. Cities and regions, as
    learning organisms, can learn much from each other, and jointly help each
    other to cope with seemingly intractable problems. For example, seniors
    can become empowered through communication with seniors elsewhere
    and become less of a burden on their city and their families. Younger people
    would need no such subtle persuasion. Indeed many schools are already
    linking with other schools worldwide. However, again, very little of this is
    in the context of learning or the learning city. Where the interaction is
    exercising the creativity of the participants in practical ways by which they
    could help their cities to become learning cities, as with the schools in the
    PALLACE example above, there are large bonuses to be had. The outward-
    looking learning cities and regions of the future will be able to harness this
    creative energy to help them achieve many of their developmental goals.

4   It is fulfilling for thousands of people
    This amounts to a huge increase in available resource through the mobilisa-
    tion of the goodwill, talents, skills, experience and creativity between cities
    and regions. It is a new resource, tapping into the knowledge of individuals,
    and turning human ingenuity and action into social and intellectual capital
    to the benefit of cities and regions. Where there is a city-ring, a group of
    cities working together in this way, the amount of available resource between
    them rises exponentially. Where the city-ring includes a mixture of muni-
    cipalities in the developed and underdeveloped world with a preponderance
    in the former, such resources can, sensitively applied, now be channelled
    into helping solve problems that have beset the world for centuries.
5   It solves previously intractable problems
    All of this would potentially mean that there would be fewer refugees. Many
    of the developing problems can be anticipated and addressed through
    cooperation between the cities at the moment of crisis. Although this may
    seem to be a long way from the city's direct area of responsibility, one by-
    product of the increased intercommunication, interaction and new under-
    standing on all sides mentioned above leads in the longer term to a
    diminution of oppression, with the consequence that people no longer need
    to migrate en masse for political reasons.
6   It is sustainable because it's so much more dispersed
    Governments and NGOs are no longer the only initiators of aid to the
    underdeveloped. Action is now shared with the cities and, through them,
    the people, who gain in understanding of the realities and problems of the
    modern world and the extent to which they ameliorate the latter. Stakeholder
    organisations and institutions in the city/region have a real world-class focus
    and raison d'être, and a contribution to make to the construction of the
    learning city at home and abroad. Certainly such idealism is out of step
    with the realpolitik of diplomacy but it is surely preferable to the military
    solutions that cause so much grief and destruction, and it represents an
    opportunity to make a real long-term difference without the baggage of
    accusations of imperialist domination. The resource needed requires less
    than 20 per cent of the money presently being spent on instruments of war
    or defence.

All of this predicates a new mission for cities and regions. No longer are they
inward-looking entities with a responsibility only to provide services for their
own citizens. They have a greater mission and a greater global responsibility,
entirely consonant with the ideals behind the learning city concept, to open up
the eyes of their institutions and their citizens to the world outside, and the
contribution they can make to improving it. This is not hopeless, blue skies,
impractical idealism. In so doing they are helping to re-create themselves into
richer entities in every way, more prosperous, more resourceful, more
knowledgeable, more sensitive, more participative and more creative, innovative

and capable. If we look at past history to the great cities of the world during their heyday – Venice, Athens, Alexandria, Constantinople, Rome, Vienna and a host more – they did not become great or prosperous by looking inwards at themselves. And of course it must be admitted that many of them achieved that state through conquest, pillage and plunder, not an option open to modern-day cities and regions. But what technology provides today is a new 21st century opportunity to expand their influence through the exchange of ideas, knowledge, experience, inventiveness, trade and practical help.

Including less-favoured cities and regions

But there is an even greater prise to be had from global cooperation. The PALLACE city-ring comprised seven cities from the developed world. As we have seen, Beijing, already making huge strides in its own development, learned a great deal from its experience among that elite. But if we now predicate a city-ring comprising six or seven cities from the developed world, for argument's, and alliteration's, sake let us say Sydney, Seattle, Southampton, Sapporo, Stuttgart and Shanghai; and we now add one or two from South America or Africa or the poverty-stricken areas of Asia, each of them linking their schools, universities, adult colleges, companies, city administrations, museums, children, parents, seniors, teachers, researchers, under the guidance of an energetic, sympathetic, persuasive and knowledgeable set of leaders; this is one way towards the elimination of world poverty much closer to the hearts, minds and capabilities of real people in real cities and regions, by-passing the need for mass migrations of unfortunate refugees.

But…

But there is also a need for a word of caution. Such links should be neither exploitative, nor patronising, nor economically imperialist. They should be used as ways of increasing genuine understanding of others, the richness of the differences in cultures, creeds and races in the participating partner cities, and not ways of breaking them down. They should be conduits for a richer and more vibrant city life, strengthening communities and expanding interactions, as well as extending opportunities and opening up new horizons. Vandana Shiva (1998) warns:

> Looking outwards without the capacity to look inwards creates competition, aggression, exploitation of nature and people, violence and insecurity. It globalises commerce and trade, not human consciousness. It creates exclusiveness rather than inclusiveness. A philosophy of inclusion can only emerge from a philosophy of intrinsic worth and self organisation – from the individual to the community (city) to the nation to the world … it is the foundation for building an Earth Democracy.

In the inevitable rush to increase profit through globalisation on this rapidly contracting planet it is the lack of a human, a social, a creative, an environmental, a cultural and, for many, a spiritual dimension that must be urgently addressed. And cities have their part to play. Take this heartfelt lament from Vidhi Jain (Jain and Chandreshsumi), of Shikshantar, an organisation to transform Udaipur (India) into a learning city:

> Over the past few months, we have learned that most people, be they teachers, city planners or people's representatives, do not understand what is a vision (or drishti). There also seems to be a lot of confusion about why we need a vision for anything, be it for our lives or for a project. Most people (be they young or old) have been conditioned to believe that all projects come with pre-planned visions and models and that meaningful people's initiatives – connected with peoples' shared visions/dreams about the city – are worthless. The majority of people are comfortable simply copying activities, plans and models without daring to imagine or go off the beaten path. It has also become very clear from our interactions that most of the people are deeply conditioned to believing that all 'good' and 'bad' in the city is due to the Government and the Politicians. Therefore, whatever needs to be done for the city will have to come from the Government, as it is its duty to think about the problems facing the city. At the same time, quite a few people were blatantly adamant in saying that the common people of Udaipur are not capable of thinking for themselves. Very few people felt that voluntary 'people-led' initiatives could work. This throws light on the low levels of self-confidence and high levels of dependency that most educated people have, and how they rationalise their apathy and try to escape thinking about their personal responsibilities and roles. Our present self-centred and mechanical lifestyles also do not encourage people to explore and engage in the different realities or opportunities that exist in the city.

Such words will be very familiar to city planners and managers in many parts of the world. They articulate the distance that cities and regions have to travel in order to overcome such feelings of inadequacy in their citizens. At the same time the volume of mistrust, misinformation, antagonism and aggression between countries, religions, cultures and peoples in cities is undoubtedly on the increase. The breakdown of stereotypes and long-standing antipathy is only possible through a combination of education and communication. It won't happen tomorrow or next week or even next year. This is a long process of learning about each other that can take as long as 20 or 50 or more years. But it must start as soon as possible, and it must include as many people of all ages, so that by the year 2020 we can point to a positive diminution of hatred, terror and mistrust, to replace it with cooperation, knowledge, understanding and wisdom. This is infinitely preferable to the use of military projects in which the lack of the creativity or will or imagination to develop more lasting solutions creates environmental, emotional, physical, political and personal disaster. Moreover, not only is it infinitely less expensive but it also provides an alternative interpretation of globalisation that celebrates cultural diversity and creative cooperation.

Five higher senses enhanced by international projects

At last we are within reach of achieving the five higher senses which educational systems, especially those for young people, must strive to create, and without which the world is a poorer place.

- sense of '*other*' – the transcendence of ego that allows individuals to appreciate, and respond to, the existence of other needs, other ideas, other peoples, other cultures;
- sense of '*planet*' – understanding the need for sustainability of the ecosystems that guarantee the future of us all, and humankind's responsibility as a planetary steward for all species;
- sense of '*together*', and its hierarchy of local, national and global community, the enthusiasm to live, work and communicate sensibly and sensitively with people from a wide variety of cultures, creeds, beliefs and races;
- sense of '*wondering*' – of envisioning one's place in the cosmic scheme of things, striving for insight, seeking self-awareness and understanding of 'higher';
- sense of '*evolving*' – of reaching for enlightenment, achieving fulfilment and realising one's own enormous potential.

These complement Gardner's eight intelligences, Goleman's work on emotional intelligence and that of Zohar and Marshall on spiritual intelligence, which has nothing to do with organised religion and everything to do with maturity of outlook, a feeling for social justice, empathy for others and the capacity for reflection. Properly managed, outward-looking, international programmes can help towards achieving these higher senses. The technology exists to make it an easily affordable exercise, but it will also need visionary drivers who can steer projects towards desired and desirable objectives.

At the same time Botkin's words of advice act as a brake.

> We need to be cautious that technologically-mediated global learning doesn't become a new force for domination. If we can imagine a kind of global learning that respects human diversity without asserting a cultural dominance over others, then e-learning opens a flood of possibilities that we have only begun to explore. The philosophical question is: industrial technology helped create the human gap, can information technology help bridge it?

In Aldous Huxley's masterpiece of the future *Brave New World*, technology had indeed taken over, people were indeed successful in their pursuit of 'happiness', and certainly healthier. Society was stable and crime-free, and poverty was non-existent. The slogan written over the entrance to each city was 'Community, Identity, Stability', aspirational words we have used frequently in this book. But also the cities were culture-free zones – the only music was in the form of jingles delivered from sponsored television, the only drama sponsored plays with happy endings, the only art, sponsored drawings and the only religion was also sponsored. The daily dose of soma for all ensured permanent addiction to mediocrity and ignorance. Perceptive readers may recognise some parallels here. Into this world came the intelligent savage, whose main source of education was an old copy of the works of Shakespeare from which he had learned all that is needed to know about love, life, grief, hate, envy, passion, delight, obsession, excitement, murder and noble aspiration...

We mentioned above John M. Eger's suggestion that cities and regions are becoming the new mini nation-states. If this is so, they will need the vision of a Mandela, the imagination of an Einstein, the administrative genius of a Hadrian, the practical capability of a Brunel, the leadership prowess of an Alexander the Great and the marketing skill of a Tom Watson. In a learning city and a learning region all of this will, of course, be easy to find.

The task is now to find a global driver for the establishment of similar city-rings. The World Initiative on Lifelong Learning, a global charitable organisation based in Edmonton, Canada and described in fuller detail in Annexe 2 of *Lifelong Learning in Action*, is one organisation that has as its mission to expand the number of city-rings. It is looking for assistance to any funding organisation, governmental or non-governmental, religious or secular, foundation or personal, that will help to create the city-rings to preserve this precious planet from its own contradictions. The contact point may be Sylvia Lee, its President, at kmi@kmintl.biz or its Vice-President, the author of this book, at longworthnorman@aol.com.

Chapter 9

Summarising, strengthening, sustaining

Putting it all together

This book contains a considerable number of justifications, quotations, recommendations, proposals, suggestions, examples, advice and action points for transforming cities and regions into learning cities and learning regions. Hopefully its point has been made that no city or region, large or small, can afford not to become a learning entity in a world that is changing rapidly. It is time therefore to summarise the previous chapters, by demonstrating how, as has been said, the education and training society, presided over by national, local and regional government throughout most of the latter half of the 20th century, is giving way to a more holistic and inclusive lifelong learning world in which local and regional government becomes fully involved in building up a culture of learning for all its citizens.

Learning cities – a practical summary

1 If you don't already have one, develop a full lifelong learning development strategy which encompasses all the recommendations shown below. Link it, and incorporate it into, the regeneration, sustainable development, marketing, wealth creation, leadership development, cultural development, security, social services and health, transport and other city plans for the future. Give it a time-line and benchmarks. Derby, Dublin, Newcastle, Gothenburg, Adelaide and Southampton are excellent examples of cities that have a clear vision of the centrality of learning to the future of the city.

2 Inaugurate a lifelong learning development committee for the city. Involve non-educational institutions as well as schools, colleges and universities. Give it teeth and a budget. Link it to the city's development board as in Dublin, Edinburgh, Beijing and Glasgow. Proliferate learning sub-committees in each neighbourhood.

3 Ensure that the world knows that you take learning seriously, learning creates wealth, it attracts industry and employment in a knowledge society. You can do this by:

- Developing a logo for your city as a learning entity. Encourage all institutions and organisations, including companies, to use it. Use it in all literature, especially marketing.
- Making reference to your city as a learning city on the web. Make sure learning providers and industrial organisations do likewise.
- Actively marketing the city as a learning city to both the outside world and to its citizens through brochures, videos, posters, media presentations etc.

4   Insert consultation procedures about learning and development. Develop a simply-worded brochure about change and the city and the importance of lifelong learning. Invite comments from all sections of society. Where bodies of people are unrepresented create the means for them to comment, e.g. neighbourhood councils and the comhairle na nóg for young people in Dublin. Especially make sure the young are involved.

5   Develop a charter which outlines the city's commitment to improving the rights of citizens to learning as has happened in Southampton, St Albert, Blackburn, Espoo and Halifax. Use the ones shown in this book as templates.

6   Encourage active citizenship actively. Extol the virtues of contribution in a leaflet and posters distributed to all organisations, institutions and citizens. Invite companies to involve their workers as in the IBM scheme shown in this book. Develop a volunteers register and a needs requirements list as in Queensland. This can be a self-funding office. Link it to the consultation process. Consider installing a time currency scheme as in the time dollars example in this book.

7   Linked to this, encourage schools and colleges to use the talents, ideas, expertise, knowledge and skills in their community to help in the learning process, as in Mawson Lakes, and in increasing resources available to them. Make new school development the centre of community so that what goes on there is seen to be linked to the needs of that community rather than a separate intellectual activity. Appoint in each school someone responsible for resource and community mobilisation in the interests of better learning. Use schools and colleges as distribution points for learning information.

8   Organise community mentoring, including telementoring, systems to help learners as in Brixton and Southampton. Do it through the volunteers register or encourage schools and colleges to develop their own. However, also ensure that potential mentors are vetted and organise courses and guidelines on mentoring as in the USA. Make sure all citizens have access to learning counsellors as in Beijing.

9   Install a continuous improvement system through learning into the management system for everyone in all departments of the city as in Southampton. Use some of the tools and techniques – learning audits, personal learning plans, radar charts etc. – described in this book. Appoint learning counsellors for every department to administer them. Above all,

ensure that all your employees know about it through courses, and are actively involved in the city's and the region's growth as a learning entity.

10 Organise a learning fair or festival for a week as in Sapporo, Glasgow, Mount Isa, Blackburn and Marion, described in this book. Make it one of the fun events of the year. Invite jugglers, choirs of all ages, stilt-walkers, comedians, fire-eaters, celebrities etc. to attract people there. Invite all organisations offering formal or informal learning to display their wares. Invite the local media to participate, e.g. through radio and TV sessions, supplements in the local newspaper etc. Publicise it well through an attractive booklet on local learning opportunities delivered to all households. Use it to gain feedback. This can be self-funding.

11 Organise seminars, workshops and courses in lifelong learning for city administrators as in Adelaide, Derby, Southampton and Birmingham. Use the learning needs analysis now being developed in the LILARA project, and the learning materials available by web from LILLIPUT and Longlearn. Use a cascade approach in which a class of 20 then becomes 20 new tutors, using these materials, in order to spread the concept.

12 Do the same within the communities to make sure that as many citizens as possible know about, and respond positively to, the challenges of a learning society.

13 Be innovative. Run competitions and events as in Espoo and Beijing. Reward outstanding achievement in learning by individuals and organisations. Initiate learning quality recognition schemes.

14 Have a technology development strategy entailing:

- the availability of cheaper computers to citizens through bulk-buying, as in Gothenburg;
- linking every student and pupil to the internet as in Norwich and many other UK cities;
- training all educators to use technology properly in a variety of ways;
- the installation of distance learning capability in learning providers and ensuring its accessibility to all;
- blueprints for a wired city and the improvements this could make to learning as described in this book.

15 Encourage the development of partnerships between all sectors and the sharing of expertise, resources, goodwill, talents and ideas. Develop partnership guidelines as shown in this book and recommend that they are adhered to.

16 Appoint at least one co-ordinator of lifelong learning and give him/her access to personnel at a high level to implement some of these recommendations. In addition re-orient other job descriptions to take into account the learning city/region component.

17 Ensure that you always have the best information available to make decisions from. Use the city's research institutions to obtain it and encourage them

to orient their research towards involving the community in it and feeding back the results to it. Use the indicators developed in the INDICATORS project, described in this book, to measure improvement in practice and performance each year.

18 Ensure that your city looks outward to the world by linking with, and learning from, other learning cities. Ensure that as many of your organisations as possible do the same through inter-school (i.e. inter-pupil, inter-teacher and inter-parent), inter-university, inter-college, inter-business, intercultural links which actively engage participants in debate and action about their own cities as learning cities. Extend it to citizens and community centres as in the Craigmillar grannies example. Use the PALLACE project as a template.

19 At the same time carry out your global responsibility to improve the less fortunate cities in the world by incorporating one of these into your network and facilitating links between organisations and people. In a globalised world, cities and regions are increasing their power to influence events. Such actions can often lead to long-term economic and employment benefits.

20 Ensure that in-service teacher training takes into account the realities of the emerging learning world as described in many places in this book and *Lifelong Learning in Action*. Ownership of learning by the learner, use of technological tools and techniques, using mentors and coaches, management of the talents, skills, knowledge and ideas of parents and people in the community, home–school agreements and many more.

Figure 9.1 therefore has been compiled from the list of learning region requirements. It is most certainly incomplete. But it contains action points as well as concepts and gives the city manager an idea of the magnitude of the task ahead. And it provides work for those people and organisations prepared to accept the challenge of change, to think outside the box and to participate in the development of their own learning regions.

These recommendations are organised in a way that encapsulates the essence of the changes that are driving cities and regions into their learning future. These are divided into organisational, enabling, pedagogical and other issues affecting the city's journey towards the learning city/region and the actions and decisions described that will need to be included in strategies and policies.

Organisational issues and actions for the learning city/region

Decision making

Good information on which to base strategy development is often difficult to find, and city managers are often to be found lamenting the lack of it. The urban studies departments of major universities have provided much of the information connected with the physical and environmental regeneration of cities and regions,

Figure 9.1 Transforming 20th century educating and training cities and regions into 21st century learning cities and regions

	20th century educating city/region	21st century learning city/region	Action points
ORGANISATIONAL ISSUES AFFECTING LEARNING CITIES AND REGIONS			
1. Decision-making	Educational decision-making in city rooted in a 20th century mass education and training paradigm	Decisions made on human potential model of individual learning needs, demands and styles of all citizens of all ages and aptitudes	Commission frequent surveys and studies. Find and satisfy customer needs for learning. Develop a learning city/region development strategy based on real need and good information
2. Joined-up local government	Cities, towns and regions foster empire-building within separate and discrete departments	Cities and regions encourage cooperation between departments	Invite all departments to submit plans for the development of lifelong learning in the local community. Include these into the learning strategy
3. The city as a Learning Organisation	Top-down provision of educational services to selected citizens. Little consultation or attention to learning styles, demands or comfort	Cities and regions become customer-oriented Learning Organisations treating each citizen as a potential customer for learning	Discover the learning needs and dreams of all citizens. Seek and act upon feedback constantly. Apply annual indicators to measure progress and performance towards learning city/regions
4. City institutions as Learning Organisations	Education and training supplied to existing and committed learners by learning providers in cities and regions as a statutory duty	All learning providers provide formal and informal learning in response to the researched needs of all citizens. Learner feedback constantly sought and acted upon	Staff obtain feedback from students for each lesson and act upon it. Administrators consistently seek feedback from teaching staff on how to improve delivery. Use annual indicators to measure progress and performance at city/region level

5. Continuous improvement	Professionals and administrators attend educational courses according to need or desire. Occasional seminars in workplace	Every professional, administrator in the city has a continuous improvement plan for personal skill and knowledge development embedded into the management system	Encourage the development of written continuous improvement plans for all city staff and for all students. Use learning needs analysis tools, audits and encourage personal learning plans. Extend these others in the community. Use mentoring
6. Outward-looking vision	Cities, towns and regions provide inward-looking educational systems to satisfy specified needs	Outward-looking systems – to open minds, encourage broader horizons, promote understanding of others and develop trading links	Twin with other learning cities. Use technology and networks to link people of all ages nationally and internationally to enhance understanding of other creeds, cultures and customs. Accept global responsibility. Help companies grow through trade delegations

ENABLING ISSUES FOR CREATING LEARNING CITIES AND REGIONS

7. Active citizenship	Education as a top-down exercise staffed by professionals with little community involvement	The city as a hive of voluntary activity involving citizens in a large variety of supportive and interactive programmes which contribute to the growth of a learning city	Encourage active citizenship by individuals, families, organisations and communities through volunteering and commitment. Mobilise city/region organisations to help. Organise and channel all the available good-will to where it is needed
8. Marketing the value of learning	Education and training as a financial investment for cities, organisations and nations	Learning as a social, personal and financial investment in and by people for the benefit of nations, organisations, society in general and themselves personally	Market the joys of learning strongly as an investment in the future – by a city in its citizens, by a workplace in its workforce, by learning providers in their students' future, by people in their own future worth and happiness. Use every aspect of the media

continued…

Figure 9.1 continued

	20th century educating city/region	21st century learning city/region	Action point
ENABLING ISSUES FOR CREATING LEARNING CITIES AND REGIONS			
9. Productive partnerships in the learning city	Each sector of the city, town and region determines its own needs and bids and acts separately for them	Holistic and inclusive – increases resources and motivation through partnerships and cooperation between each sector of the community	Facilitate fruitful partnerships between sectors as an investment in new resources and knowledge. Adopt a total service budget approach which acknowledges the synergy between stakeholders and desired outcomes
10. Breaking the barriers to learning	Laissez-faire approach in top-down education system	Cities and regions identify learning barriers as well as learning needs and address them	Find the barriers to learning and develop a strategy to dismantle them. Provide learning counsellors. Create a culture of learning through a strategy based on support for lifelong and life-wide learning for all
11. Access to learning	Take it or leave it courses developed and delivered by city learning providers on their own premises	Learning made available where, when, how and from whom the learner wants it with the learner's consent	Encourage providers to provide learning where people are – homes, housing estates, workplaces, pubs, sports stadia, church halls etc.
12. Technology and networks	Most teaching based on traditional methods of classroom delivery	Increasing use of distance learning, multimedia and networks	Invest in technology provision in all learning providers. Provide email addresses for all students. Encourage use of email, the internet and collaborative learning with international learning providers. Employ distance learning techniques, develop multimedia software. Commission research into the wired city concept etc.

13. Joined-up learning	Education is compartmentalised according to age, aptitude and purpose	Learning is lifelong in concept and content, providing links vertically and horizontally between age groups in buildings open to the whole community	Open up learning to the whole community. Provide community-based facilities which encourage links between learning providers and people of all ages. Community schools, lifelong learning centres etc.
14. Promoting employability	Educates and trains for employment and short-term need	Promotes learning for employability in the long term	Carry out regular skills surveys leading well into the future. Cooperate with industry to determine needs
PEDAGOGICAL ISSUES IN LEARNING CITIES AND REGIONS			
15. Giving ownership to the learner	Ownership of the need to learn and its content is with the educator	Learner, as customer, rules. As far as possible ownership of the need to learn and its content is given to individuals	Develop and use techniques and tools to help individuals of all ages understand their own learning needs and styles, e.g. audits and personal learning plans
16. Role of examinations and assessment	Examinations used to separate successes from failures at specific times	Examinations as failure-free learning opportunities confirming progress and encouraging further learning	Influence development of innovative assessment tools embedded into personal learning programmes, and examined when the student feels ready
7. Skills-based curriculum	Education in city institutions is knowledge and information based – what to think	Learning in city institutions and the community is understanding, skills and values based – how to think	Redevelop content dominated curricula into personal skills-based learning programmes that expand the capacity of people to engage in learning

continued…

Figure 9.1 continued

	20th century educating city/region	21st century learning city/region	Action point
PEDAGOGICAL ISSUES ON LEARNING CITIES AND REGIONS			
18. Active learning	City education providers deliver passive classroom based education, founded on tested memory development	Learning is an active, creative, exciting journey into the future involving learners in new experiences and developing positive values and attitudes	Encourage active learning methods – brainstorms, data collection and analysis, creative discussion, case studies and simulations, visits etc. to make learning fun, pleasurable and an expression of the most natural human instinct. Borrow ideas from the best industry education methods
19. Focus on the learner	Education is uniformity – content is based on the needs of national governments to provide evidence of progress	Learning is based on the need to develop human potential, creativity and response to change and uncertainty in an unknown future	Influence curricula etc. to develop education for competence, flexibility, adaptability and versatility. Develop individual support services and more sophisticated indicators of progress
OTHER ISSUES FOR LEARNING CITIES AND REGIONS			
20. Learning and culture	Cultural life of city kept separate from education life and facilities	Education and culture synonymous in a glorious mixture of learning opportunities from all parts of the community	Turn all community buildings – libraries, museums, theatres, galleries, shopping malls etc. – into new-look educational adventure playgrounds for everyone
21. Celebrating learning	Citizens see learning as a difficult chore and as received wisdom	Citizens see learning as fun, participative and involving, and as perceived wisdom	Celebrate, reward and recognise learning frequently at all ages and stages of learning
22. Use of available resources	Educators as providers – sole distributors of information, knowledge and resource to learners. Community remote	Educators as managers – of all the resources and expertise available in a community, city or region	Discover and use the talents, skills, expertise and knowledge within the community from all sources. In-service training to empower educators to use this. Appoint resource manager

Figure 9.2   Decision-making in learning cities and regions

	20th century educating city/region	21st century learning city/region	Action points
Decision-making	Educational decision-making in city rooted in a 20th century mass education and training paradigm	Decisions made on human potential model of individual learning needs, demands and styles of all citizens of all ages and aptitudes	Commission frequent surveys and studies. Find and satisfy customer needs for learning. Develop a learning city/region development strategy based on real need and good information

though to date the issues concerning social and community aspects of learning cities and regions have been in shorter supply. However, with the new European and national government focus on lifelong learning, a number of academic establishments have now opened up research centres concentrating on implementation issues, while some of them are also expanding into real learning city matters, fuelled by grants from the European Commission and others. Those cities and regions containing universities with such departments are at an obvious advantage, and the projects and research described in earlier chapters have helped to build up expertise networks organised from such places as the Centre for Research into Lifelong Learning at Stirling University and Napier University in Scotland and others too numerous to mention (the names of those in the LILLIPUT, INDICATORS, TELS and PALLACE networks are to be found on the project websites listed in Annexe 1). The OECD sponsored PASCAL project (www.obs-pascal.com) has been established to provide an information observatory for cities and regions. Other good information can be commissioned from organisations created for the purpose.

Joined up local and regional government

Japan has recognised the holistic nature of lifelong learning for many years. Each national and local government department is required to produce plans for expanding the incidence of lifelong learning in its own region and in the country as a whole. This iswhy the Research Department of Lifelong Learning at Japan's National Institute for Educational Research says:

> Regarding the community framework for the promotion of lifelong learning, Lifelong Learning Centres should be established in the prefectures, whose function is to provide information concerning lifelong learning, to perfect the system of consultation on learning, and to devise all kinds of learning and co-operation among educational institutions.

Figure 9.3 Joined-up local and regional government

	20th century educating city/region	21st century learning city/region	Action points
Joined-up local government	Cities, towns and regions foster empire-building within separate and discrete departments	Cities and regions encourage cooperation between departments	Invite all departments to submit plans for the development of lifelong learning in the local community. Include these into the learning strategy

It is also why, as described in *Lifelong Learning at Work*, 'Yashio city in the East of Japan has originated more than 70 lifelong learning programmes for its citizens from kindergarten to 3rd age'. Other local and regional authorities in other parts of the world are now following suit and using the concepts behind the construction of a learning city to break down the artificial and claustrophobic barriers between administrative departments.

Cities and regions as learning organisations

Chapter 2 has raised the issue of the city/region as a learning organisation and suggested some exercises by which progress towards it can be measured. The example of how Southampton has defined the professional responsibilities of its staff along learning organisation lines is also outlined in Chapter 2. Many other cities have followed suit. Customer-orientation is of course not a new concept. It arose from the total quality management concepts being followed by every successful large company during the late 1980s and 1990s, and many local and regional authorities have adapted these to operate within their own environments.

Figure 9.4 Cities and regions as a learning organisation

	20th century educating city/region	21st century learning city/region	Action points
The city as a *Learning Organisation*	Top-down provision of educational services to selected citizens. Little consultation or attention to learning styles, demands or comfort	Cities and regions become customer-oriented *Learning Organisations* treating each citizen as a potential customer for learning	Discover the learning needs and dreams of all citizens. Seek and act upon feedback constantly. Apply annual indicators to measure progress and performance towards learning city/regions

In the UK the Investors in People kitemark is another set of quality indicators in which some authorities have invested their time and money, and this is rapidly spreading around the English-speaking world. But quality indicators need to be consistently monitored after the first flush of enthusiasm has waned. The local authority Stakeholder Audit developed in the INDICATORS project led by the Centre for Lifelong Learning Research at the University of Stirling, and described in Chapter 4, provides a tool for doing this.

Figure 9.5 City/region institutions as learning organisations

	20th century educating city/region	21st century learning city/region	Action points
City institutions as *Learning Organisations*	Education and training supplied to existing and committed learners by learning providers in cities and regions as a statutory duty	All learning providers provide formal and informal learning in response to the researched needs of all citizens. Learner feedback constantly sought and acted upon	Staff obtain feedback from students for each lesson and act upon it. Administrators consistently seek feedback from teaching staff on how to improve delivery. Use annual indicators to measure progress and performance at city/region level

Stakeholders as learning organisations

Equally city institutions need to prove themselves as learning organisations, as was discussed in Chapter 6. These are not just the traditional learning providers such as schools, adult colleges and universities but anywhere where learning takes place – hospitals, large and small companies, professional update centres, community centres and many others. They may learn from the habit of successful industry education departments where constant feedback from students (often described as happiness sheets) is a sine qua non of every lesson in order to maintain a high standard of learning and comprehension. Again, the stakeholder audits for schools, universities, small companies and adult colleges will help to maintain awareness and quality, and also serve as staff training templates, while the LILLIPUT and Longlearn websites contain excellent learning materials on this aspect of learning cities and regions.

Continuous improvement

One important characteristic of any learning organisation is the willingness of its staff to stay up to date with developments not only in their own field but also

Figure 9.6 Continuous improvement in cities and regions

	20th century educating city/region	21st century learning city/region	Action points
Continuous improvement	Professionals and administrators attend educational courses according to need or desire. Occasional seminars in workplace	Every professional, administrator in the city has a continuous improvement plan for personal skill and knowledge development embedded into the management system	Encourage the development of written continuous improvement plans for all city staff and for all students. Use learning needs analysis tools, audits and encourage personal learning plans. Extend these others in the community. Use mentoring

in the general field of the organisation for which they work. Multinational companies, for example, work hard to inculcate a company culture on their employees which makes them all, in the words of the chart in Figure 2.2, ambassadors of the organisation to its customers, clients, audiences and suppliers. Total quality management has moved on in recent years to continuous improvement programmes requiring all staff in all departments to become lifelong learners. Similarly educators of all ages cannot fulfil their professional responsibilities to their students if they are not aware of the recent research into how people learn or acquainted with the new tools and techniques – for example, Personal Learning Audits, Personal Learning Plans – that allow them to improve their own and their students' performance. Some of the tools discussed in Chapter 3 are very relevant here as aids to management efforts to encourage the culture of continuous improvement, particularly the Personal Learning Audits and Personal Learning Plans. Mentoring is a particularly useful tool now dramatically increasing in use in learning cities and regions.

Looking outward to the world

As we have shown in Chapter 8 modern information and communications technology has made the possibility of links with other cities, regions, cultures, creeds and countries easy to attain. Multicultural communities are especially fortunate in this respect. Increasing numbers of cities and regions, for example Dublin, Espoo, Adelaide and Barcelona are accepting that not only do they have global, as well as local, responsibilities but also that these links can be fruitful in many ways – socially, economically, environmentally, culturally and as learning opportunities for all their citizens. They are enjoined therefore to contact existing networks that can not only put them in touch with other cities for information

Figure 9.7 Outward-looking cities and regions

	20th century educating city/region	21st century learning city/region	Action points
Outward-looking vision	Cities, towns and regions provide inward-looking educational systems to satisfy specified needs	Outward-looking systems – to open minds, encourage broader horizons, promote understanding of others and develop trading links	Twin with other learning cities. Use technology and networks to link people of all ages nationally and internationally to enhance understanding of other creeds, cultures and customs. Accept global responsibility. Help companies grow through trade delegations

exchange but also have the creativity and imagination to engage in meaningful projects on a global basis. The PALLACE project has led the way, as Chapter 8 demonstrates.

Learning city/region enabling issues and actions

This second set of learning city and region issues deals with those actions that cities and regions will need to take in order to create the culture of learning so important to their future. Individually they represent a series of actions that any city or region would want to take in order to grow with the 21st century. Collectively they help to define learning cities and regions and fuel that growth.

Active citizenship

Active citizenship is not just an add-on to learning, but an essential by-product of it as well as a mobiliser of the huge volume of human resource within every community. Many examples have been given in Chapter 7 of those cities that have improved inter-personal, inter-family and inter-community relations and social stability by releasing the creativity and commitment of their citizens. However, this vast store of goodwill should be formalised, much in the way that Brisbane has established a register of volunteers and matched it with the needs of individuals, organisations and the city itself. While this is sometimes a function of the social services department, it can be a stand-alone facility run by the volunteers themselves with the help of a powerful figure in the city hierarchy. Care should be taken to ensure that the activities met a genuine need, and do

Figure 9.8 Active citizenship in learning cities and regions

	20th century educating city/region	21st century learning city/region	Action points
Active citizenship	Education as a top-down exercise by city institutions staffed by professionals with little community involvement	The city as a hive of voluntary activity involving citizens in a large variety of supportive and interactive programmes which contribute to the growth of a learning city	Encourage active citizenship by individuals, families, organisations and communities through volunteering and commitment. Mobilise city/region organisations to help. Organise and channel all the available good-will to where it is needed

not lead to unemployment of the artisans who would normally carry out these tasks for payment. The idea of time currency, described in Chapter 7, is also an attractive way of increasing volunteering.

Information and communication

In the modern world of powerful and persuasive communication, citizens are beset with a plethora of potent and sometimes conflicting messages from TV, radio, video, the press, posters, the internet, post, advertising agents, the workplace, and national and local government. Very few have been given the mental tools to cope with the information overload that this eclectic mixture of the trivial and the important imposes upon us all. Competing with this, broadcasting the learning message of the learning city both internally to its citizens and externally to its suppliers, customers and potential investors, is therefore no trivial task. And yet one key element of strategy emphasised in this book is the importance of letting people know how important learning is to the development of their own city and/or region and hence their prosperity within it. For this it will need to use the stakeholder organisations themselves – the schools, the workplaces, the colleges, the hospitals, the museums and libraries etc. – as messengers, as happens in Espoo. It will need to transmit the learning city news by displays, exhibitions and posters in surgeries, restaurants, shopping malls and public places; by electronic means on the city and stakeholder websites; by broadcasting means on TV, radio and videotape as in the excellent videos produced in Glasgow and Dublin; by the printed word in leaflets, brochures and in the local newspapers. Above all, this should be a message of the joy of learning, in Finland the title of the country's national lifelong learning strategy.

Figure 9.9 Marketing learning

	20th century educating city/region	21st century learning city/region	*Action points*
Marketing the value of learning	Education and training as a financial investment for cities, organisations and nations	Learning as a social, personal and financial investment in and by people for the benefit of nations, organisations, society in general and themselves personally	Market the joys of learning strongly as an investment in the future – by a city in its citizens, by a workplace in its workforce, by learning providers in their students' future, by people in their own future worth and happiness. Use every aspect of the media

Productive partnerships

Partnerships between stakeholders in the city/region, including local and regional government, have a multiplicity of purposes and outputs. Many of them are not so well-organised or productive as the IBM/Woodberry Down twinning scheme, described in Chapter 2, was. A good synergetic relationship between organisations would establish facilitating links at many levels, have the imprimatur of powerful people in all participating organisations, employ someone to drive it (volunteers from either or all organisations?), break down stereotypes, solve problems for participating partners and engage a large number of people in interaction with each other. Good partnerships act as human, physical, intellectual and financial

Figure 9.10 Productive partnerships in the learning city

	20th century educating city/region	*21st century learning city/region*	*Action points*
Productive partnerships in the learning city	Each sector of the city, town and region determines its own needs and bids and acts separately for them	Holistic and inclusive – increases resources and motivation through partnerships and cooperation between each sector of the community	Facilitate fruitful partnerships between sectors as an investment in new resources and knowledge. Adopt a total service budget approach which acknowledges the synergy between stakeholders and desired outcomes

resource generators for each partner. There is also another dimension at city/ region level in which a total service budget approach, first pioneered in some parts of the United States, addresses social issues in the community through a collective budget to partnerships of several stakeholders and services.

Figure 9.11 Breaking down the barriers to learning

	20th century educating city/region	21st century learning city/region	Action points
Breaking the barriers to learning	Laissez-faire approach in top-down education system	Cities and regions identify learning barriers as well as learning needs and address them	Find the barriers to learning and develop a strategy to dismantle them. Provide learning counsellors. Create a culture of learning through a strategy based on support for lifelong and life-wide learning for all

Breaking down the barriers to learning

The TELS survey identified a number of barriers to learning common to all cities and regions. Of these the three that were deemed to be the most intractable were based on personal and emotional factors such as lack of self-esteem, low aspirations and a poor family culture of learning. Embryo learning cities and regions, in their need to develop a metropolitan learning culture, will need to address this deficit. There is no short-term answer. Their roots have been set down over many years in the history of depressed communities, failure oriented education systems, community and family sub-cultures and many more. But a number of strategies, based on the range of recommendations made at the beginning of this chapter and in Chapter 1, exist. Identification and action at an early age by surrounding kindergartens and primary schools with the experts – counsellors, psychologists, logopedists, mentors etc. as happens in Espoo – who can work with teachers to solve problems immediately when they occur, and build up self-esteem in young children, is one possible route for city administrations. It is described in fuller detail in *Lifelong Learning in Action*. Others lie in the empowerment of vital and vibrant communities around the schools and the use of local expertise, skills and knowledge, as in Mawson Lakes. Tools and techniques, for example the Personal Learning Audits and Plans described in Chapter 5, can be used to rekindle a lifelong interest in learning.

Figure 9.12 Improving access to learning

	20th century educating city/region	21st century learning city/region	Action points
Access to learning	Take it or leave it courses developed and delivered by city learning providers on their own premises	Learning made available where, when, how and from whom the learner wants it with the learner's consent	Encourage providers to provide learning where people are – homes, housing estates, workplaces, pubs, sports stadia, church halls etc.

Access to learning

One barrier that is relatively easy to break down is access to learning. *Lifelong Learning at Work* tells the story of the learning shop and centre in the Metro shopping mall in Gateshead and the courses given by Sunderland University in more than 30 locations in the city. These initiatives have been copied in several other UK, Canadian and Australian towns and cities. Citizens who would otherwise have to spend time travelling to a college on the other side of town can find the courses they want in the local area. Some cities have created second chance opportunities in places where reluctant learners feel more comfortable – such as the football and rugby stadia in the UK's 'Learning through Sport' programmes. Yet others, for example Ilkley College in West Yorkshire, have taken their courses into the pubs. A learning city focusing on the needs and demands of individual learners will encourage its learning providers to be creative in their delivery of learning – why not a learning restaurant where diners also receive education with their meals? Or mobile education centres visiting outlying villages in hard to reach areas as the mobile library does, and as happens in many rural areas of the UK and Australia?

Using technology

From *Lifelong Learning in Action*:

> Despite a hard-fought rearguard action by professional teacher associations intent on preserving the image of an all-knowing and all-powerful teacher, the idea that one person can fulfil the hopes, ambitions and demands of more than 30 young individuals in the same space over the same time now looks as ridiculous as the notion that Canute could hold back the waves.

As most city managers are now aware the future lies in the use of the technological tools at our disposal, at the marriage of the information, communications and broadcasting technologies into powerful pedagogical tools. No educator can compete with the internet as an information source. No lesson

Figure 9.13 Using technology wisely

	20th century educating city/region	21st century learning city/region	Action points
Technology and networks	Most teaching based on traditional methods of classroom delivery	Increasing use of distance learning, multimedia and networks	Invest in technology provision in all learning providers. Provide email addresses for all students. Encourage use of email, the internet and collaborative learning with international learning providers. Employ distance learning techniques, develop multimedia software. Commission research into the wired city concept etc.

can have a more powerful impact than one which is carried out in collaboration with a student from the other side of the world, or one which uses the immediacy of satellite transmission to depict, say, French farmers rebelling in Brussels against agricultural imports, as was described in Chapter 2. But look into the technological future and there are yet more wonders to behold. For example, the wired city concept, which potentially allows say a school to broadcast the school play on local cable to parents and the community, or a college to carry out a survey of learning preferences. The possibilities are endless. This is where learning cities and regions, especially, as we have seen in Chapter 2, those in North America, will invest many of their financial resources for learning in the future, not forgetting that they have the support of companies wishing to implement their corporate social responsibilities in a field with which they are familiar. As we have also seen in Chapter 7, however, there are wise and unwise uses of education technologies – as multimedia page-turners they are no more motivating than the driest of books. Nor can technology replace educators. But a good educator will turn the technology to his/her, and the students', best advantage.

Inter-generational learning

The Gothenburg example of how the island of Hisingen, a former shipbuilding and dockland area of the city, has been transformed into a vibrant technology park and living community is described in *Lifelong Learning at Work*. Here the

Figure 9.14 Creating community learning spaces

	20th century educating city/region	21st century learning city/region	Action points
Joined-up learning	Education is compartmentalised according to age, aptitude and purpose	Learning is lifelong in concept and content, providing links vertically and horizontally between age groups in buildings open to the whole community	Open up learning to the whole community. Provide community-based facilities which encourage links between learning providers and people of all ages. Community schools. Lifelong learning centres etc.

catalyst was a large fully equipped modern learning and technology centre used by small companies, schools, colleges, universities and by the community in the evenings. Here too people of all ages and callings mingled and exchanged ideas and experiences, knowledge and skills to foster the sort of creative interaction and output that would satisfy the 21st century need for new products and services. Of course, technology and business parks are now an essential feature of many cities and regions though not all include the young and the community in their interactions. But the out-of-box thinking that questions the homogenisation of education into age and aptitude groups will continue to be debated. Among the results of the introduction of lifelong learning implementation by local and regional authorities, Kearns (2004) cites 'the progressive harmonisation and integration of the sectors of education in a more seamless and holistic approach to learning in many contexts'. Already, as we have seen in Chapter 8, the central adhesive in new community developments now being planned and built by public/private consortia in Australia and elsewhere is the ubiquitousness and interdependence of learning provision to and from university centres, community facilities, schools, homes and small companies. Mawson Lakes is a fine example, but also there are others in Springfield in the Brisbane Learning Corridor and on the outskirts of Melbourne. Not only are they examples of how the availability of learning is becoming part of the estate agent's armoury of inducements, they also point towards a future where inter-generational and inter-institutional learning is the norm.

Promoting employability

In the 20th century, cities and regions in the Western world have sought the nirvana of full employment through manufacturing industry. All of this changed from the 1980s. Fuelled by free-market economics and globalisation, most of the manufacture of goods has moved from mass-employment factories in the developed world to the developing world where labour is cheaper and costs are

Figure 9.15 Promoting employability in learning cities and regions

	20th century educating city/region	21st century learning city/region	Action points
Promoting employability	Educates and trains for employment and short-term need	Promotes learning for employability in the long term	Carry out regular skills surveys leading well into the future. Cooperate with industry to determine needs

lower. Into the gap have flowed service industries based on an ever-increasing need for knowledge and creativity, rapid and accelerating change and the demand for more highly educated citizens. As *Lifelong Learning in Action* and other chapters in this book have suggested, future citizens can expect to have several jobs, and sometimes careers, in a lifetime, and to keep themselves continuously updated. Companies, and increasingly local authorities, now aspire to world-class standards simply in order to survive. As most local and regional governments are aware, employability is now the watchword, leading to the need for such personal attributes as adaptability, flexibility, creativity, imagination, and the ability to think outside the box, hardly the type of school graduate our mass-producing, subject dominated examination systems are providing. Most authorities and companies now invest in regular skills and knowledge-needs surveys in order to be able to anticipate needs in advance. Some, such as Newcastle in the North-East of England, have appointed employability managers. However, employability is as much an attitude of mind as a specific strategy and this is much more difficult to inculcate in city and region populations.

Pedagogical issues and actions in learning cities and regions

There are, in addition, a number of pedagogical issues affecting the construction of learning cities and regions, and originating in the need for new outlooks as described above. While they are mainly outside of the detailed scope of this book, and some of them are possibly outside of the ability of cities and regions to influence, the rapid growth of lifelong learning concepts and ideas throughout the world is engendering a long overdue and serious look at the values, methods, procedures, organisation and content of traditional education. Thanks to the research on multiple intelligences by Howard Gardner, on emotional intelligence by Daniel Goleman and on spiritual intelligence by Zohar and Williams, we know so much more about how people learn, and more importantly how to harness this knowledge in the service of better learning. And yet, even though industry has been adopting its principles for years, so little of this priceless knowledge and action finds its way into public education systems. In a learning city such insight would be the fuel that releases the energy and increases the self-esteem of the people. Learning city managers will therefore need to at least know what the pedagogical issues are so that they can apply those measures for which they have the capability. Equally the city's learning providers, often the last organisations to adopt new ideas and methods, will benefit from new knowledge of how to administer the tools and techniques that they can administer on behalf of themselves, their students and the city.

Figure 9.16 Who owns the learning?

	20th century educating city/region	21st century learning city/region	Action points
Giving ownership to the learner	Ownership of the need to learn and its content is with the educator	Learner, as customer, rules. As far as possible ownership of the need to learn and its content is given to individuals	Develop and use techniques and tools to help individuals of all ages understand their own learning needs and styles, e.g. audits and personal learning plans

Ownership of learning

Perhaps the most important by-product of the change from a focus on teaching to a focus on learning is the transfer of power from educator to learner, from receiving preordained education to ownership by the student of the learning itself. It is also the basis of motivation in those for whom learning is difficult or uninteresting. Industry educators have recognised this for many years and have adopted methodologies that involve small and large group discussion, individualised tuition, brainstorming, mentoring and coaching, and embedded testing and feedback. When the learner is customer his or her needs and demands are at the forefront and this puts a premium on sophisticated support services, a knowledge of learning styles, the facility to learn at a personal pace and a greater self-knowledge, obtained through the application of tools such as Personal Learning Audits and Personal Learning Development Plans. Some, not nearly enough, adult education providers are changing their methods to fit the new paradigm, and even some schools are now making attempts to justify the curriculum to their pupils. However, there is a long way to go before the principles of learning ownership are fully understood by educators understandably reluctant to cede power. Once again the LILLIPUT and Longlearn materials are designed to facilitate this process.

Figure 9.17 The role of examinations

	20th century educating city/region	21st century learning city/region	Action points
Role of examinations and assessment	Examinations used to separate successes from failures at specific times	Examinations as failure-free learning opportunities confirming progress and encouraging further learning	Influence development of innovative assessment tools embedded into personal learning programmes, and examined when the student feels ready

Assessing learning

From *Lifelong Learning in Action*:

> An examination process designed to fail a good proportion of its students is surely wasteful. A value system setting greater store on academic and intellectual performance over personal attributes such as self-esteem, self-knowledge and tolerance for others is surely misguided. An assessment procedure testing only the skill of the memory to regurgitate facts and information, and ignoring the importance of other high order skills such as information-handling, decision-making, communicating, thinking and others is surely inappropriate for the 21st century.

An increasing number of educationists are recognising the truth in these words. It should not be beyond the capability of governments and universities to devise an assessment system which treats every examination as a non-threatening learning opportunity for each examinee, leading to a report on where he/she is on his/her own learning curve and pointing to the learning needs for the future. In this there are no failures – only opportunities for further development. However, such is the resistance of teachers, parents and often the students themselves to the idea of taking failure out of the system, and such is the power of the examinations industry backed by a conservative media, that it will probably take a long time before anything is done – at the schools level anyway. Local and regional government authorities should nevertheless be aware of the issue as a pedagogical time bomb that will ultimately find its time to explode.

Skills and competence-based curricula

Countless reports and papers emphasise the changing role of 21st century educators from being purveyors of knowledge and information to facilitators of learning through a variety of means. Further, the knowledge explosion in many

Figure 9.18 Skills and competence-based curriculum

	20th century educating city/region	21st century learning city/region	Action points
Skills-based curriculum	Education in city institutions is knowledge and information based – *what* to think	Learning in city institutions and the community is understanding, skills and values based – *how* to think	Redevelop content dominated curricula into personal skills-based learning programmes that expand the capacity of people to engage in learning

subject areas has rendered obsolescent much of what is traditionally taught in schools and adult education. The modern alternative is a 'competence or skills-based' curriculum similar to that proposed by the UK Royal Society of Arts (RSA) 'Opening Minds' project where solid improvements in both learning and motivation have been reported (see *Lifelong Learning in Action*) in the participating schools. Students move from being told what to think to learning how to think creatively. According to Ian Nicol, in Scottish Business in the Community's list of ten priorities for employability in the 21st century, educational certificates only come in at number ten after such skills and attributes as the ability to work in teams, open-mindedness, adaptability, learning to learn etc. Clearly, he says, a credibility gap exists between schooling and the wider world of employment. Other similar conclusions are to be found elsewhere. While cities and regions can do little to influence what happens in the schools and vocational education colleges in the immediate future, they do have the possibility, and perhaps the responsibility, of making authoritative representations to government bodies, based on their perceptions of their own needs for skills development.

Active learning

Similarly there is a wide variety of tools and techniques for stimulating learning that can make learning a more pleasurable experience for all, many of them used in industry to develop professionals, technicians and managers. The geographer Fairgrieve (1926) commented that 'Geography is not to be found in a classroom', and took his students out on field trips whenever he could. The same is true of many other subjects traditionally taught within those four walls. The Crick committee on the teaching of citizenship recommended active methods such as visits to the city hall to see democracy in action (or not). Schools in Ontario, and those investing in the International Baccalaureate throughout the world, are expected to complete a minimum number of experiential learning days in the outside community. But even within the classroom there are methods that energise the creativity of the learner rather than expecting him/her to sit passively

Figure 9.19 Active learning

	20th century educating city/region	21st century learning city/region	Action points
Active learning	City education providers deliver passive classroom based education, founded on tested memory development	Learning is an active, creative, exciting journey into the future involving learners in new experiences and developing positive values and attitudes	Encourage active learning methods – brainstorms, data collection and analysis, creative discussion, case studies and simulations, visits etc. to make learning fun, pleasurable and an expression of the most natural human instinct. Borrow ideas from the best industry education methods

absorbing book- or talk-based knowledge for regurgitation in examinations. The LILLIPUT and Longlearn materials referred to frequently in this book adopt this approach.

Learner needs

Professor Sir Graham Hills (2005), leader of the Royal Society of Arts project team on 'Visions for a More Capable Society', laments that the UK government's drive for accountability in education has created examination systems that simply develop conformity and uniformity, and argues that an education for competence would be a much more useful approach for both schools and adult education. From the comments above about employability, ownership, active learning and

Figure 9.20 Focusing on learner needs

	20th century educating city/region	21st century learning city/region	Action points
Focus on the learner	Education is uniformity – content is based on the needs of national governments to provide evidence of progress	Learning is based on the need to develop human potential, creativity and response to change and uncertainty in an unknown future	Influence curricula etc. to develop education for competence, flexibility, adaptability and versatility. Develop individual support services and more sophisticated indicators of progress

the skills-based curriculum, it will be obvious that this book supports that view. But we also argue that lifelong learning concepts impose a 180 degree change of focus from the needs of the educator to the satisfaction of the needs and demands of the learner. Most local and regional authorities are not in a position to influence government education policies, but they are able to support their own citizens as learners by installing advice and support services that will encourage each individual to work out his/her own learning pathway. In addition they have enough influence over the learning providers to require them to assess the personal needs, styles and requirements of every learner and relate these to personal indicators of progress.

Figure 9.21 Raising the value of culture

	20th century educating city/region	21st century learning city/region	Action points
Learning and culture	Cultural life of city kept separate from education life and facilities	Education and culture synonymous in a glorious mixture of learning opportunities from all parts of the community	Turn all community buildings – libraries, museums, theatres, galleries, shopping malls etc. – into new-look educational adventure playgrounds for everyone

Other learning city/region issues and actions

Culture and learning

Mary Pinard reports:

> For the past ten years at Babson Management College in the United States, a creativity stream has been part of the module that first-year students must take during their first five weeks on campus. They're randomly assigned to one of seven classes where they learn poetry, painting, fiction-writing, theatrical improvisation, puppeteering, movement, or music. Each module is taught by a 'creativity consultant' who is a working artist proficient in that field. From their very first session with their creativity consultant, students are immersed in the principles of the creative process

In the 1980s customer engineers at IBM were sent on courses on art and music appreciation to improve their leadership skills and to transform them into more rounded people. Evidently, enlightened business and industry leaders recognise that culture is a vital part of the learning process, a view that has been lost in our more utilitarian national and local education policies, resulting in a loss of knowledge and interest in matters cultural among younger people.

Cities and regions are in a position to change this and to see the potential of their cultural services Cinderellas – museums, libraries, galleries, theatres and so on – as essential parts of the educational process at all levels. In the PALLACE project they were also used as information and feedback centres for passing on the message of the learning city to citizens. But why stop at those four? A learning city will be a vibrant place where street theatre abounds, where surgeries, hairdressing salons and drinking places, to name but a few, show the work of local artists, where the civic halls become a focus for outdoor artistic and musical events, where sports and leisure clubs are also cultural centres, where individual streets compete or cooperate with each other to show exhibitions of cultural heritage from around the world. High, popular and local cultures become the focus of learning opportunities free from the trammels of the need to demonstrate examination competence or the threat of failure. Moreover, more citizens themselves begin to participate in these activities, societies, choirs, drama groups and special interest groups multiply, enhancing cultural life and adding stability to the locality.

Figure 9.22 Celebrating learning

	20th century educating city/region	21st century learning city/region	Action points
Celebrating learning	Citizens see learning as a difficult chore and as received wisdom	Citizens see learning as fun, participative and involving, and as perceived wisdom	Celebrate, reward and recognise learning frequently at all ages and stages of learning

Celebrating learning

The participation theme is continued in celebration. The learning festivals in Marion and Sapporo, described in Chapter 3, were successful in bringing thousands of people back into the learning fold. They were happy events, presenting an image of learning often missing from the grim purpose in traditional learning establishments, and emphasising the fun of acquiring and using new knowledge, skills, experiences and talents in whole communities. Or of simply participating in events like 'Learning at Work' or 'Family Learning Weeks', initiatives started by the UK Campaign for Learning and now an integral part of the learning scene in more than 40 countries. However, this does not preclude the satisfaction to be gained from receiving rewards and awards for learning success in traditional diploma ceremonies. The more that lifelong learning concepts of ownership, active learning, empowerment, local culture, mentors,

Figure 9.23 New resources in cities and regions

	20th century educating city/region	21st century learning city/region	Action points
Use of available resources	Educators as providers – sole distributors of information, knowledge and resource to learners. Community remote	Educators as managers – of all the resources and expertise available in a community, city or region	Discover and use the talents, skills, expertise and knowledge within the community from all sources. In-service training to empower educators to use this. Appoint resource manager

technology usage, partnerships and celebration take hold, the more cities and regions become vibrant, self-regulating, celebratory places for joyful living.

New resources

It may seem that new financial resources needed to create learning cities and regions are endless, and indeed aspiring municipalities will need to invest additional financial capital in helping them grow. But much of this lies in the re-alignment of existing budgets. In addition, there are other existing resources that are very much under-used. As we have seen in Chapter 7, every community has a vast store of untapped human, physical, intellectual, financial and organisational potential within its boundaries. From the parents to church congregations, from workplaces to community centres, from individual enthusiasts to policemen, firemen and nurses, there are talents, skills, knowledge, experiences, insights – all of it potentially at the service of education to enrich the everyday experiences of children and adults alike. The burgeoning *Universities of the 3rd Age* are an example of citizens getting together to share their knowledge and experiences. The story told in Chapter 7 of the unrequited efforts of ex-patriate brits wanting to help language, music and mathematics learning in Southern France is another. The trick is how to make it happen, how to manage the richness of the available resources in the interests of the richness of learning, which we have said is now the primary task of every teacher as facilitator of learning. Certainly every learning organisation should employ someone, whether paid or as a volunteer, to energise the resource.

Suggestions for further work from this chapter

1a Give a copy of Figure 9.1 to a selection of key managers and educators with columns 3 and 4 blanked out. Ask them to complete column 3.

1b Give a copy of Figure 9.1 to the same selection with column 3, but not column 4, completed. Ask them to compare their answers with those given. Then ask them to complete column 4.

1c Give them the full chart and ask them to complete the following exercises.

2 Use Figure 9.1 to estimate the extent to which the vision of your city or region takes each point into account. Estimate the percentage of a) city managers, b) elected representatives, c) educators and d) the total number of citizens, who:

    i)   would be aware of the transformations suggested in columns 2 and 3 and

    ii) would agree with the transformations suggested in columns 2 and 3 and

    iii) have taken any of the proposed actions in column 4.

3 For each of the 22 proposed actions in Figure 9.1 give a mark to estimate the extent to which the city has implemented the recommendation: 1 = not even aware of it, 2 = aware but has done very little, 3 = is in the strategy and has started to make some effort to implement this, 4 = has made considerable progress in implementing this, 5 = has implemented it in full in all institutions and aspects of city/region life.

4 Read the rationales – give an example of:

    a)   an action that has been taken in your city or region in this field;

    b)   a further action that could be taken in your city or region;

    c)   a key enabling action that needs to be taken in your city or region to make it happen.

Annexe

A list of useful websites

1 Projects and results

www.appui.esc-toulouse.fr (for LILLIPUT learning materials)
www.pallace.net (for PALLACE project)
www.tels.euproject.org (for TELS project)
newtels.euproject.org (for NewTELS project)
www.ioe.stir.ac.uk/Indicators/ (for INDICATORS Stakeholder Audits project)
r3l.euproject.net (for R3L projects)
www.obs-pascal.com (for PASCAL Observatory project)

2 Lifelong learning and learning city networks

www.campaign-for-learning.org.uk
www.lc-network@ntlworld.com (UK Learning Cities Network)
www.edcities.bcn.es (Educating Cities Network)
www.eurocities.org
www.niace.org.uk (National Institute for Adult and Continuing Education)
www.oecd.org
www.lcc.au (Victoria (Australia) Learning Cities Network)
www.anta.gov.au (Australian National Training Agency)
www.cittaslow.net (Slow Cities Network)
www.regionalstewardship.org (Alliance for Regional Stewardship, USA)
www.iap2.org (International Association for Public Partnership)
www.smartcommunities.org/

3 Useful learning city and region websites

www.dublin.ie
www.intoreal.com (Glasgow)
www.edinburghlearning.com
www.hume.vic.gov.au (Hume Global Learning Centre)
www.cll.bham.ac.uk (Birmingham, UK)

www.brisbane.qld.gov.au

www.marion.sa.gov.au (South Australia Centre for Lifelong Learning and Development)

4 Other useful lifelong learning information

www.newhorizons.org

www.volunteeringqueensland.org.au

www.strategis.gc.ca (Knowledge Management International, Canada)

www.iipuk.co.uk/IIP/Internet/InvestorsinPeople/ (Investors in People)

www.longlearn.org.uk (for learning materials related to the chapters of this book that can be used by local and regional authorities for staff continuous improvement courses)

Bibliography

Adin, V. and McDowell, R. (2004) 'New Zealand PALLACE Report on Adult Learning and Learning Communities', in N. Longworth and S. Allwinkle (eds) *PALLACE Report to the European Commission*, Edinburgh: Napier University.

Alliance for Regional Stewardship (2001) 'Empowering regions: strategies and tools for community decision making', available from 350 Cambridge Avenue, Suite 200, Palo Alto, CA.

Allison, J. and Nystrom, S. (2003) 'From smart state to learning communities: learning festivals as a strategy to stimulate and foster learning communities', in N. Longworth and S. Allwinkle (eds) *PALLACE Report to the European Commission*, Edinburgh: Napier University.

Argyris, C. (1991) 'Teaching smart people how to learn', *Harvard Business Review*, 69(3): 99–109.

Australian National Training Authority (2002) *Learning Communities Project* [online] http://www.anta.gov.au.

Ball, C. (1995) 'Learning does pay', in D.C.A. Bradshaw (ed.) *Bringing Learning to Life: the Learning Revolution, the Economy and the Individual*, London: Falmer Press.

Ball, C. and Stewart, D. (1995) *An Action Agenda for Lifelong Learning for the 21st Century*, Report from the First Global Conference on Lifelong Learning (ed. N. Longworth), Brussels: World Initiative on Lifelong Learning.

Berkeley, J. (1993) 'Recording achievement and lifelong learning', in COMMENT 7, Oct. 1993, Brussels: European Lifelong Learning Initiative.

Bernstein, S. (1999) *Learning to Do It Together: A Review of New Tools for Regional Decision Making, Information Access and Improved Democracy*, Center for Neighborhood Technology, 2125 W. North Avenue, Chicago, IL 60647.

Best Value Victoria (2002) *Community Consultation Resource Guide*, Melbourne: Victorian Local Governance Association (VLGA).

Botkin, J. (2002) *Towards a Wisdom Society* [online] http://www.swaraj.org/shikshantar/ls2_botkin.pdf.

Campaign for Learning (1995) 'Make it happen, a Personal Development Plan', available from 19 Buckingham Street, London WC2N 6EF.

Candy, P. (2005) 'Lifelong learning: critical, desirable or just a good idea', address to Adult Learning Australia's Adult Learners' Week [online] www.ala.gov.au.

Cannon, T., Nathan, M. and Westwood, A. (2003) 'Welcome to the Ideopolis', Work Foundation Working Paper, London: The Work Foundation.

City of Helsinki (2002) *Helsinki, an Educating, Training and Learning City*, City of Helsinki Urban Facts, available from P.O. Box 5500, 00099 Helsinki.

Cochinaux, P. and De Woot, P. (1995) *Moving Towards a Learning Society*, A Forum Report by European Round Table of Industrialists (ERT) with Conference of European Rectors (CRE), Brussels.

Coffield, F. (ed.) (1999) 'Breaking the consensus: lifelong learning as social control', Newcastle: Department of Education, University of Newcastle.

Commission of the European Union (1996) *Accomplishing Europe through Education and Training*, Luxembourg: Study Group on Education and Training, EC Publications Office.

Commission of the European Union (1996) 'Communiqué of the Dublin Meeting of the Education Committee of the Council of the EU Strategy for Lifelong Learning', Luxembourg: EC Publications.

Commission of the European Union (1998) 'Territorial employment pacts: examples of good practice', Luxembourg: EC Publications.

Commission of the European Union (2000) 'Communiqué of the Lisbon Summit of the Education Committee of the Council of the EU Strategy for Lifelong Learning', Luxembourg: EC Publications.

Commission of the European Union (2001) *Memorandum on Lifelong Learning for Active Citizenship in a Europe of Knowledge*, Brussels: DG Education and Culture.

Commission of the European Union (2002) *Realising a European Area of Lifelong Learning*, Brussels: DG Education and Culture.

Commission of the European Union (2002) Call for proposals for the R3L programme, DG Education and Culture, Brussels [online] europa.eu.int/comm/education/policies/lll/life/regio/index_en.html.

Crick, B. (1998) *Education for Citizenship and the Teaching of Democracy in Schools*, Report of the Advisory Group on Citizenship, London.

Department for Education and Employment (DfEE) (1998) *Learning Communities: A Guide to Assessing Practice and Processes*, Learning City Network Secretariat, 111 Grantham Road, Bingham, Nottingham NG13 8DF.

Dick, B. (1997) 'A beginners guide to action research', Action Research Papers [online] http://www.scu.edu.au/schools/sawd/arr/guide.html (2 February 1999).

Dryden, G. and Vos, J. (2005) *The Learning Revolution*, Stafford: Network Educational Press.

Dublin City Development Board (2002) 'Dublin, a city of possibilities 2002–2010: Dublin's learning city strategy', available from DCDB, Dublin [online] www.dublincity.ie.

Eckersley, R. (2001) 'The end of the world (as we know it)', *Sydney Morning Herald*, 20 January: 5.

Eckersley, R. (2004) 'A new world view struggles to emerge', *The Futurist*, 38(5), September–October: 20–4.

Eger, J.M. (1996) 'Building smart communities: a new framework for an Americas information initiative', address to the International Telecommunication Union, Rio de Janeiro, June [online] http://www.smartcommunities.org/library_newframe.htm.

Eger, J.M. (2001) 'Cyberspace and cyberplace: building the smart communities of tomorrow' [online] www.smartcommunities.org/wf/cyberspeech.htm.

Ellis, W.N. (2000) 'Community lifelong learning centers', in R. Miller (ed.) *Creating Learning Communities*, Washington, DC: Foundation for Educational Renewal.

European Round Table of Industrialists (ERT) (1996) *Investing in Knowledge: Towards the Learning Society*, Brussels: ERT.

Fairgrieve, J. (1926) *Geography in School*, London: University of London Press.

Finland Ministry of Education (1997) *The Joy of Learning: A National Strategy for Lifelong Learning'*, Committee Report 14, Helsinki: Finland Ministry of Education.

Florida, R. and Gates, G. (2002) 'Technology and tolerance: diversity and high-tech growth', *Brookings Review*, 20(1).

Gardner, H. (1993) *Multiple Intelligences: The Theory in Practice*, New York: Basic Books.

Goleman, D. (1998) *Working with Emotional Intelligence*, New York: Bloomsbury.

Guinness (2000) 'Learning and growing', employee brochure available from Guinness Centre, Taylors Lane, Dublin 8, Ireland.

Handy, C. (1992) *Managing the Dream: The Learning Organisation*, London: Gemini Consulting Series on Leadership.

Hills, G. (2005) 'Developing a capable population', *RSA Journal*, February: 20–3.

Holford, J., Jarvis, P. and Griffin, C. (1998) *International Perspectives on Lifelong Learning*, London: Kogan Page.

Horgan, J. (1995) 'The learning organization', Foreword in T. Stahl, B. Nyhan and P. D'Aloja (eds) *A Vision for Human Resource Development*, Brussels: European Centre for Work and Society.

Huxley, A. (1931) *Brave New World*, London: Perennial Classics.

IBM, (2005) 'IBM's on-demand community', *IBM in the UK 2005*, available from IBM UK Ltd, P.O. Box 41, North Harbour, Cosham.

International Association for Volunteer Effort (IAVE) (2001) *Universal Declaration on Volunteering*, Washington, DC: IAVE.

Jain, V. and Chandreshsumi, M. (2000) 'A search for meaning: Udaipur as a learning city', *Vimukt Shiksha*, special issue: 56–62.

Jilks, B. (1998) Interview with Bruce Jilks [online] http://www.designshare.com/Research/Jilk98/JilkInterview.htm.

Kearns, P.S. (2004) 'Towards a learning revolution in Australia: a consultation paper on future directions for lifelong learning', available from Adult Learning Australia, Canberra, ACT 2601.

Keating, J., Badenhorst, A. and Szlachetko, T. (2002) *Victoria as a Learning Region*, background report for OECD Victoria Learning Cities and Regions Conference, Melbourne 14 –15 October, Melbourne: RMIT.

Kenny, D. (2003) *Politics and Religion in a Creative Cosmology*, Canberra: Centre for Progressive Religious Thought.

Korhonen, K. (1997) *Educating Engineers of the 21st Century: The Challenges of Higher Engineering Education in Finland*, Helsinki: Helsinki University of Technology.

Korthagen, F. (1996) 'Lifelong learning by teaching and the role of teacher educators', IVLOS Institute of Education, Utrecht University, *COMMENT*, September (18): 14–15, Brussels: ELLI.

Landry, C. (2000) *The Creative City: A Toolkit for Urban Innovators*, London: Earthscan.

Larsen, K. (2001) 'Learning cities: the new recipe in regional development', *OECD Observer*, p. 73.

Learning Cities Network (1998) *Learning Towns, Learning Cities*, Sudbury: DfEE Publications.

Lee, S. (2004) 'Creating our futures', Report on the PALLACE Canadian Conference, Edmonton, in N. Longworth and S. Allwinkle (eds) *PALLACE Report to the European Commission*, Edinburgh: Napier University.

Loader, D. (1993) 'Restructuring an Australian school', *The Computing Teacher*, March.

Longworth, N. (ed.) (1995) *Community Action for Learning, Proceedings of the WILL World Conference on Lifelong Learning, Rome*, Brussels: ELLI.

Longworth, N. (1996) *Skill Europe, Final Project Report to the European Commission FORCE Programme*, Brussels: DG Education and Culture.

Longworth, N. (1998a) 'Learning communities for a learning century', *Jolli Magazine*, March/April (5): 7.

Longworth, N. (1998b) *Proceedings of the Southampton Conference on Learning Cities*, [online] www.pallace.net.

Longworth, N. (1999) *Lifelong Learning at Work: Learning Cities for a Learning Century*, London: Kogan Page.

Longworth, N. (2001) *Lifelong Learning: Creating Learning Cities, Towns and Regions*, European Policy paper, Brussels: DG Education and Culture.

Longworth, N. (2001) *The Local and Regional Dimension of Lifelong Learning: Creating Learning Cities, Towns and Regions*, a European Policy Paper from the TELS project, Brussels: DG Education and Culture.

Longworth, N. (2003a) *Lifelong Learning in Action: Transforming 21st Century Education*, London: Taylor & Francis.

Longworth, N. (2003b) 'PALLACE futures' [online] www.newhorizons.org.

Longworth, N. (2005) 'Learning cities, learning regions, lifelong learning implementers', in J.Crowther and P. Sutherland (eds) *Aspects of Lifelong Learning for All*, London: Routledge (forthcoming).

Longworth, N. and Allwinkle, S. (2005a) *The LILLIPUT Project: Developing Learning Materials on Learning Cities and Regions*, final report to the European Commission, Edinburgh: Napier University.

Longworth, N. and Allwinkle, S. (2005b) *The PALLACE Project: Linking Learning Cities and Regions in Europe, North America, Australasia and China*, final report to the European Commission, Edinburgh: Napier University [online] www.pallace.net.

Longworth, N. and Davies, W.K. (1996) *Lifelong Learning: New Visions, New Implications, New Roles for Industry, Government, Education and the Community for the 21st Century*, London: Kogan Page.

Longworth, N. and De Geest, L. (eds) (1995) *Community Action for Lifelong Learning for Developing Human Potential*, part 2 of report of First Global Conference on Lifelong Learning, Rome, Brussels: World Initiative on Lifelong Learning.

Longworth, N. and Franson, L. (2001) *The TELS Project: Towards a European Learning Society*, final report to the European Commission [online] tels.euproject.org.

Longworth, N., Osborne, M. and Sankey, K. (eds) (2005) *INDICATORS – Developing and Testing Indicators for Monitoring and Measuring Stakeholder Organisations in Learning Cities and Regions*, final report to the European Commission. Stirling/Glasgow: Centre for Research in Lifelong learning.

LTScotland (2005) 'Assessment is for learning' project [online] http://www. ltscotland. org.uk/assess/casestudies/index.asp.

Martin, J. and Norman, A. (1973) *The Computerised Society: An Appraisal of the impact of Computers on Society over the Next 15 years*, Harmondsworth: Pelican.

McPherson, K. (1991) 'Learning through service', *Learning Revolution*, Winter: 50 (IC 27).

Muirhead, B. (2002) 'Communicate', Projects and Activities of University of Queensland Community Service and Research Centre, Ipswich, Queensland.

Naisbitt, J. (1985) *Megatrends*, Paris: Organisation for Economic Cooperation and Development (OECD).

Nicol, I. (2005) 'A new design for education', *RSA Journal*, April: 35.

National Institute of Educational Research (NIER) and UNESCO Institute of Education (1997) *Comparative Studies on Lifelong Learning Policies*, Tokyo: NIER.

Nyhan, B. (1991) *Developing People's Ability to Learn, A European Perspective on Self-learning Competency and Technological Change*, Brussels: European Interuniversity Press.

Nyhan, B., Attwell, G. and Deitmer, L. (eds) (2002) *Towards the Learning Region: education and Regional Innovation in the European Union and the United States*, Thessaloniki: CEDEFOP.

Organisation for Economic Cooperation and Development (OECD) (1973*) Recurrent Education: A Strategy for Lifelong Learning*, Paris: OECD/CERI.

Organisation for Economic Cooperation and Development (OECD)(2000) *Cities and Regions in the New Learning Economy*, Paris: OECD.

Paquet, G. (1999) *Governance through Social Learning*, Ottawa: University of Ottawa Press.

Plato (350 BC) *The Republic*, trans. Allan Bloom (1991), New York: Basic Books.

Ralph, D. (2000) 'Discovering and celebrating learning in communities' [online] www.lcc.edu.au/.

Regenzhani, D. (2002) Address to seminar of Brisbane Educationists, 20.6.2002, unpublished, University of Queensland.

Richardson, J. (2002) 'Reach for the stars: individual learning plans allow teachers to take charge of their own learning', *Tools for Schools*, February [online] http://www.nsdc.org/library/publications/tools/tools2-02rich.cfm.

Robertson, P. and Dakers, J. (2002) *Personal Learning Plan Programme 2002–04: Evaluation* [online] www.literacytrust.org.uk/ Database/secondary/personalised.htm.

Roddick, A. (2000) 'Beautiful business', *RSA Journal*, cxlviii(5495): 54–9.

Salagaras, S. (2004) 'The South Australia PALLACE report on schools and learning communities', in N. Longworth and S. Allwinkle (eds) *PALLACE Report to the European Commission*, Edinburgh: Napier University.

Schuller, T. (1998) 'Three steps towards a learning society', *Studies in the Education of Adults*, 30(1) (April): 11–20.

Scottish Power Learning (1998) 'Personal Development Plan', Cumbernauld: Scottish Power Learning.

Shi Long (2004) 'Beijing learning city', address to PALLACE Canadian conference, Edmonton 2004, in N. Longworth and S. Allwinkle (eds) *PALLACE Report to the European Commission*, Edinburgh: Napier University.

Shiva, V. (1998) 'Rebuilding an earth democracy: a 50th anniversary perspective', in Rukmini Sekhar*, Making a Difference: A Collection of Essays*, New Delhi: Spic-Macay.

Simpson, S. (1994) 'Profiting from business in higher education', in *Capacity Building for the 21st Century*, Proceedings of the 4th UNESCO–NGO Collective Consultation on Higher Education, 26–28 September, Paris: UNESCO, pp. 115–22.

Southampton City Council (2003) *Southampton: The Renaissance of the City*, Southampton: Southampton City Council.

Southee, S. (2004) 'Ford Employee Development Assistance Programme (EDAP)', address to Whitehall college [online] http://www.poptel.org.uk/whitehall-college/whitehall/enter/news/edap.htm.

Steele, R.L. (1992) 'Schools of the 21st century', *Time Magazine*, April.

Swift, N. (2003) 'Slow cities movement offers alternative to global mediocrity' [online] http://www.citymayors.com/environment/slow_cities.html.

Taylor, L. (2005) 'The Australian Centre for Lifelong Learning situated within Education City, Springfield Gateway', email (26 May 2005).

Thorne, M. (1995) 'Strategic future of FE and HE links', address to Scottish Further Education Funding Council (SFEFC) bulletin 2/102/1995, Edinburgh: SFEFEC.

Toffler, A. (1980) *The Third Wave: The Revolution that will Change our Lives*, London: Collins.

UNESCO (1973) *Objectives for the Future of Education (Fauré report)*, Paris: UNESCO.

UNESCO Commission on Education for the 21st Century (1996) *Learning: The Treasure Within*, Paris: UNESCO.

UNESCO (1998) *Higher Education in the 21st Century*, World Conference on Higher Education, Towards an Agenda 21, working document ed/98/conf.202/CLD.19, Paris: UNESCO.

Vystrcilova, R. and Komenda, T. (2004) 'Report to the LILLIPUT project on language learning and law in learning cities', in N. Longworth and S. Allwinkle (eds) *LILLIPUT Report to the European Commission*, Edinburgh: Napier University.

Wain, K. (2000) 'The learning society: post-modern politics', *International Journal of Lifelong Education*, 19(1) (January–February): 36–53.

Westfield Washington Schools (1996) *New Dimensions in Education*, booklet available from Westfield Washington Schools, 322 West Main Street, Westfield, IN 46074.

Wheeler, G.K. and Bernier, K.R. (2002) 'Giraffe club in the classroom: engaging and empowering students: a framework for teaching about global issues and solutions' [online] www.newhorizons.org.

Williamson, B. (1998) *Lifeworlds and Learning: Essays in the Theory, Philosophy and Practice of Lifelong Learning*, Leicester: NIACE.

Yarnit, M. (2000) *Towns, Cities and Regions in the Learning Age: A Survey of Learning Communities*, London: UK Local Government Association.

Young, S. (2003) 'Passive consumers or co-creators?: listening to learners', address to Australian College of Educators, Melbourne, 11 July.

Zohar, D. and Marshall, I. (1999) *SQ – The Ultimate Intelligence*, London: Bloomsbury.

Index